BANK CONFIDENTIALITY

This book is to be returned on
or before the date stamped below

2 4 NOV 2003

BANK CONFIDENTIALITY

FRANCIS NEATE

Slaughter and May

ROGER McCORMICK

Freshfields

International Bar Association

Butterworths

London, Boston, Dublin, Edinburgh, Hato Rey,
Kuala Lumpur, Singapore, Sydney, Toronto, Wellington
1990

United Kingdom	Butterworth & Co (Publishers) Ltd, 88 Kingsway London WC2B 6AB, and 4 Hill Street, Edinburgh EH2 3JZ
Australia	Butterworths Pty Ltd, Sydney, Melbourne, Brisbane, Adelaide, Perth, Canberra and Hobart
Canada	Butterworths Canada Ltd, Toronto and Vancouver
Ireland	Butterworth (Ireland) Ltd, Dublin
Malaysia	Malayan Law Journal Sdn Bhd, Kuala Lumpur
New Zealand	Butterworths of New Zealand Ltd, Wellington and Auckland
Puerto Rico	Equity de Puerto Rico, Inc, Hato Rey
Singapore	Malayan Law Journal Pte Ltd, Singapore
USA	Butterworth Legal Publishers, Austin, Texas; Boston, Massachusetts; Clearwater, Florida (D & S Publishers); Orford, New Hampshire (Equity Publishing); St Paul, Minnesota; and Seattle, Washington

A CIP Catalogue record for this book is available from the British Library.

ISBN 0 406 17948 4

Typeset by Phoenix Photosetting, Chatham
Printed and bound by Bookcraft (Bath) Ltd
Midsomer Norton, Avon.

Preface

Most of the papers in this publication were first delivered in May 1989 at the Sixth Annual International Financial and Banking Law Seminar of the Section on Business Law of the International Bar Association. The other papers were written subsequently and the original papers were revised in the light of the discussion at the seminar.

Each contributor has been responsible for his own paper, although as joint editors we have tried to introduce an element of uniformity of approach. Our thanks are due to all the contributors, who have responded to our requests with unfailing promptness and courtesy.

Although some of the papers were written and others revised after May 1989, the reader should not assume that they take account of any changes in law occurring after that date.

March 1990   Francis Neate
                                                          Roger McCormick

Contents

The IBA, the Section on Business Law and its Committee on Banking Law

The International Bar Association (IBA) is the world's foremost international association of lawyers, with a membership of some 12,500 individual lawyers in 130 countries, as well as 113 Bar Associations and Law Societies. Its principal aims and objectives are:

to encourage the discussion of problems relating to professional organisation and status;
to promote an exchange of information between legal associations world-wide;
to support the independence of the judiciary and the right of the lawyers to practice their profession without interference;
to keep abreast of developments in the law, and help in improving and making new laws.

Above all, though, it seeks to provide a forum in which individual lawyers can contact, and exchange ideas with, other lawyers.

The IBA has three sections, of which the Section on Business Law (SBL) is the largest with 9,610 members. This section is divided into 26 specialist committees, of which Banking Law is the biggest with over 1,800 members.

This committee aims to study and discuss the legal and practical aspects, particularly from the international viewpoint, of issues related to banking and financing.

Members of the committee are typically partners of law firms practising in national and international banking matters, or in-house lawyers of banks active in international financial transactions.

The committee meets annually at conferences of the IBA and SBL; organises the Annual International Financial and Banking Law Seminars, which usually take place in May each year; publishes a quarterly newsletter with latest developments in banking law world-wide to which members are invited to submit news items; and arranges regional meetings through its regional sub-committees.

A subsidiary, and very successfully accomplished, aim is that of enabling committee members to become personally acquainted with qualified colleagues in other countries, specialising in the same or similar areas, to whom they may turn for professional assistance in their own international practice.

Further details of the IBA are available from:

2 Harewood Place,   Telephone: 071 629 1206
Hanover Square,   Telex: 8812664 INBAR G
London   Fax: 071 409 0456
W1R 9HB.

Contributors

FRANCIS NEATE

Francis Neate was educated at St Paul's School, London, from which he gained an Exhibition in Classics at Brasenose College, Oxford. After changing from the study of Classics to that of Law, he was awarded a BA in Jurisprudence in 1962 by Oxford University, where he was also a Cricket Blue in 1961 and 1962. He was a Commonwealth Scholar at the University of Chicago Law School for the academic year 1962/63, being awarded a JD. After working briefly for Davis Polk & Wardwell in New York, he joined Slaughter and May in London in 1964, qualified as a solicitor in 1966 and became a partner of Slaughter and May in 1972. He is Chairman of Committee E (Commercial Banking) of the Section on Business Law of the International Bar Association.

ROGER McCORMICK

Roger McCormick is a partner of Freshfields, currently working in their Paris office. He was educated at Manchester Grammar School and Wadham College, Oxford, and qualified as a solicitor in 1975. He became a partner in Freshfields in 1981 and has worked in Paris since 1988.

Like Francis Neate, Roger is a member of Committee E of the IBA and the Chairman of that Committee's Publications Sub-Committee. He is also Vice-Chairman of the City of London Law Society's Banking Law Sub-Committee.

Australia

EW WALLACE

Bill Wallace is a banking and corporate finance lawyer at the Sydney office of Mallesons Stephen Jaques and an authority on Australian stamp duties law and federal financial institutions duty. He is co-author of the standard textbook on Australian Stamp Duties Law. He practices principally in banking and in corporate financing fields, acting for major leaders, companies and financial intermediaries across a broad spectrum of financing transactions. He also acts for banks and merchant banks in developing new banking products.

Bill Wallace completed his Bachelor of Economics and Bachelor of Laws degrees at Monash University in 1971. After working with law firms in Melbourne and London, and as an associate to a High Court judge, he joined the Sydney office of the firm in 1975. He became a partner in 1980. In 1985, he compiled a Report for the New South Wales Government on restructuring the State's Taxes on Financial Transactions, aspects of which were subsequently enacted through Parliament.

Wallace is a past chairman of the Australian Law Council's Banking and Finance Law Committee and member of the Business Law Executive of the Council.

Austria

MICHAEL KUTSCHERA

Born: 10 October 1957, Vienna.

Education: Dr jur, Mag jur University of Vienna, Law School (1979); MCJ, New York University, Law School (Fulbright Fellow) (1983).

Bar Membership: New York (1985) Vienna (1987).

Profession: Assistant at the Institute of Commercial Law at the University of Vienna, Law School (1978–1982); Clerk with the District Court of the City of Vienna, the Commercial Court Vienna and the Criminal Court Vienna (1979–1980); Foreign Associate, Shearman & Sterling (New York and Paris offices) (1985–1987); Partner, Binder Grösswang & Partners, 1010 Vienna, Tuchlauben 7a (since 1989).

Publications: Gruson, Hutter, Kutschera *Legal Opinions in International Transactions: Foreign Lawyers' Response to US Opinion Requests* (2nd ed) (Graham & Trotman, 1989)
Gruson, Kutschera *Opinion of Counsel on Agreements Governed by Foreign Law* 19 Vand J Transnat 1 L 515 (1986)
Kutschera, *Zur Haftung des Geschäftsführers gemäß* § 25 GmbHG, GesRZ 1982, 243

Belgium

CHRIS SUNT

Born: Lier, Belgium, 5 February 1955.

Bar Membership: Brussels (1980).

Education: University of Antwerp (PhB, 1975); University of Ghent (LLB, 1978); Harvard Law School (LLM, 1980).

Publications: Legal Aspects of the ECU (Butterworths, London, April 1989).

Profession: Assistant Professor of Commercial Law, University of Ghent (1979–1982).

JACQUES RICHELLE

Born: Brussels, Belgium, 29 May 1962.

Bar Membership: Brussels (1989).

Education: Université Libre de Bruxelles (LLB, 1988); Duke University School of Law, Copenhagen, Denmark, International Law Seminar (summer 1988); Southern Methodist University School of Law, Dallas, Texas (LLM, 1989).

Canada

DAVID W DRINKWATER

David W Drinkwater (age 41) studied business at the University of Western Ontario, London, Ontario, Canada obtaining an Honours BA in Business in 1970. He studied law at Dalhousie University, Halifax, Nova Scotia, Canada, obtaining an LLB in 1973. He also studied post graduate law at the London School of Economics obtaining a LLM in 1974. He joined Osler, Hoskin &

Harcourt in Toronto, Canada in 1974 and moved to the United Kingdom to become partner in charge of their London office in 1986. He is now partner in charge of the London office of Osler Renault, the international partnership of Osler, Hoskin & Harcourt and of Ogilvy, Renault.

His practice has concentrated on corporate finance and mergers and acquisitions with an international emphasis. He is a past Chairman of the Policy Advisory Committee to the Ontario Securities Commission and has been a lecturer in securities law at Osgoode Law School and in Business Planning at the University of Toronto Law School. He was co-author of the text *Private Placements in Canada* (Carswell, Toronto, 1985).

JAMES E FORDYCE

After graduation with a Bachelor of Arts degree in 1970 from the University of Toronto, Canada, James E Fordyce (age 44) studied law at Osgoode Hall Law School at York University in Toronto and obtained an LLB degree in 1973. He joined Osler, Hoskin & Harcourt in Toronto in 1973 and became a partner of the firm in 1980. The main focus of his practice is in mergers and acquisitions and banking. In 1989 he was seconded to the Paris office of Osler Renault, the international partnership of Osler, Hoskin & Harcourt and of Ogilvy Renault of Montreal, Canada.

Denmark

PER OVERBECK

Per Overbeck was born on 16 February 1946 in Denmark. He obtained a Master of Law in 1971 and a Master of Economics in 1976 from the University of Copenhagen. His appointments include: Deputy judge at the Greenland High Court in 1970; Principal in the Ministry of Industry (the Danish Export Credit Guaranty Department) in 1972–73; Principal in the Ministry of Foreign Affairs in 1973–79; Assistant Professor of Law of Contracts at the University of Copenhagen in 1976–1979; First Secretary at the Danish Embassy in Paris in 1979–83 (he received the Ordre National du Mérite on 26 July 1983); Deputy General Manager with the Danish Bankers Association in 1984–86.

Since 1984, he has been a member of the Legal Committee of Fédération Bancaire de la Communauté Européenne. Since 1986 he has been Senior Vice President of Den Danske Bank and Secretary to the Board of Directors and Director of Legal Affairs. And since 1988 he has been a member of the Danish Financial Institutions' Board of Appeal. He was elected to the Board of Association Bancaire pour l'Ecu in June 1989.

England

RICHARD GRANDISON

Richard Grandison was educated at Fettes College, Edinburgh, from which he gained an Exhibition in Classics at Pembroke College, Cambridge. He changed to study law and was awarded a BA by Cambridge University. He qualified as a solicitor at Slaughter and May in 1978 and became a partner in 1987.

France

PHILIPPE GIROUX

Born: Paris, France, 7 January 1929.

Bar Membership: 1953.

Education: Stanislas College, Paris; University of Paris Law School (Master of Law, 1950; Doctor of Law, 1952); Paris Institut des Hautes Etudes Internationales (Graduate, 1952).

Profession: Senior Partner of Giroux, Buhagiar et Associés, Paris; Officer of the International Section of Confédération Syndicale des Avocats; specialised in corporate and commercial law with an emphasis on securities and banking transactions.

Germany (Federal Republic)

WOLFGANG HAUSER

Born: 3 August 1952.

Legal education: Universities of Göttingen and Frankfurt (1971–1976); Harvard Law School, Cambridge, Mass (LLM) (1977–1978); Doctor of laws (Dr jur) University of Frankfurt (1982).

Professional activities: admission to the Frankfurt Bar (1980); research fellow at the Institute for Foreign and International Trade Law, University of Frankfurt (1980–1982).

In 1982 Wolfgang Hauser joined Westrick & Eckholdt, one of the largest law firms in the Federal Republic of Germany of which he is a partner. He works mainly on commercial banking and corporate law matters.

Greece

YANOS GRAMATIDIS

Born: Larissa, Greece, 12 May 1952.

Bar Membership: Supreme Court, Greece (1977).

Member: Athens Bar; International Bar Association (Business Law Section, Section on General Practice); American Bar Association; Inter-American Bar Association; Law Society of London; Solicitors European Group; Hellenic-American Chamber of Commerce; British-Hellenic Chamber of Commerce; Anglo-Hellenic Law Association (Chairman 1988–1989); Board of Governors of the London Hellenic Society; Institute of Directors, London.

Education: University of Athens Law School (LLB; Department of Political Sciences); The Hague Academy of International·Law; Institut International des Droits de l'Homme, Strasbourg.

Profession: Partner of the Greek law firm Bahas, Gramatidis & Associates (Resident Partner, London, England Office).
   Special Representative in Greece of the International Franchise Association.
   He participated as speaker in various seminars and conferences and as Chairman in the 1990 April McGeorge School of Law Conference in Austria.

Author: Acquisition of Real Property in Greece by Aliens (1985); *The new Law on Leasing in Greece* (1987); *Hotel Contracts in Greece* (1987); *Timesharing in Greece* (1987); *The establishment of Lawyers in the EEC* (1983); *Franchising: The Greek legislation* (1988); *Investment Incentives in Greece* (1988); *Mergers & Acquisitions in the EEC* (1988); *Acquisition of Greek Securities* (1988).

Italy

MARCELLO GIOSCIA

Marcello Gioscia graduated from the Law School of Genoa in 1961 and was admitted to the Italian Bar in 1964. He received a Master of Laws at the Columbia University Law School in 1971 and, since then, has specialised in corporate and financing matters. He is Vice-Chairman of the Banking Committee of the Business Section of the International Bar Association and is a partner in the Italian law firm Studio Legale Ughi e Nunziante, which he joined when it was founded in 1968.

Luxembourg

ALEX SCHMITT

Education: Licencié en Droit, University of Brussels (1978); Licencié en Droit Européen, University of Brussels (1980); LLM, Harvard Law School (1981).

Profession: Lecturer at the University of Brussels Law School; Partner, Bonn & Schmitt, Luxembourg.

LUC FRIEDEN

Education: Maître en Droit, University of Paris-Sorbonne (1986); Master of Comparative Law, University of Cambridge (1987); Master of Laws, Harvard Law School (1988).

Profession: Partner, Bonn & Schmitt, Luxembourg.

Netherlands

VPG DE SERIERE

Mr De Serière was admitted to the bar in Amsterdam and is a partner of the law firm Loeff & Van der Ploeg (shortly, following the merger with the Brussels law firm of Braun Claeys Verbeke & Sorel, to be renamed Loeff Claeys Verbeke). Mr De Serière was born in 1949. He studied Netherlands civil and commercial law at the State University of Leiden, the Netherlands. He holds a LLB degree of Cambridge University in public international law and EEC law. In 1976 he joined the firm in Amsterdam. Since then, he has worked in Indonesia and in the offices of the firm in New York. He is a co-author of various publications, including *Dutch Business Law*, *Tax Treatment of Cost-Contribution Arrangements*, and *Commercial Arbitration in Asia and the Pacific*. He is now resident in Amsterdam and specialises in financial and corporate transactions.

Norway

OLE CHRISTIAN HOIE

Born: 1943.

Bar Membership: 1971.

Education: Oslo University Law School (1968).

Profession: Partner Advokatfirmaet Wiersholm, Bachke & Helliesen (1983). Joined WBH in 1981.

Spain

JUAN FERNANDEZ-ARMESTO

Juan Fernadez-Armesto is chaired Professor of Commercial Law at the Universidad de Comillas in Madrid (ICADE), and a partner of Uria & Menendez.

LINDA HINIKER

Linda Hiniker received a JD degree from Stanford University, was foreign consultant to Uria & Menendez, and is currently associated with Cleary, Gottlieb, Steen & Hamilton in New York.

Switzerland

DR HANS RUDOLF STEINER

Born: Zurich, Switzerland, 3 November 1942.

Bar Membership: 1970.

Education: Kantionales Literar Gymnasium, Zurich and University of Zurich (Dr jur, 1968); Harvard Law School (LLM, 1971).

Profession: Secretary to District Court (1969); Partner of Walder Wyss & Partner, Zurich (since 1974); Chairman of the Zurich Bar Association (1982–84); Member of the Board of the Swiss Federal Bar Association (since 1985); Co-Chairman of the Subcommittee on recent developments in securities laws (QI) of IBA/SBL.

Dr Steiner is engaged mainly in advising and representing finance companies, brokers and banks and in international arbitration as counsel and arbitrator.

United States

DAVID R SLADE

David Slade is a resident partner of Milbank, Tweed, Hadley & McCloy in the London office, where he has practiced since 1983. He has extensive knowledge of Euromarket financings, and related areas of US securities, banking and tax laws. He is also experienced in project financings and leveraged lease financings.

Mr Slade is a graduate of Dartmouth College, the Fletcher School of Law & Diplomacy where he received his MALD, and Harvard Law School. He also studied at the University of Mainz, West Germany and the University of Leningrad, USSR.

Mr Slade is a member of the Association of the Bar of the City of New York, the New York State Bar Association, the American Bar Association and the Massachusetts Bar Association. He is also a member of the Council on Foreign Relations.

Introduction

Francis Neate

In September 1979 at the Biennial Conference of the Section on Business Law of the International Bar Association, the Banking Committee (Committee E) conducted a comparative survey of the laws relating to banking confidentiality in a wide variety of jurisdictions. A large number of papers were read and subsequently published.[1] Switzerland, of course, led, followed by Austria, Germany and a number of other continental European jurisdictions. Then came the US, a stark contrast to Switzerland. The common law countries—England, Australia, New Zealand, Canada—brought up the rear. It was an interesting exercise. I delivered the English law paper at that conference. I emerged from the conference with a recollection of two striking contrasts.

The first contrast was the one between those countries, notably Switzerland, also Austria, in which breach of the banker's duty of confidence was enforced by the criminal law, and those where it was merely a civil obligation. In the former, enforcing the duty seemed to be straightforward. Everything was nicely cut and dried. One does not, after all, hesitate long when the choice is between performing one's duty and going to gaol. In the latter jurisdictions, by way of contrast, much doubt and uncertainty seemed to exist in some of the grey areas thrown up by the increasing internationalisation of banking business: to take one example, how should the branches or subsidiaries of a bank in one country respond to demands for information from the supervisory authorities in another country? There was an attractive simplicity to the certainty engendered by the harsh Swiss approach to these issues. On the other hand, it also seemed to encourage a rigidity which did not always make a lot of sense; whereas the greater flexibility permitted by those laws which provided merely for a civil duty appeared to me to permit a more pragmatic approach. After all, is serious harm likely to result to customers (unless they are criminals) from the disclosure of information to responsible supervisory authorities? Or, as an alternative way of looking at the problem, is there not greater risk overall to customers in general if the supervisory authorities are unable to do their job properly because of their failure to obtain information which is withheld in the interests of the few who might be damaged by its disclosure?

The second contrast lay in the extreme isolation of the US from most of the other countries. One of the principal causes of this was the very considerable resentment engendered in other countries by the recurring US tendency to extend its jurisdiction beyond its shores. The US representatives were themselves so sensitive to this resentment that one heard them apologising on more than one occasion for their authorities' behaviour; indeed, I cannot recall anyone during the 1979 conference trying to defend the US approach to the issue of jurisdiction.

However, another strong element contributing to the US isolation was the strong European feeling that the US banking and securities industries were over-regulated. The US Securities Exchange Commission was the body we all loved to

1 'Banking Secrecy' published by the International Bar Association in January 1980.

hate. The European view seemed to be that our longer history had enabled us to develop systems of regulation and supervision which allowed for pragmatism and greater flexibility for sensible bankers and securities firms to conduct sensible business efficiently and quickly, without being trammelled by detailed regulations or the necessity of having a lawyer at their side every step of the way. In the English context, after the Financial Services Act and the 'Guinness' and 'Blue Arrow' scandals (among others) of the last decade, one might view this attitude with some amusement; alternatively, one might hark back to the 1970s, when this attitude was prevalent, with nostalgia for a golden age. But there is no doubt that such an attitude was widespread and was encouraged by many of the US bankers, lawyers and others then operating in Europe. It was natural enough for the US lawyer in private practice to look upon the SEC (or, in the case of banks, the Comptroller of the Currency) as the organisation primarily responsible for making his and his clients' lives so difficult; and to contrast this with the apparent freedom in Europe. In addition, he must have been worn down by the chore of endlessly explaining to his European counterparts the detailed ramifications of the activities of powerful regulatory organisations of which they had no experience and knew no equivalents. As to the US bankers and securities dealers, the experience of coming to Europe in the 1970s was a culture shock which many found liberating. I can remember many questions from US bankers in the early 1970s as to whether there was any fundamental legal impediment to the transaction being proposed; to which often the reply would be—why should there be? What do you have in mind? In consequence, there were few articulate defendants of the US approach to whom Europeans were exposed; rather, they were encouraged in their faith in their own systems by the majority of US practitioners in Europe. Scandals such as the IOS affair were conveniently forgotten.

One wonders also how far this divergence in attitude was reinforced by more deep-rooted historical and cultural attitudes. Certainly, it is a commonplace assertion that to declare an act a criminal offence is to reinforce the underlying belief that it constitutes a moral wrong. Everyone knows the historical reasons why Switzerland takes so seriously the banker's duty of confidence and treats breach of it as a criminal offence. In the paper on Swiss law delivered in 1979, these reasons were stated proudly and unequivocally. It may be a sign of the times that, in the equivalent paper in this publication, the statement is more muted. There can be no doubt that in 1979 the stringency of Swiss law on this subject was highly respected and the reasons for it well understood. In a sense, Switzerland was regarded as the acme of banking rectitude.

No doubt, there was (as there still is) a strong competitive element also. There always has been and always will be a huge quantity of international money, owing allegiance to no particular country, looking for a home where secrecy is guaranteed. Switzerland's assumed success in attracting a large proportion of this money has long been regarded with envy by bankers in other countries.

There may also have been an element of assertion of cultural superiority by the old world over the new, a recurring tendency in many parts of Europe after (if not also before) the Second World War.

Many of these factors were contributing to the apparent isolation, during the 1970s, of US attitudes to banking regulation and banking secrecy from the European attitude. Certainly, this isolation was apparent from the papers delivered and views expressed at the conference in 1979. Yet, even then, the discerning observer might have perceived the beginnings of a convergence in those attitudes. The most concrete indication was, perhaps, the Treaty of 25 May

1973 between Switzerland and the US concerning mutual assistance in criminal matters, which was mentioned in almost apologetic terms by the Swiss speaker at the 1979 conference as a minor tear in the enveloping fabric of Swiss banking secrecy, yet to some appeared to drive a coach and horses through the principle. In the United Kingdom, the Banking Act 1979 was strengthening the powers of the banking supervisors; legislation against insider trading was also mooted. This first came into effect in the Companies Act 1980.

Ten years later, one can see that a distinct shift in European attitudes has taken place. There appear to be several reasons for this. First, and perhaps foremost, the increasing globalisation of the banking and securities businesses presents a whole new range of problems to the domestic supervisors. It has become clear to them that the traditional concept of jurisdiction limited by territorial boundaries is wholly inadequate in the context of the developing global market. Simultaneously, there has been an increasing recognition of and determination to tackle the money laundering which is an inherent feature of international and organised crime. Finally, there has been a growing appreciation and acceptance, in the securities industry, of the principle of the 'integrity' of the market; in other words, that confidence in financial markets can only be preserved by the provision of simultaneous and, where possible, instantaneous access for all to all relevant information. The principal source of all these ideas has been the US. It is no longer isolated.

In the United Kingdom, the legal effect has been dramatic. As already mentioned, insider trading became a criminal offence in 1980. The attack on organised crime (particularly drug- or terrorist-related) has been stepped up to such an extent that, in one case today, a bank which merely suspects that it is handling the proceeds of crime itself commits a criminal offence if it fails to report its suspicion.[2] The investigatory powers of the authorities have been strengthened or, in the case of inquiries instituted by the Department of Trade under the Companies Acts, utilised to an extent never seen before. Market practices which, in the past, might have been considered dubious but would certainly have gone unpunished, if not undetected, have been ruthlessly stamped on. Finally, 'Big Bang'—presented as the 'deregulation' of the securities industry—has been accompanied by the Financial Services Act, under which the securities industry is now regulated to an extent it has never known before.

Although the United Kingdom would, no doubt, claim that it has worked out (and is still working out) its own solutions, the similarities between the approach of the United Kingdom and that of the US are far more striking than the differences. No doubt many reasons can be offered for this convergence of attitudes, but I will limit myself to suggesting two. The first is obvious: the much-trumpeted 'victory' of the philosophy of the free market. There is no need to enter the debate over whether or not the philosophy is right, or whether or not it has been victorious over competing ideologies. It is sufficient to acknowledge that in the United Kingdom, in the last decade, this philosophy has been dominant and that the one field of activity to which its principles have been applied most vigorously has been the financial sector. This is not to say that the financial sector has been opened to unrestricted free enterprise. Rather, as already noted, it has been subjected to greater regulation than ever before. There have been substantial borrowings from the longer US experience of running an economy dedicated to the free enterprise principle. The paradox is that maintenance of the free market appears to require the strictest regulation of the market participants.

2 Drug Trafficking Offences Act 1986.

The second reason is more complex, but also represents a borrowing, albeit less conscious, from US experience. The increasing internationalisation of the banking and securities industries is rapidly eroding the cultural homogeneity of local financial markets. In the United Kingdom this process is already almost complete. Twenty years ago, the financial system in the United Kingdom was the preserve of the middle class 'establishment'. This is not to say that it was a closed shop. Many successful careers in the City of London started at the level of 'office boy' or the like. But the values of the City and its (unwritten) codes of conduct were those of the establishment and even those who did not 'belong' when they started aspired to join. The cynic would, of course, say that one reason why this way of doing things endured for so long was that, as with any system organised and run by and for the establishment, abuses of the system were ignored—at least until one section of the establishment began to disapprove of the activities of another, as happened in the insurance market at Lloyd's in the late 1970s. But that was not the whole story. The system enabled financial business to be conducted quickly and efficiently, with the minimum of regulation and relatively modest paper-work, because it was based to a considerable extent upon trust between the majority of participants engendered by shared standards and mutual understanding. However, much of this has been lost as a result of the internationalisation of the City of London which has been taking place over the last 20 years, considerably accelerated by 'Big Bang'.

Once again, one has to look to the US for the longest experience of organising a society comprising a mix of widely different cultures. Once again, one finds that the solution lies in the promulgation of regulations spelling out in great detail what behaviour is and is not permitted. When there are no shared assumptions, written rules are the only recourse; alternatively, if the only common understanding is that what is not forbidden is permitted, then a detailed list of what is forbidden must be provided.

All these factors have been at work in the United Kingdom over the last ten years and all have contributed to a very substantial shift in attitudes towards regulation of the banking and financial industries, which have been reflected in legislation. To return to the narrower scope of this book—the banker's duty of confidence—the same trend has occurred. In the paper on English law on this subject which I delivered to the conference in 1979, I said that the basic principle of English law was that the law will not permit you to keep your secrets by hiding them in a bank. At the time, this seemed to be a bold over-statement. Today, it is clearly right.

It was because I believed that there had been, over the last ten years, so clear a convergence of attitudes between the United Kingdom and the US, that I thought it would be interesting, in 1989, to revisit the subject of banking secrecy on a comparative basis, if only to discover to what extent a similar convergence might be found in other countries. Accordingly, at the Sixth Annual International Financial and Banking Law Seminar of the Section on Business Law of the International Bar Association, held in Copenhagen in May 1989, a session was devoted to this subject. A number of panellists, mainly but not exclusively from European jurisdictions, were invited to submit papers and a variety of case studies were discussed. The title of the topic was changed—from 'Banking Secrecy' to 'Use and Abuse of Confidential Information'. This change was deliberate, in order to ensure that two topics were dealt with which had scarcely featured in the 1979 papers. The first was insider trading. The second was the subject of conflict of interests. It is ironic that the principal reform associated with 'Big Bang'—the removal of enforced dual capacity in securities dealing—has introduced a whole league of new problems of this nature. Today, you may well find your trusted broker, whom you have instructed to buy shares for you, selling you his own at a considerable profit. In the banking context, the most interesting field in which these problems have started to arise is in the context of take-over bids. Target companies have been alarmed to find their own bank representing, or lending money to, the bidder. The Take-over Panel has addressed this kind of problem but, if the law also has a role to play, it seems likely that this will be found in the law relating to abuse of confidence. Similarly, the new fashion among banks and others of offering a 'one stop' service to customers, ranging from traditional banking to estate agency, stockbroking, merchant banking, equipment leasing, etc has introduced the temptation to weaken the duties of confidentiality traditionally owed by commercial banks in order to maximise 'cross-marketing' opportunities within the enlarged group of which the commercial bank forms part. It is relatively easy for banks to include standard terms in documentation with their customers in order to achieve this; if this practice is to be curbed, legislation will be required and the matter becomes one of public policy.

Insider trading, of course, has been given wide coverage in the media during the last decade. Some still see it as a 'victimless crime' or as merely 'an Anglo-Saxon obsession'. Many complain that, although laws have been enacted in various jurisdictions, they are not applied with much rigour. Indeed, insider trading is a classic example of the inherent weakness in 'harmonisation' measures in the international community. Legislative bodies do not actually catch international criminals by passing sophisticated new laws: it is how the laws are applied that matters.

The quality of the papers and of the discussion at the seminar in 1989 was uniformly excellent and it seemed worth while to repeat the 1979 experiment by producing a publication. A number of other contributors were, therefore, also approached and the original contributors revised their papers in the light of the discussion at the seminar. The results are contained in the following chapters. All European jurisdictions are covered except Sweden, together with the other leading common law jurisdictions: Australia and Canada, and, of course, the US.

It is for the reader to judge whether, and to what extent, the trends suggested above can be seen to be more widespread. I write merely from a United Kingdom perspective. Certainly, the jurisdictions covered in the following chapters vary considerably in their experience of the problems and the level of sophistication with which they have so far been addressed, and this is reflected to some extent in the papers in question. I would suggest, however, that the trends suggested above can be discerned in many of the countries in question; and further that, if the factors underlying and compelling those trends continue to exist, each country will eventually be forced to choose. One option will be to join the global market; in which case one would expect increasingly rigorous supervision of the financial industry, coupled with more exchanges of information and standardisation of supervisory criteria among the supervisors; an ever more vigorous attack on the money laundering activities of international crime; and ever more detailed rules designed to preserve the 'integrity' of the financial markets. Insider dealing will be made a criminal offence (if it is not already) and more strenuous efforts made to catch the offenders. The alternative is to join the 'off-shore haven' club, among whose members, no doubt, the concept of banking secrecy will be elevated to an ever higher moral plane. Members of the European Community will all have to make the same choice and it seems clear that this will be for the first option.

5th March 1990   FRANCIS NEATE

1   Australia

E W Wallace

NATURE AND EXTENT OF BANKER'S DUTY OF CONFIDENCE

Source of Duty in Australia

Australia is a federation of six states and two territories, together with a federal (commonwealth) government. The Australian constitution gives to the federal government the power to legislate throughout Australia with respect to banking (other than 'State banking', which covers the business of banking engaged in by a State itself as banker), together with power to legislate with respect to the incorporation of banks and the issue of paper money. This is not an exclusive power, so that each of the states and territories can also legislate with respect to banking where there is a proper territorial connection with its local geographic area.

Each of these nine governments hence has the power to legislate in respect of the banker's duty of confidence. However, in Australia there is no legislation which enshrines or codifies the duty. There are many federal and state statutes which impinge on aspects of the banker's duty of confidence, but these mainly require disclosure in certain circumstances and hence represent exceptions to the duty. Those statutes do also often provide some 'exceptions to the exception', by prohibiting disclosure in some cases for privacy and related reasons.

In the absence of legislation setting out the banker's duty of confidence, and given that the commonwealth and each of the Australian states and territories is a separate common law jurisdiction, the basis for the banker's duty of confidence in Australia rests in common law. The principles set out in the leading case of *Tournier v National Provincial and Union Bank of England* [1924] 1 KB 461, still succinctly summarise for Australian law purposes the scope of the duty and the category of exceptions to it.

This chapter does not repeat the principles arising out of *Tournier*'s case, but rather concentrates on the extent to which Australian cases have amplified or qualified the principles and on the Australian legislative and regulatory provisions which relate to the banker's duty of confidence.

Nature and Extent of Australian Banker's Duty of Confidence

Contractual duty; equitable duty of confidence

Given the source of the Australian law on the banker's duty of confidence as summarised above, it is clear that the duty is based on contract.

However, it is important to emphasise that the duty also has a strong basis in equitable principles. The general duty of confidence has matured only over recent decades into the broad equitable rule that 'he who has received information in confidence shall not take unfair advantage of it. He must not make use of it to the prejudice of him who gave it without obtaining his consent': *Seager v Copydex Ltd* [1967] 1 WLR 923 at 931. The application of this rule to professional persons, including bankers, is clear, so that it is now settled that 'a professional man is to keep his client's affairs secret and not to disclose them to anyone without just cause': *Parry-Jones v Law Society* [1969] 1 Ch 1 at 7, and likewise in Australia, *Crowley v Murphy* (1981) 34 ALR 496.

The fact that the duty of confidence is based in contract does give it a certain 'fragile' character. This is particularly so where, as in Australia, the duty is not codified by statute, yet there is much legislation, often in draconian terms, which does require disclosure and hence makes exceptions to the duty.

It is true that, where a contractual right, whether express or implied, is disputed, the court should concentrate on determining the obligations of the party as a result of that express or implied right, and the introduction of equitable concepts should be resisted: *Deta Nominees Pty Ltd v Viscount Plastic Products Pty Ltd* [1979] VR 167 at 191.

However, there have been a number of cases involving contractual rights where the courts have emphasised the concurrent underlying equitable principles based on a breach of confidence: for example, *Surveys & Mining Ltd v Morison* [1969] Qd R 470; *Mense v Milenkovic* [1973] VR 784. Further, the fact that the duty also derives from important equitable principles, based on a fiduciary duty of confidence, can assist in giving more substance to the duty—or in allowing it to withstand legislative pressures chipping away at the duty.

This can be as important to a banker as to a customer, particularly in the international sphere. Some of the cases where a court has resisted a foreign court's attempts to require disclosure of confidential information have referred to the protection under local law of the duty of confidence as being in the public interest and not merely as protecting a private right: see pp 18–19. This dovetails neatly into the important equitable origins of the duty of confidence.

Policy Considerations

Again, the international implications which are arising more frequently with the banker's duty of confidence make it necessary to examine the policy behind giving to the banker–customer relationship the duty of confidence. There is currently a debate in Australia, in the context of a proposed expanded credit reporting system, about whether finance companies and other financial institutions, which are not strictly speaking 'banks' but which may perform similar tasks for customers, should have some duty of confidence along the lines of the *Tournier*'s case principle.

As has been observed by Finn, 'Confidentiality and the Public Interest' (1984) 58 ALJ 497 at 502, the necessary or crucial consideration why confidentiality is perceived to be an integral element in particular relationships is:

'in the recognition that in some but not in other types of relationship there intrudes or is to be fostered some important individual, social or public value, some public interest, the preservation or promotion of which warrants or requires in some degree enforced confidentiality. Enforced confidentiality, in other words, is a means for securing an end. And it may be necessitated by a number of factors amongst which can be numbered: (a) the maintenance of privacy; (b) the promotion of information flow; (c) the prevention of possible information abuse, or of abuse of a position of dominance; and (d) an encouragement to the full and effective utilisation of some types of professional service.

In those relations in which secrecy is an imposed obligation there will often, in fact, be strong and reciprocal expectations that confidentiality is to be maintained, and this, commonly, for privacy reasons. But save where confidence is actually agreed, the presence of a public interest of the type suggested is itself sufficient, it is submitted, to transform confidentiality from a privacy expectation or from a matter of ethics, into a legal obligation . . . in banking it has been suggested—perhaps oddly—that "[t]he credit of the customer depends very largely upon the strict observance of . . . confidence" (*Tournier*'s case at 474).'

Legislation overrides contractual duty

There is an important practical consequence arising from the fact that the duty is based in contract. If legislation, expressed in general terms, on its ordinary interpretation is inconsistent with the duty of confidence, then that legislation is to be so interpreted, unless the legislation itself specifically states otherwise. In this respect, the contractual duty of confidence can differ from, say, legal privilege.

This is illustrated by the decision of Stephen J in the High Court of Australia in *Smorgon v Australia and New Zealand Banking Group Ltd* (1976) 134 CLR 475. The Commissioner of Taxation served on the bank a notice under s 264(1)(b) of the Income Tax Assessment Act 1936, which is discussed in more detail at pp 9–10, requiring it to produce certain documents which had come into its hands pursuant to the relationship of banker and customer. Stephen J at 489 rejected an argument that the general words of s 264(1)(b) should be read as not intended to override the contractual duty of confidentiality:

'If the legislature plainly says that those having information shall disclose it to the Commissioner then no mere contractual duty of confidentiality can stand in the way. In my view it is just such language which appears in s 264 and I regard it as effective to require the Bank to make such disclosure as the Commissioner may require.'

Remedies for breach

Since the duty of confidence is a contractual one within the banker–customer relationship, the basic remedy is an action for breach of contract, apart from any possible allegation of defamation. Australian cases have regarded it as axiomatic that wrongful disclosure of information by a bank can result in an action for breach of contract: *Commissioner of Taxation v Australia and New Zealand Banking Group Ltd* (1979) 143 CLR 499.

Tournier's case was an action for both slander and breach of contract, but because a new trial was ordered, the case does not assist in determining how to calculate damages for the contractual breach.

In *Sunderland v Barclays Bank Ltd* (1938) 5 Legal Decisions Affecting Bankers 163, du Parc LJ stated that if his judgment had been in the plaintiff's favour he would have awarded only nominal damages. Special damage would need to be proved in order to substantiate an award of other than nominal damages.

There is no reason in principle why an injunction should not be granted in respect of the breach in appropriate circumstances. For example, in 1989, in an unreported case, the New South Wales Supreme Court granted injunctive relief to a customer against a bank and restrained disclosure of details of the customer's banking transactions, in the light of an allegation that the bank was intending to disclose the information during negotiations for the sale of part of its business to another entity.

Where an action for a breach of the duty of confidence is based more on the equitable duty of confidence rather than contract or is based in tort, for example where a third party is bringing a claim (see further in this regard the discussion later in this chapter in the context of banker's opinions), then other equitable remedies, such as an account of profits and an order for delivery up of documents embodying or containing the confidential information, would be available in appropriate circumstances.

· Legislation requiring disclosure (discussed below) often creates criminal offences which can lead to criminal remedies, both for a failure to disclose and for wrongful disclosure where the legislation provides an exception to the obligation to disclose.

Where a bank defaults in a statutory obligation to produce documents or disclose information, then even where the legislation only prescribes a fine for breach, it has been held that, if the default continues, an injunction can lie to compel obedience to the requirement: *Attorney General v Thomas* (1983) 13 ATR 859 (relating to s 264 of the Income Tax Assessment Act, discussed on pp 9–10).

EXCEPTION—DISCLOSURE UNDER COMPULSION BY LAW

It is clear from the authorities, originating from *Tournier*'s case, that an exception to the bank's duty of confidence is a case where disclosure is required under compulsion by law. Weaver and Craigie *Law Relating to Banker and Customer in Australia* (1975) p 167 comment that although 'the power to compel disclosure is certainly more widely conferred now than it used to be, it is still by no means universally conferred on governmental and law enforcement agencies, a fact which officials do not always seem to appreciate'. However, there are in Australia numerous examples where in particular situations disclosure is required under compulsion by law. Most practical problems with the duty of confidence arise in determining whether the law does compel disclosure. This is particularly so in the international sphere, as discussed at pp 14–22.

Subpoena

Since the courts do not give to banking secrecy a higher degree of protection than other types of confidential information, in any court proceedings where evidence concerning a person's banking arrangements is relevant, that evidence can be obtained by subpoena. It is then disclosed only to the court, not directly to the party calling for the evidence. Much has been written about the principles applying to production of evidence by subpoena in this area. It is sufficient to say that these general principles are applicable in Australia, and see below concerning the bankers' books provisions.

One interesting principle has been referred to in Australian cases which can be important in corporate and banking transactions. In *Re ACI International Ltd* (1986) 11 ACLR 240, the Supreme Court of Victoria refused to set aside subpoenas directed to a bank, requiring it to produce information about customer's records and the bank's role in a corporate takeover. The court made at 246 the following observation:

'The parties involved in such litigation are usually large corporate bodies with wide experience in the field of commerce and commercial law. Many of such corporate bodies have their own legal departments and/or are advised and assisted by experienced bankers and legal advisers. Whilst to a layman the terminology used in the subpoenas the subject of the present applications, terminology which in some instances is taken directly from the Companies (Vic) Code, may appear formidable, it should be well understood by those who venture into this particular arena. If it is not, then they would be well advised to leave take-overs to those possessing the appropriate knowledge and expertise.'

Search Warrants

Search warrants, to obtain evidence in a criminal investigation before charges have been laid, can only be issued in relation to a specific statutory provision. There can be difficulties for a bank where the bank surrenders confidential documents and the warrant is later held to be invalid. The issue of a search warrant by a magistrate represents an exercise of a judicial discretion and in some situations a warrant can be set aside: *TVW Ltd v Robinson and Cant* [1964] WAR 33; *Tillett*'s case, below.

The bank should not accede to a request from the police to delay informing a customer or to fail to inform the customer, as this could be a breach of the duty owed by the bank to its customer.

Search warrant must set out reasonable grounds

In an Australian Capital Territory case, the court set aside certain search warrants which empowered commonwealth police officers to search premises including specific bank premises, holding that the fact that a search warrant had been executed did not preclude relief by way of certiorari. It was also held that a search warrant granted under the Commonwealth Crimes Act involved must show on its face that the justice was satisfied by information on oath that there was reasonable ground for suspecting that the relevant evidence was on the premises named in the warrant: *R v Tillett* (1969) 14 FLR 101.

'Negative search' not permitted

In a decision of the Federal Court of Australia, it was held in relation to a search warrant of solicitors' premises that a 'negative search' could not be undertaken; that is, an examination of every file and paper in order to ascertain that it was relevant to the search: *Crowley v Murphy* (1981) 34 ALR 496. Similar results would apply to a search conducted on banking premises.

Duty on Certain Trustees and Agents to Disclose

In some of the Australian states and territories, legislation requires solicitors and certain agents to conduct trust accounts, and moneys held on behalf of clients must be deposited into those accounts. The provisions often require banks to report to the relevant authorities the fact that such an account has become overdrawn (or would be overdrawn if all cheques presented had been paid). These statutes can also provide that the inspectors or auditors, who check whether the account holders have complied with the statutory requirements, can obtain information from the bank at which the trust account is kept.

Disclosure under Companies Legislation

Corporate investigations—'Officer' of company includes bank

The uniform Australian Companies Codes, which is uniform legislation enacted in each Australian state and territory, under a commonwealth–state co-operative scheme which is currently under review, allow for the appointment of inspectors to investigate the affairs of companies and to make enquiries from their 'officers'. The definition of 'officer' includes 'a person who acts, or has at any time acted, as . . . banker . . . for the corporation'. The inspector may give to the officer (the banker) written notice requiring:

(I)   the production of books;
(II)   the giving of 'all reasonable assistance' to the inspector 'in connection with the investigation'; and
(III)   the officer 'to appear before the inspector for examination on oath'.

It has been held in relation to a similar former provision that, with these provisions, the reference to a banker 'describes the banking corporation with which the company conducts its banking business. The word does not extend to officers or employees of that banking corporation': *Australia and New Zealand Bank Ltd v Ryan* (1968) 88 WN (NSW) (Pt 1) 368 at 371. The judge considered that this interpretation would not deprive the provision of its effect, because:

'the requirement imposed upon the banker to give "all assistance in connection with the prosecution which he is reasonably able to give" extends to imposing upon the banker the obligation, if it is reasonably able to do so, to make available for interview such of its employees as have information falling within the scope of subs (6) and, without attempting to specify every instance, the obligation to render such other assistance as it is reasonably able to give, whether by way of production of documents, inspection of records, entry on to premises, or otherwise, as may be sought by the Minister or the Registrar in connection with the prosecution'.

The current provision refers to assistance 'in connection with the investigation', rather than 'in connection with the prosecution' as formerly, and hence also requires assistance to be given prior to the institution of legal proceedings. It was also held in *Ryan*'s case at 373 that the statutory obligation 'will override any express or implied contractual obligation' to the customer.

Corporate investigation—disclosure of bankers' books

Section 12(2) of the Companies Codes provides that the Corporate Affairs Commission may at any time by notice in writing give direction to a person who is or has been a banker for or on behalf of a corporation, to produce specified banker's books relating to specified affairs of the corporation. Section 12(1) outlines the ambit of the power of the Commission to request production. Those purposes are:

(I)   the performance of a function or exercise of a power by the Corporate Affairs Commission under the Companies Code or the Securities Industries Code;
(II)   preventing a contravention or failure to comply with a provision of the Code;
(III)   ensuring compliance with a provision of the relevant Code; and
(IV)   where the information and/or documents are required for an offence relating to a company which involves fraud, dishonesty or concerns the management of the affairs of a company.

Prosecution on liquidation—banker to give information and books

Subsections 457(2) and 457(5) of the Companies Code provide that the Commission may require, by notice in writing, that a person who has acted as a banker for a company is to give all assistance in connection with a proposed prosecution instituted by the Commission consequent upon a report to the Commission by the liquidator of a company pursuant to s 418. Where the Commission has decided to investigate a matter reported to it by a liquidator it may, pursuant to s 541(2) and (3), apply to the court for an order requesting a person capable of giving information concerning the promotion, formation, management etc of a company to attend before the court and to be examined on matters that relate to the promotion, formation, management, administration or winding up of the corporation or matters that otherwise relate to the affairs of the corporation concerned. This can apply to a banker.

Section 384(1) of the Code provides that the court may require any banker to pay, deliver, convey, surrender or transfer to the liquidator or provisional liquidator forthwith or within such time as the court directs any money, property or books in his hands to which a company is prima facie entitled. There was a recent example of the use of this provision in Australia, where the Western Australia Supreme Court ordered that the National Australia Bank give to the provisional liquidators of the Rothwell's group of companies access to confidential bank documents.

Disclosure Under the 'Bankers' Books' Evidence Provisions

Summary of provisions

The statute law of each of the Australian states and territories includes provisions under which bankers who are called on to produce their books in evidence may tender verified copies. There are also provisions empowering the courts to make orders permitting the inspection of bank records and the taking of copies. This legislation, although not completely uniform between the states and territories, is based on the United Kingdom Bankers' Books Evidence Act 1879. Section 7 of that Act has its counterparts in all the Australian Acts and Ordinances, and reads (in part) as follows:

'On the application of any party to a legal proceeding a court or judge may order that such party be at liberty to inspect and take copies of any entries in a banker's book for any of the purposes of such proceedings.'

To take the New South Wales provisions as an example (the Evidence Act 1898, ss 44–51), s 45 of the Act provides that the copy of an entry in a banker's book shall not be received in evidence unless it is proved:

(I)   that the book was, at the time of the making of the entry, one of the ordinary books of the bank;
(II)   that the entry was made in the usual and ordinary course of business; and
(III)   that the book is, or at the time of the making of the copy of the entry was, in the custody or control of the bank.

The term 'bankers' books' is defined in s 3 to include ledgers, day books, cash books, account books and other accounting records used in the ordinary business of the bank.

A banker or officer of a bank shall not, in any legal proceeding to which the bank is not a party, be compelled to produce the banker's book the contents of which can be proved under s 45, or to appear as a witness to prove the matters, transactions and accounts therein recorded, unless by order of a judge made for a special cause: s 49.

Section 46 covers the procedure for verification of a copy of an entry in a banker's book. Proof is required that the copy has been examined with the original entry and is correct. This proof is to be given by the person examining the copy, either orally or by affidavit.

By s 50, any party to a legal proceeding may apply to a court for an order to inspect and take copies of any entries in a banker's book relating to the matters in question in those proceedings. This order may be made either with or without calling the bank, but the order must be served on the bank two clear days before it is to be obeyed, unless the court directs otherwise.

Court Rules

In each jurisdiction, the Court Rules recognise the special position of bankers. For example, Part 37 rule 5 of the New South Wales Supreme Court Rules states that where, in any proceedings, the person named in a subpoena is a bank and the bank is not a party to those proceedings, and the subpoena requires the bank to produce a banker's book, the contents of which can be proved under the Evidence Act provisions, the subpoena shall, unless the court for special cause otherwise orders, permit the bank to produce proof of the relevant entries in the banker's book in accordance with the Evidence Act provisions, instead of producing the banker's book.

Discretionary remedy

The English cases demonstrate that a wide discretion will be exercised in applications for orders under s 7 and that an application is more likely to succeed where there is cogent, independent evidence of criminal activity and the banking evidence is really needed in order that the prosecution may proceed. On the other hand, where these considerations are not present it is more likely that the applicant will be refused an order and left to use the subpoena procedure. The Australian position accords with this.

Customers should be informed

Where an order is served on a bank, it would be regular banking procedure to inform the customer as soon as practicable, especially where the order has been obtained ex parte.

Irregular practices do not overcome disclosure duty

Disclosure will be required under the provisions, even though, because of irregular practices (eg by a bank official), certain transactions did not pass through the usual channels and were not recorded: *R v Mitchell* [1971] VR 46.

Bank need not be a party to the litigation

While there must be an existing 'proceeding' before an order can be sought, a court does have power under the statute to order production of the original books of a bank at the trial of an action although the bank is not a party to the litigation: *Hay v Paterson; Re Colonial Bank* (1899) 15 VLR 360. Again, a judge can make an order for the production of a bank's books in legal proceedings, notwithstanding an undertaking by the bank to produce verified copies to the applicant for such an order: *Darling v Carter Co* (1903) 29 VLR 135. In that case, the Supreme Court of Victoria ordered a bank to supply copies of the account of a man who had absconded, for the purpose of proving the entries in the account.

In *MacKinnon's case* [1986] 1 Ch 484, discussed in more detail at pp 17–21 below, Hoffmann J held at 492 that an order under s 7 of the 1879 Act 'therefore has strong analogies with a subpoena, tailored to meet the convenience of banks. It would be illogical if the bank had no locus standi to apply to discharge it'. He considered that the bank did not need to be joined as a party to the action: 'if any person affected may apply to discharge an injunction . . . I do not see why the same should not be true of an order under the Bankers' Books Evidence Act 1879'.

'Fishing' expeditions not permitted

An order allowing a party to inspect and take copies of entries in a banker's book will not be made where there is reason to believe that the inspection is sought merely for 'fishing' purposes; i e where a person is attempting to discover evidence to build up a case: *Gordon v Kerr* (1916) 33 WN (NSW) 55.

No new discovery powers

The bankers' books provisions do not give any new power of discovery of documents: see, for example, *Commissioner of Railways v Small* (1938) 38 SR (NSW) 564, and *Dewley v Dewley* [1971] 1 NSWLR 264, where it was held that the issue of a subpoena requiring the production of an excessively wide range of documents would be an abuse of the process of the court. Accordingly, the bankers' books provisions of the Evidence Act do not alter the principles of law and practice with regard to discovery or take away any previously existing ground of privilege for non-disclosure: *Hart v Minister for Lands* (1901) 1 SR (NSW) 133.

Applies to criminal proceedings

The statutory provisions relating to bankers' books apply to criminal proceedings as well. Section 415 of the Crimes Act 1900 (NSW) states that where it is necessary to prove the state of an account or the entries in bankers' books or other documents, it is not necessary to produce such books, so that the evidence may be given orally or by affidavit.

Disclosure under Income Tax Legislation

The Federal Income Tax Assessment Act 1936 gives the Commissioner of Taxation very wide powers to require any person, whether a taxpayer or not, to attend and give evidence concerning his own or any other person's income or assessment of taxation. Section 264(1) provides that:

'The Commissioner may by notice in writing require any person, whether a taxpayer or not, including any officer employed in or in connection with any department of a Government or by any public authority—

(a) to furnish him with such information as he may require; and
(b) to attend and give evidence before him or before any officer authorized by him in that behalf concerning his or any other person's income or assessment, and may require him to produce all books, documents and other papers whatever in his custody or under his control relating thereto.'

No dispute of fact required

Section 264(1) does not require that there be a dispute of fact before the Commissioner. In effect, the provision allows the Commissioner to 'fish' for information so that he can determine the taxable income of any person. However, he is only entitled to documents that relate to a person's income or assessment, so that he may request the holder of the documents to supply him with information to enable him to identify the relevant documents. That is, in a preliminary enquiry, the Commissioner is only entitled to a general description of the documents and not to complete details of their contents. However, once he has that information he may then require production of the appropriate documents: *Goesman Investments Pty Limited v ANZ Banking Group Ltd* [1979] 79 ATC 4418.

Further aspects of s 264(1) are discussed below.

'Custody or control' involves physical not legal possession

In *FCT v Australia and New Zealand Banking Group Ltd* (1979) 143 CLR 499, the High Court considered the meaning of the words 'custody' and 'control', with a request to the ANZ Bank under s 264 of the Income Tax Assessment Act quoted above.

The taxpayer, the customer, had four safe deposit boxes or lockers at a branch of the bank. Each locker was double locked, two keys being needed to open it. One of these keys was held by the bank. The other was made in duplicate and both of the duplicates were issued to the customer. The customer retained one of these duplicates and lodged the other with the bank in a sealed envelope. The agreement between the customer and the bank was that the bank was to keep the sealed envelope in safe custody and to use it only to replace the key held by the customer, upon his written request, in the event of the loss or destruction of his key.

At first instance, Stephen J held that the contents of the four safe deposit lockers were not in the custody or control of the bank, having regard to the arrangements between the bank and the customer.

However, the full court upheld the Commissioner's appeal. Gibbs ACJ held at 521 that the bank had 'the custody, or physical control, of the documents in the lockers', because it had in its possession the keys which enabled it to open the locker and gain access to the documents. Gibbs ACJ held at 521 that

'any agreement or arrangement made by the Bank with the depositor does not affect the question whether the Bank has the documents in its control and is able to produce them. The Bank has actual custody or physical control of the contents of the locker, even if it has bound itself by contract to refrain from exercising the power which it has in fact. It can open the locker and produce its contents even if it has agreed not to do so.'

Gibbs ACJ held at 520 that s 264(1)

'is not concerned with the legal relationship of the person to whom the notice is given to the documents which he is required to produce: it is concerned with the ability of the person to whom the notice is addressed to produce the documents when required to do so. Therefore, in my opinion, a notice can be given under the section to any person who has physical control of the documents in question, whether he has or has not legal possession'.

The other members of the court came to similar conclusions. Mason J held that the bank had 'control' over the documents in the lockers within the meaning of that word as used in the Act. He did, however, concede that the bank had the ability to open the boxes without damaging them.

This question of physical damage is really one of degree: to extract the key the bank has to damage the envelope. The position may be different where the bank does not hold the duplicate of the customer's key, so that it would need to destroy the lock to open the locker.

Gibbs ACJ did recognise the banker's dilemma: if he produces documents to which the Commissioner is not entitled, the bank can be liable to the customer for breach of contract; yet failure to produce documents, to which the Commissioner is entitled to have access, may make the bank liable to the fine imposed by the tax legislation.

Corruption, Tracing Criminal Proceeds

There is a growing trend in Australia for Commissions and Royal Commissions, appointed to investigate alleged criminal conspiracies and to trace financial proceeds from criminal activities, to be given broad powers of inspection and investigation, which would cover documents held by banks on behalf of customers. For example, in New South Wales, a new body, the Independent Commission Against Corruption, has been given broad powers in its legislation. Section 22(1) of the Act provides that the Commission may, for the purpose of an investigation conducted by it, require a person to attend before the Commissioner or an Assistance Commissioner and produce a document specified by the Commission (see also ss 35 and 37).

In the Federal sphere, s 79(1) of the Proceeds of Crimes Act (Commonwealth) 1987 provides that when a financial institution (which is defined to include banks) has information about an account held with that institution, and has reasonable grounds for suspecting that the information may be relevant to a prosecution of the person for an offence against the law of the commonwealth or a territory, then that institution may give the information to a police officer or a member of staff of the National Crime Authority. However, it is also provided that no action will lie against the financial institution by reason of the financial institution taking these steps.

Disclosure of Cash Transactions

Another recent example of a major incursion requiring disclosure of bankers' records is the Commonwealth Cash Transaction Reports Act 1988. The Act is modelled on the United States' Bank Secrecy Act. By s 71 of the Act, a bank is required to report to the Director of the Cash Transaction Reports Agency a broad range of details about a significant cash transaction. The information includes details of name, address, occupation, nature of transaction. Certain transactions are exempt but these exemptions are not broad. See further, Walter and Erlich 'Confidences-Bankers and Customers' (1989) 63 ALJ 404 at 412–414.

Tax File Number Legislation—Banker's Obligations to Disclose and Privacy

This federal legislation requires all taxpayers and potential taxpayers to be given a tax file number. The legislation is a compromise, following the collapse of the government's original plan to issue identification cards, the 'Australia Card', to all Australian citizens. The move is designed to assist the Tax Office with 'its efficiency and effectiveness in detecting tax cheats'. The system enables the Tax Office to match up information supplied by taxpayers in their income tax returns with information which banks, building societies, credit unions and other financial institutions are required to give about customer's accounts. When Phase 2 of the system comes into operation, it will not be possible to open a bank account without giving a tax file number, and the Tax Office is then entitled to require from the banks information about customers' accounts.

While the legislation gives the Tax Office power to require disclosure of information by the banks, the Tax Office cannot disclose that information to other persons or to other government bodies; it can only use it in checking the accuracy of tax returns and then taking action against taxpayers for any discrepancies.

Parallel with this legislation is the introduction of the Commonwealth Privacy Act 1988. This Act gives the Privacy Commissioner broad powers to investigate complaints about interferences with privacy arising out of the tax file number system, and court proceedings can be brought in respect of breaches of privacy. Under the legislation, the Privacy Commissioner is required to set detailed guidelines, which elaborate upon the interim guidelines set out in Sch 2 to the Privacy Act.

The Privacy Act protects a customer from unauthorised disclosure of information obtained by the Tax Office from the bank about the customer's accounts and provides that, 'except to the extent that it does so expressly or by necessary implication', the Act shall not limit or restrict the operation of laws imposing an obligation of confidence and shall not limit or restrict laws prohibiting disclosure, whether civil or criminal. However, no recognition is given in the legislation to the banker's duty of confidence to a customer, and on the principles discussed earlier in this paper, the obligation on the bank to disclose information to the Tax Office overrides that duty.

Disclosure under Anti-Trust Legislation

In the Federal Trade Practices Act (which is anti-trust legislation), s 155 gives the regulating authority, the Trade Practices Commission, wide powers to call for production of documents and information which relate to a matter which may constitute a contravention of the legislation. The provision is wide enough to require a bank to produce evidence which may be used in, for example, prosecuting a customer of the bank in relation to a price fixing arrangement or a similar practice.

Other Statutory Obligations to Disclose

Section 62 of the Banking Act 1959 (Cth) allows the Australian central bank, the Reserve Bank, to direct the banks (other than state banks) to furnish information, but provides that any such direction shall not require the giving of information which identifies any individual customer (see also ss 81 and 69). For an interesting use of such a provision in allowing a 'public interest' defence to be raised, see the reference to the *Libyan Bank* case at p 18–19.

Section 125(1) of the Bankruptcy Act (Commonwealth) 1966 obliges the banker to inform the trustee in bankruptcy in writing of the existence of the account of an undischarged bankrupt, provided that the banker is satisfied that the account is not held on behalf of some other person.

A number of other federal and state statutes empower public authorities and some professional bodies to call upon bankers (among others) to supply them with information regarding the bank's customers and the bank's affairs.

EXCEPTION—DISCLOSURE IN PUBLIC INTEREST

Weerasooria *Banking Law and the Financial System in Australia* (1988) 19.29 concludes as follows in relation to this exception:

'While the right to disclose under this exception should not be lightly assumed, it would appear that it would apply in the following cases: (a) during time of war where the customer's dealings indicate that he is trading with the enemy; (b) during time of national emergency where a customer is reasonably suspected of treasonable activities against the state; (c) to prevent the perpetration or aid the detection of serious frauds and crimes.'

A bank's duty to its customer does not prevent it from volunteering information to police investigating serious criminal offences. That is, a banker may have a public duty to give information to police or to an authority engaged in the investigation of serious criminal offences, but this would not usually be a duty enforceable by legal sanction, unless the legislation provides a sanction (see the examples at pp 10–12 above). In the absence of a legislative requirement, a bank should not volunteer information to the police or these authorities unless it is satisfied that there are reasonable grounds for believing (a) that a serious crime had been committed involving the customer and/or the use of his account or other transactions by him as a customer, and (b) that the information would provide evidence to the proof of the commission of that offence. It would be difficult for a bank to satisfy itself that these pre-conditions had been met.

The public interest factor can become important in the international context and see particularly the discussion at p 18–21 and the reference there to the *Libyan Bank* case.

EXCEPTION—DISCLOSURE IN INTERESTS OF BANK

This really covers disclosure required by the legitimate interests of the bank, or for the legitimate protection of the bank. This would cover, for example, disclosure to the extent necessary to prosecute legal proceedings initiated by the bank against the customer, and disclosing information by a bank as to its customer's banking affairs in the course of dishonour.

Disclosure to Guarantors

In *Ross v Bank of New South Wales* (1928) 28 SR (NSW) 539, it was held that a guarantor who had mortgaged property to the bank as a collateral security was entitled to be told, and the bank was obliged to disclose, the amount of the account, the rate of interest being charged, and the amount realised on the collateral securities. The following propositions come from the case:

(I)   a guarantor who has mortgaged property by way of collateral security to a bank (ie a third party mortgagor) is not entitled to obtain the same full account that a bank is obliged to give to its customer,

(II)   or demand a copy of the customer's account,

(III) but is entitled to demand information as to the balance then owing, the rate of interest charged and the amount, if any realised by the bank in respect of collateral securities.

If the debt exceeds the amount of the guarantee, then the bank should state that the guarantor is liable for the full amount of the guarantee. However, if the debt is less than the amount of the guarantee, then the bank may inform the guarantor of the actual amount of the debt, including bank charges. The ideal situation would be to hold a meeting between the guarantor, the customer and the banker, where the guarantor in the customer's presence can ask for information on any matters concerning the customer's affairs.

EXCEPTION—DISCLOSURE BY CONSENT, BANKERS' OPINIONS

Concept of 'Consent'

Despite suggestions to the contrary in some Australian texts, it seems fairly clear that in *Tournier*'s case the exception was intended to apply to both express consent and implied consent (see particularly [1924] 1 KB 461 at 473 per Bankes LJ and at 485 per Atkin LJ). In practice, the difficult distinction is usually not between 'express' and 'implied' consent, but rather between (a) 'actual' consent of the customer (whether given by express words or implied from his conduct) and (b) a 'consent' based on no more than the custom of bankers in giving information as to the affairs of their customers and knowledge of that custom.

Legal Basis for Giving a Status Opinion

The issue is whether the practice is so universal, and so notorious, that a totally implied term permitting it forms part of the contract between banker and customer unless the customer had inserted into his contract an express term to the contrary. *Paget* p 177 expresses doubts as to the custom being so widely known, especially among non-trading persons, as to give the bank protection in all cases, notwithstanding the universality of the practice of giving other banks such information.

Weaver and Craigie p 171, suggest that in Australia the practice may be sufficiently notorious to bind all customers. Mr Justice Kitto has referred to 'the multitudinous inquiries of this kind that everyone knows are constantly made of bankers': *Mutual Life and Citizens' Assurance Co Ltd v Evatt* (1968) 122 CLR 556 at 588–589.

In *RH Brown & Co v Bank of New South Wales* [1971] WAR 201 at 207, Virtue SPJ of the Western Australian Supreme Court commented that it was 'a matter of some notoriety that it has long been the practice for banks to perform services of this nature both for their own customers and other banks'. The court referred to a brochure to customers which included a statement that the bank would perform these services for its customers. The case did not turn on this issue and the court made no express finding, although it seems reasonable to assume that it would have found an implied term in the contract between banker and customer had it been necessary to do so. In the appeal to the High Court, apart from recognising that there was a practice among banks of supplying opinions, the High Court expressed no view as to whether the practice had any, or if so what, legal basis: (1972) 46 ALJR 297.

INTERNATIONAL ASPECTS OF DUTY OF CONFIDENCE

Methods for Obtaining Information in Australia for Overseas Proceedings

Australian courts have the usual machinery for taking evidence in civil proceedings on behalf of the courts in other countries. These procedures include the examination of witnesses and the production of documents. Evidence relating to bank accounts and other banking transactions are treated in the same way as any other evidence.

One method to obtain information on an international basis is of course by 'letters of request' or 'letter rogatory'. This involves a request for the provision of the evidence, made by a court in the country which seeks the information, to a court in the place at which the records are maintained. This request approach can enable the requesting court to obtain information without being accused of infringing the sovereignty of the other company. If, instead, the approach of issuing a subpoena is used, this can raise issues of international comity and sovereignty. It gives the bank a difficult choice: defy the subpoena and be at risk of being held in contempt of court in the foreign jurisdiction, or obey it and be at risk of having infringed the duty of confidence applying in the country where the information is maintained.

Foreign Proceedings (Prohibition of Certain Evidence) Act 1976

Questions of whether the foreign tribunal has a right to obtain the evidence can lead to difficulties. The Australian government passed the Foreign Proceedings

(Prohibition of Certain Evidence) Act 1976. Section 5 of the Act empowers the federal Attorney-General to make written orders prohibiting (except with his written consent) the production of documents, or evidence concerning them. Australian citizens or residents can also be prohibited by such an order from giving evidence before a foreign tribunal about documents in Australia.

The Attorney-General may only use these powers when he is satisfied that a foreign tribunal may be acting inconsistently with international law or comity, or where the restrictions are desirable to protect the national interest. In both cases he may act only in matters involving the laws or the executive powers of the commonwealth.

The definition of a 'tribunal' is wide and includes a court or grand jury and any authority, officer, examiner or person having authority to take or receive evidence.

Foreign Proceedings (Excess of Jurisdiction) Act 1984

By this Commonwealth Act, in certain cases the federal Attorney-General can make an order prohibiting the right of a foreign court to call for documents to be produced from Australia or persons within Australia to be called in proceedings involving a foreign court.

This is broad enough to apply to matters within the constitutional power of the federal government and hence could apply to any federal laws concerning banking. However, duty of confidence is a common law, not a Federal statute law, matter.

Circumstances when Australian Court Would Refuse Assistance to Foreign Tribunal

There have been no direct authorities on the point in Australia. There is no reason why the English and Commonwealth cases would not apply to Australia, and these are analysed at pp 17–21.

On the basis of the authorities, therefore, it is possible, even without the intervention of the federal Attorney-General under the Foreign Proceedings (Prohibition of Certain Evidence) Act, for an Australian court to refuse assistance to the foreign tribunal.

In *Re Westinghouse Uranium Contract* [1978] AC 547, the House of Lords held that an attempt by the United States Department of Justice to convert letters rogatory into a request for evidence for purposes of a grand jury investigation was an infringement of United Kingdom sovereignty. The conclusion of the House of Lords in that case suggests that a request from a foreign court, which could expose local subjects to proceedings conducted in the foreign country in respect of acts performed outside that foreign country, would be denied, if an order giving effect to that request would then involve an infringement of a privilege recognised in English law (in that case, the freedom of a person not to incriminate himself). It is therefore likely that other privileges will be equally recognised, such as a bank's duty of confidence. The exception to this duty, compulsion at law, does not seem wide enough to force disclosure required in respect of a local subject or company under foreign law, and see further the later cases discussed below.

The problem of course can arise in two ways. The assistance of an Australian court may be sought, to conclude that the information or documents requested from a foreign tribunal need not be produced. Most of the cases concern this situation. Secondly, in reverse, the Australian court may be asked to consider the validity of a request or requirement to produce documents or information imposed locally on the bank where that order would require production of documents or information in a foreign jurisdiction. This was the situation in *Mackinnon*'s case, discussed below.

Attitude of US Courts

The traditional view in the United States has been that, when a subpoena is served on the office of a foreign bank in the United States, that subpoena can validly require the production of information concerning a customer of the bank from anywhere in the world. However, the views of the US courts have changed from case to case and over time.

The US courts do take into consideration a prohibition imposed by the law in force where the records are maintained. In *Société Internationale Pour Participations Industrielles AET Commerciales SA v Rodgers* 357 US 197 (1958), the United States Supreme Court refused to order a Swiss bank to produce documents, because disclosure of those documents was contrary to Swiss bank law and the bank had not acted in bad faith.

In *Ings v Ferguson* 282 F 2d 149 (1960), the court refused to order New York officers of two Canadian banks to produce records from Canadian branches: the Canadian banks were only witnesses and not parties, and the court observed the laws and both the US and Canada procedures were available for securing evidence by letters rogatory. The judge doubted whether the New York manager could direct Canadian officers to send branch records out of Canada in violation of a statutory provision in Quebec; but the judge emphasised more 'fundamental principles of international comity', holding at 152 that courts 'should not take such action as may cause a violation of the laws of a friendly neighbour or, at the least, an unnecessary circumvention of its procedures'.

This principle should apply to Australia, even though the duty of confidence does not itself involve a statutory breach. The Attorney-General may also make an order under the Foreign Proceedings (Prohibition of Certain Evidence) Act 1976: see above.

In the later case of *United States v First National City Bank* 396 F 2d 897 (1968), the court refused to allow a bank to justify its refusal to disclose documents by reason of German bank secrecy laws. It was held that German law did not impose an absolute prohibition and, further, that the bank had not taken bona fide steps to seek permission to disclose. The bank's customer could have obtained injunctive relief in Germany and, during the US court hearings, the judge adjourned to enable a bank to ascertain whether its customer would seek an injunction. If an injunction had been obtained, a breach of it would have made the bank subject to criminal penalties in Germany. It is clear US law that courts will not make orders which will result in a breach of criminal law in a foreign country.

The modern trend of US law is that the prohibition of disclosure under the foreign law must be absolute before this justifies the US court in refusing to make the order against the bank.

In *SEC v Banca Della Svizzera Italiana* 92 FRD 111 (1981), the US court did not allow the Swiss bank operating in the US to rely on Swiss bank secrecy law to justify its refusal to disclose information required to prosecute some of its customers for insider trading offences.

However, where a bank has made genuine attempts, even if unsuccessful, to seek the permission of local authorities to comply with the foreign order, or where it cannot be accused of seeking to use the foreign secrecy law as a mere shield, an order for a subpoena will be refused: see, for example, *US v Bank of Nova Scotia* 691 F 2d 1384 (1982).

Consequences for Australia

If an Australian bank, in answer to a subpoena addressed to its US agency, supplied evidence relating to a customer's account or other banking arrangements in Australia, the bank could be faced with an action in Australia for breach of contract. It would seem unlikely that the bank could successfully plead compulsion of law as a defence. But if the bank were restrained by injunction in Australia from divulging the information to the United States court, then presumably the latter would withdraw the subpoena on the basis of the dicta in the *First National City Bank* case. It was concluded at p 3 that injunctive relief should be available in Australia in appropriate circumstances.

A common sense approach would be for the US courts to follow the decision in *Ings v Ferguson* and require the party seeking the information to proceed through the Australian courts by letters rogatory.

Impact of Recent Cases in Australia

It is likely that the Australian courts, like the English courts, will not always be sympathetic to attempts by the US courts to obtain information within Australia for a US proceeding. The US orders are often seen as an invasion of local jurisdiction, and the economic interests of the US which are being enforced are seen as different from Australia's. The existence of the Foreign Proceedings (Prohibition of Certain Evidence) Act 1976, referred to above, could be seen as an instance of this.

X AG *case*

In *X AG v A Bank* [1983] 2 All ER 464, an injunction was granted restraining the bank from disclosing its records kept in England, which disclosure was required by a subpoena served on the US bank's head office for production in the US of the London records, in relation to investigations by the US Department of Justice into the crude oil industry, for which the investigators wished to produce before a Federal grand jury documents belonging to the customer. The records related to a customer who did not carry on business in the US and which had accounts with the London branch of the defendant, a US bank.

Mackinnon's *case*

In *Mackinnon v Donaldson Lufkin and Jenrette Securities Corp* [1986] Ch 482, the plaintiff had brought an action against the defendant for international fraud. The plaintiff had obtained in the UK:

(I) an order against the defendant's bank (a US bank with branch offices all over the world, including London), under s 7 of the UK Bankers' Books Evidence Act 1879, requiring the bank to allow the plaintiff to take copies of the bank's books relating to the defendant's account; and

(II) a subpoena requiring the bank to attend by its proper officer to give evidence at the trial and produce documents.

The order and the subpoena were directed to and served on the bank at its London branch. The relevant books and papers relating to the defendant's account were located in the US where the account was maintained. The bank moved to have the order and the subpoena set aside on the grounds that in principle they exceeded the international jurisdiction of the court and infringed the sovereignty of the US. The court acceded to the bank's request and discharged the subpoena and order.

Hong Kong—FDC *case*

In *FDC Co Ltd v Chase Manhattan Bank* (17 October 1984, unreported), the plaintiff, an American firm, maintained an account with the Hong Kong branch of the defendant, an American bank. The American revenue authorities, while investigating the plaintiff's income tax position, demanded information from the defendant's head office in New York about the plaintiff's account in Hong Kong.

The Hong Kong Court of Appeal affirmed the trial court's decision to grant the plaintiff an injunction to enjoin the defendant from complying with this request and stopping it transferring the information to the US. The court held that the bank's duty of confidence was not subject to territorial limits. The defendant, accordingly, was not entitled to divulge information about the plaintiff's account either in the Colony or overseas.

Propositions from these cases

Some of the propositions which arise from these cases, and which would apply to Australia, are as follows.

Which law applies?

It was held in the *X AG* case that as the accounts of the companies were opened and maintained in London, the proper law of the contract was English law, so that the confidentiality of the contract of banker and customer (recognised in English law) applied to the relationship of the members of the group within the bank. London was where the relationship started and where the contract was made, and the circumstances were that the contract must be taken to have had a proper law from its inception. See also *Libyan Arab Foreign Bank v Bankers Trust Co* [1988] Ll LR 259, and *Libyan Arab Foreign Bank v Manufacturers Hanover Trust Co* [1988] 2 Ll LR 494.

Duty of confidence can be a 'public interest' matter

The banker's duty of confidence to a customer is, in an international dispute, a matter of public and not just private interest. Thus, in the *X AG* case, Leggatt J noted at 477 that if the US court order were obeyed, it

'would take effect in London for the production of documents in breach of what might be termed a private interest in the sense that what is directly involved is a contract between banker and customer. But this indubitably is also a matter of public interest, because it raises issue of wider concern than those peculiar to the parties before me.'

That is, in the case of a foreign bank, the courts pay particular attention to the principle of the sovereignty of others, because documents in the custody of a bank concern not only their own business but also that of their customers and they owe their customers a duty of confidence regulated by the law of the country where the documents are kept.

It is clear from the conclusion in the *FDC* case that the Hong Kong Court of Appeal was anxious to protect the secrecy laws governing the interests of the banks in Hong Kong. Huggins VP observed:

'All persons opening accounts with banks in Hong Kong, whether foreign or local banks, are entitled to look to the Hong Kong courts to enforce any obligation of secrecy which, by the law of Hong Kong, is implied by virtue of the relationship of banker and customer.'

In *Libyan Arab Foreign Bank v Bankers Trust Co* [1988] 1 Ll LR 259 at 285–286, the US bank argued that it had not breached a duty of confidence by disclosing information, because it had acted 'pursuant to a higher public duty', quoting the public interest exception recognised in *Tournier*'s case. The disclosure was to the Federal Reserve Board of New York. The court was assuming that the New York law was on this issue the same as English law, and referred to the power in the UK of the Bank of England to obtain information from banks. See, in Australia, the provisions of the Banking Act referred to at p 12 above. The court concluded at 286 that:

'presuming (as I must) that New York law on this point is the same as English law, it seems to me that the Federal Reserve Board, as the central banking system in the United States, may have a public duty to perform in obtaining information from banks. I accept the argument that higher public duty is one of the exceptions to a banker's duty of confidence, and I am prepared to reach a tentative conclusion that the exception applied in this case.'

Foreign court unlikely to resort to contempt proceedings if bank prohibited from disclosing by local court

In the *X AG* case the court, in considering whether, on a balance of convenience, the injunction ought to be vacated or continued, held that the important factors were that the American order would lead to a breach of secrecy, and the fact that the US court would be unlikely to resort to contempt proceedings if the bank was prohibited from making disclosure by a court at the place where the records were maintained. The court also referred at 480 to the exercise by the United States court in London 'of powers which, by English standards, would be regarded as excessive'.

Thus, in the case, expert evidence showed that it is

'highly unlikely that a United States bank or its officers will be held in contempt for conduct in compliance with the order of a British court in the circumstances stated, that is an injunction restraining the transfer or disclosure of records kept in London in respect of a bank account maintained by a non-American corporation at the bank's London branch' (at 473).

Authorities were cited for this proposition, referring to the doctrine of foreign government compulsion, accepted in the US, which depends on a prohibition in one state conflicting with a command in another. It was noted that in the *First National* case, it was held that the defence based on German law was speculative, based on exposure to civil liability or loss of standing in the financial community, and on appeal the distinction was made between the Swiss bank secrecy law, which is a mandatory law backed by criminal sanction, and German law for breach of which there was at most a civil liability.

Therefore, 'the bank, having properly pursued its good faith efforts to relieve itself from the consequences of an injunction in this country, ought not to be held liable for contempt and any proceedings brought to that end in New York' (at 474).

What constitutes 'disclosure'—secrecy

It was argued in the *FDC* case that the transfer of the information by the Hong Kong office to the head office in New York could not be regarded as disclosure, as the data would initially remain available to the defendants alone. Huggins VP conceded that this might be the case if the information were transmitted to the United States office as a matter of routine. But he thought that

'it would be closing your eyes to the reality of the situation to allow the [defendants] to make an internal transfer of information which it would not make in the ordinary course of business when that transfer is designed for no other purpose than to bring the information within the jurisdiction of the foreign court'.

In the *X AG* case, it was held at 471 that disclosure of the documents to the grand jury would constitute or create a breach of the bank's duty,

'not merely in the technical sense of the grand jury itself constituting a third person to whom disclosure of confidential documents would constitute a breach of that confidentiality, but also in the far wider and more material sense that, as it would appear, there is in practice no secrecy in relation to matters entrusted to grand juries'.

Is there an extra-territorial effect? Substance of matter considered

The Court of Appeal in the *FDC* case was not influenced by the fact that the American order was on its face directed to the bank's head office in the United States. The order was 'aimed unashamedly' at information which was within the jurisdiction of the Hong Kong court and, accordingly, had an extra-territorial effect. The court concluded:

'The Hong Kong courts could enjoin the [defendants] against disclosing the information to the United States Government in Hong Kong and I am satisfied that they can restrain a transfer which is nothing more nor less than a device to avoid the enforcement in Hong Kong of the orders of a foreign court.'

Recognition of bank's dilemma

The Court of Appeal in the *FDC* case expressed concern about the difficulty faced by the defendants. If they transferred the information to the US they may be prosecuted in Hong Kong; if they refused to transfer the information, they may be held in contempt in New York. Nonetheless, the court felt obliged to give effect to the laws of Hong Kong. The other cases also have recognised this dilemma.

As Professor Ellinger has argued on a number of occasions, the only solution to this conflict would seem to be an international convention.

Presence within jurisdiction not sufficient

In *Mackinnon*'s case, the court held at 493 that 'It does not follow from the fact that a person is within the jurisdiction and liable to be served with a process that there is no territorial limit to the matters upon which the court may properly apply its own rules or the things it can order such a person to do'. The court rejected the plaintiff's argument that because the bank had registered under the UK Companies Act and obtained recognition as a bank under the Banking Act, the bank had submitted itself to the jurisdiction of the English courts.

Court reluctant to impose obligation on foreigner to disclose documents outside jurisdiction

In *Mackinnon*'s case, the court considered that it is an established principle 'that a state should refrain from demanding obedience to its sovereign authority by foreigners in respect of their conduct outside the jurisdiction'. This is 'a self-imposed limitation upon a state's sovereign authority' (at 494). It is distinct, not only from the enforcement of private right arising out of matters properly within the court's jurisdiction, but also from discovery required by order of the court to be given by ordinary parties to English litigation including foreigners. It is also different from discovery under the Supreme Court Rules in respect of ordinary parties to English litigation who happen to be foreigners, because: 'If you join the game you must play according to the local rules.'

It was held that a subpoena or an order under the 1879 Act did not involve the enforcement of a private right but was an exercise of sovereign authority to assist in the administration of justice. Therefore a court would not, save in exceptional circumstances, impose on a foreigner, and in particular a foreign bank, which is not a party to the proceedings, any requirement to produce documents which were outside the jurisdiction and concerning business which had been transacted outside the jurisdiction.

Therefore, because the effect of the subpoena and the order was to require the bank to produce documents held at the bank's head office in New York, the subpoena and order would take effect in New York and accordingly would be an infringement of the sovereignty of the US.

The court further noted at 494 that the bank's duty of confidence

'is in some countries reinforced by criminal sanctions and sometimes by "blocking statutes" which specifically forbid the bank to provide information for the purpose of foreign legal proceedings. (Compare s 2 of our Protection of Trading Interests Act 1980). If every country where a bank happened to carry on business asserted a right to require that bank to produce documents relating to accounts kept in any other such country, banks would be in the unhappy position of being forced to submit to whichever sovereign was able to apply the greatest pressure.'

While an enforcement of private rights can be made by injunction or specific performance, even though this requires the performance of acts abroad (e g where a foreigner may have agreed by a contract over which the court has jurisdiction to perform acts abroad), 'a subpoena does not involve the enforcement of a private right. It is an exercise of sovereign authority to require citizens and foreigners within the jurisdiction to assist in the administration of justice' (at 494).

It was further held at 498–499 that

'the authorities on *Bankers Trust Co v Shapira* [1980] 3 All ER 353 discovery against a bank are consistent with that seems to me to be correct in principle, namely, that its international jurisdictional limits are the same as those of a subpoena duces tecum or an order under the Bankers' Books Evidence Act 1879'.

Courts reluctant to infringe sovereignty

In the *Mackinnon* case, there were unusual circumstances, in that the corporate customer had ceased to exist and therefore compliance with the order was highly unlikely to involve the bank in any civil liability in New York, and the banks had already complied with similar orders in the case. However, the court held at 499 that 'it would be wrong to undertake a process of weighing the interests of this country in the administration of justice and the interests before its courts against those of the United States.' Again, it was stated at 499 that

'it is likewise inappropriate to decide the matter on a balance of convenience between the plaintiff and the bank. It seems to me that in a case like this, where alternative legitimate procedures are available, an infringement of sovereignty can seldom be justified except perhaps on the grounds of urgent necessity relied on by Templeman J in *London and County Securities v Caplan* (26 May 1978, unreported).'

Data Protection Legislation

In Europe, data protection laws keep in check applications of technology and exist in the laws of members of the Council of Europe who are signatories to and have ratified its Convention for Protection of Individuals with regard to the automatic proceeding of personal data.

The laws generally relate to automatic processing of information and restrict the collection, use and transfer of personal data, that is, data relating to natural persons.

The Council of Europe Convention urges nations not to obstruct transborder data flow unless the domestic legislation of another nation does not provide equivalent privacy protection. Countries with data protection laws permit transfers of personal data amongst countries with similar data protection legislation but prohibit the transfer to non-data protection countries.

The US Right to Financial Privacy Act 1978 only deals with the provision of access to the financial records of any customer of a financial institution to a federal authority and does not in any way come close to the European Convention.

If a bank has a global data base capable of access by the branch bank in the US, there will be no need to resort to letters rogatory or a subpoena on the head office of the bank in another country if the information in question is contained in that data base. A US court will be able to require the branch bank to produce such information as the branch bank is able to call up on its terminal. This still leaves the foreign bank in a conflicting position—should it obey the US order, or observe its duty of secrecy; yet the customer is jeopardised to the extent that it would probably find it difficult to obtain an injunction restraining the release of information by the branch bank in the US.

INSIDER TRADING

Control of Insider Trading in Australia

Insider trading involves the dealing in a company's shares by a person who is in possession of price-sensitive information which is not generally available. In Australia, the practice is regulated in all states and territories. The primary regulatory control is contained in ss 128–130 of the Securities Industry Code, which is legislation which exists in all states and territories in relatively uniform terms.

There has been some discussion of the significance of insider trading in the context of bank and merchant banking activities: see A Black 'Policies in the Regulation of Insider Trading and the Scope of Section 128 of the Securities Industry Code' (1988) 16 MULR 633 at 658. The issue of insider trading has particular impact upon banks or merchant banks having multiple functions, even if those functions are divided across several divisions. Clearly, a bank or merchant bank in dealing with a corporate client may obtain information which could be material to the making of investment decisions as to the client's shares. At the least, such information may be likely to affect the trading decisions of the reasonable investor.

It appears, however, that the prohibition upon insider trading in s 128 of the Securities Industry Code only applies to information which is material in the stronger sense of being likely to affect the price at which the shares are traded on the market. A bank placed in a situation of conflict of interest will have to take into account the statutory prohibition upon communicating price sensitive information to other persons contained in s 128(5) of the Securities Industry Code, a duty of confidence owed to the client from which information was received, and the duty owed to any client of the bank who is relying upon the bank for investment advice.

The operation of the doctrine of agency involves further difficulties, since it is possible that inside information possessed by one employee of a bank or merchant bank will be attributed to the bank, with the result that s 128 would be contravened if another employee of the bank engaged in investment advising in areas where such inside information was material.

Australian Common Law

The traditional statement of the common law, in *Percival v Wright* [1902] 1 Ch 421, has been subject to a good deal of criticism. However, it was followed by the Victoria Supreme Court in *Esplanade Holdings Pty Ltd v Divine Holdings Pty Ltd* (1980) 4 ACLR 826, where it was affirmed that the relationship between a company's directors and the company's members as individuals is not fiduciary in its character, and that therefore there is no duty of disclosure.

It is not clear from the report of the *Esplanade* case whether the decision of the New Zealand Court of Appeal in *Coleman v Myers* [1977] 2 NZLR 225 was discussed. In the New Zealand case, it was held that a director of a small family company, whose shareholders looked to the directors for guidance, did owe a duty to those shareholders. The court decided that while *Percival v Wright* may have been correct on its facts, there could be no general rule that a director never owes a fiduciary duty to an individual shareholder.

If *Coleman v Myers* is to be reconciled with *Percival v Wright*, the reconciliation lies in the special circumstances of the New Zealand case, where it was clear that the shareholders relied upon the advice of the directors. This can require a director to have regard to the position of an individual shareholder, and so give rise to a duty not to take advantage of inside information. In a similar situation, in *Allen v Hyatt* (1914) 30 TLR 444, where the directors of a company held themselves out as acting as the agents of the shareholders in the disposal of shares, it was again held that a duty of disclosure did exist.

The common law situation still governs a face to face dealing, where it is always up to the parties themselves to protect themselves by contractual remedies. The statutory provision under s 128 of the Securities Industries Code, discussed at pp 23–28, is not really directed at correcting a face to face dealing. Rather, it only acts in a market situation. Directors may be subject to further duties of disclosure on the issue of a 'Part B statement' in the context of a corporate takeover.

Prohibition on Employee or Officer Disclosing Information—Companies Codes

Section 229(3) of the uniform Companies Codes is directed to ensuring performance by an officer or employee of a corporation of his duty to the corporation in respect of information obtained by virtue of his position. Thus if, by virtue of his position, an officer or employee of a bank acquires inside information, he is prohibited from making 'improper use' of that information to gain an advantage for himself or for another or to cause detriment to the bank. There are two main elements to the offence:

(I) the information must be acquired by virtue of the employee's position; and
(II) the employee must make 'improper' use of the information.

Clearly, use of information derived by a person's role as officer of a company would be improper where that person used it for trade in securities in breach of a duty of confidence owed to the company, or in breach of an express term of his employment contract which prohibited trading upon information obtained from the company.

Regulation of Insider Trading—s 128 of Securities Industry Code

Section 128 of the Securities Industry Code is the most significant and comprehensive regulation of insider trading. It is re-enacted in the new

Corporations legislation, which is the proposed new statute for the companies and the securities market: that legislation is presently the subject of much debate within Australia, and it raises difficult issues of state/federal relations.

Types of insider trading prohibited

The section is primarily directed at persons who are or, at any time in the preceding six months, have been 'connected with' a company. The phrase 'connected with' is widely defined in s 128(8). A person is connected with a company if:

(I)   he is an officer or substantial shareholder of the company or of a related company; or

(II)   he occupies a position that may reasonably be expected to give him access to inside information by virtue of any professional or business relationship with the company or a related company; or

(III)   he is an officer of a substantial shareholder.

A substantial shareholder is a person or company entitled to not less than 10% of the voting shares of a listed company: ss 136(1) and 136(9) of the Companies Codes.

Such an insider is prohibited from doing four things:

(I)   If, by reason of his connection with a company, the insider is in possession of inside information relating to that company, he is prohibited from dealing in that company's securities: s 128(1). This prohibition is aimed at preventing a person from trading in the securities of his own company if, because of his connection with that company, he has inside information. The information must be obtained 'by reason of' the connection with the company.

(II)   If by reason of his connection with one company, the insider is in possession of inside information which relates to any transaction involving that company and another company, the insider is prohibited from dealing in any securities of that other company: s 128(2). This prohibition is aimed at preventing a person from trading in the securities of another company if, because of his connection with his own company, he has information regarding a transaction between his own company and the other company. The situation may involve knowledge of a contract between the two companies or of a proposed take-over or of a merger, for example.

(III)   The insider is, where he would himself be precluded from dealing in any securities, also prohibited from causing or procuring anyone else to deal in those securities: s 128(4). This section is designed to prevent insiders from avoiding an insider trading prosecution by instructing someone else to buy securities.

(IV)   The insider is also prohibited from communicating any inside information to anyone whom he knows, or ought reasonably to know, will make use of the information: s 128(5). This applies only if the securities are listed on a stock market, by reason of s 128(5)(a). It seems designed to prevent 'loose talk', by establishing a de facto duty of care on the insider not to disclose inside information to people who are likely to use it. It also covers a situation where an insider communicates information to someone expecting that person to use the information where the situation would not be caught by the previous 'cause or procure' prohibition.

'Tipping'

Section 128 does not apply only to insiders. A person who has inside information but who has no connection with any relevant company will still be precluded from using the information if:

(I)   he obtained the information from someone who was prohibited from using it (s 128(3)(a)); and

(II)   he knew or ought reasonably to have known that person was so prohibited (s 128(3)(a)); and

(III)   he was associated with or had some arrangement with that person (s 128(3)(b)).

Such a person is frequently referred to as a 'tippee'.

The aim of this prohibition is exactly the same as that of the prohibitions on 'causing or procuring' and on 'loose talk'. The difference is that the problem is tackled from the side of the tippee (that is, the person receiving the information) rather than from the side of the insider (that is, the person giving the information). There must be some arrangement or association between the insider and the tippee before the prohibition will operate. Section 128(3)(b) refers to an arrangement 'for the communication of [inside] information . . . with a view to dealing in securities'. Thus, the arrangement between an insider and a tippee must be of a particular type. Section 6 of the Securities Industry Code refers to certain types of association for the purposes of determining the nature of the association required under s 128(3). The difficulties of proving an association or arrangement still remain.

There is also a prohibition on a tippee causing or procuring another to deal in the relevant securities, and (if the securities are listed) from communicating his information to anyone he knows or ought reasonably to know will make use of the information. Sub-tipping is also regulated from the side of the sub-tippee (that is, the person who receives the inside information). A sub-tippee may not trade in securities if he knows or ought reasonably to know that the original source of the inside information was an insider. This prohibition applies all the way down the tipping chain.

Prohibition on corporation dealing in securities

Where a corporation has an officer who is an insider or a tippee, then that corporation may not deal in any securities to which the inside information relates. Thus, s 128(6) provides that, subject to s 128(7) and (7A), a body corporate shall not deal in any securities at a time when any officer of that body corporate is precluded by s 128(1), (2) or (3) from dealing in those securities.

Certain defences are available to corporations in certain situations. These are dealt with in s 128(7), which establishes a Chinese Wall defence (see p 28), and s 128(7A), concerning takeovers.

Section 128(7A) exempts a company from the prohibition upon dealing in securities in another company under s 128(6) where the company would be within that prohibition only because an officer of the company possesses information which was obtained in performing his duties as an officer of the company, and the information relates only to proposed dealings by the company in securities of the other company.

Section 128(7A) avoids the unintended consequence of s 128(6) that a company making a takeover bid might, in the absence of s 128(7A), have been prohibited from trading in the shares of the target company because an officer of the bidder was possessed of information that the bid was under consideration. Such information is almost certainly material price-sensitive information for the purposes of s 128.

The result of s 128(7A) is that in such circumstances, the officer would be prohibited from trading on his own behalf in the shares of the target company, but the potential bidder company would be entitled to trade in those shares prior to making its takeover bid.

Types of 'information' to which insider trading legislation applies

Section 128 refers to information which is not generally available, and which would be likely materially to affect the price of particular securities if it was generally available. Such information could, in shorthand form, be termed price-sensitive, non-public information. However, beyond these requirements, it is not completely clear what 'information' is. In *Ryan v Triguboff* [1976] 1 NSWLR 588, the New South Wales Supreme Court was dealing with the now repealed s 75A of the New South Wales Securities Industry Act, which referred to 'specific information'. The court held that the words 'specific information' could not be attracted to a situation in which the defendant had by way of a 'generalised deduction' from other facts effected a sale of securities at a higher price. Lee J considered that 'the specific information' must be capable of being pointed to and identified, and must be capable of being expressed unequivocally.

Section 128 refers to 'information', rather than 'specific information'. In *CAC v Green* [1978] VR 505, 'information' was held not to be restricted to factual knowledge of a concrete kind, but to extend to information obtained by means of a hint or a veiled suggestion.

If a person creates a piece of knowledge, by research or deduction from publicly available facts or by planning some course of action in the future, for example a take-over, then that knowledge would normally be considered to amount to 'information', in the sense that the concept is understood, for example, in the law of breach of confidence. The reason that a person who has undertaken research may act on that research without breaching s 128 is that, in most circumstances, that information has not been obtained by reason of the person being connected with the body corporate. It therefore falls outside the scope of the prohibition in s 128(1). Where the person came into possession of the results of that research because of his connection with the company, then s 128(1) would usually prohibit that person from dealing in securities, although the information had not been obtained directly from the company.

The reason that a person planning a take-over may buy shares before announcing the bid is that s 128(7A) was inserted to allow a take-over bidder to do so. The doubt that existed prior to the insertion of s 128(7A) as to whether a takeover bidder might have been prohibited by operation of s 128 from purchasing shares prior to making the bid itself suggests that knowledge of a course of action for the future is information, and that in the absence of s 128(7A) this knowledge when possessed by an officer of the bidder could have the result that the bidder was prohibited from trading.

There is a further requirement: to be classified as 'inside' information, the information must be non-public.

There is also a materiality requirement. Information must be 'likely materially to affect the price' of the relevant securities. The test is an objective one, being for a court to deal with in each particular case. The difficulty, with regard to the materiality requirement, lies in its proof, rather than its definition.

Types of 'dealing' prohibited

The prohibitions of s 128 all involve 'dealing in securities'. The term 'dealing' is widely defined, in s 4(1), to include 'acquiring, disposing of, subscribing for or underwriting securities', as well as making or offering to make an agreement for the purpose of securing a profit by acquiring, disposing of, subscribing for or underwriting securities.

However, in *Hooker Investments* (1986) 10 ACLR 524, it was held by McHugh JA that s 128 is 'directed to people who are trading in the market place and is not directed to an underwriting agreement to subscribe for shares proposed to be issued'. Obiter in the *Hooker Investments* case suggests, further, that s 128 is concerned with securities which are already issued, and therefore that the section does not regulate the issue of securities.

The *Hooker Investments* case is also authority for the proposition that the possession of inside information relevant to one or more securities of a company does not preclude dealing in other securities of that company. It is limited to dealing in 'those securities' in respect of which the information 'would be likely materially to affect the price'.

Defences

There are several defences available to those charged under s 128. It is a defence if the insider can show that the other party to the deal knew (or ought reasonably to have known) about the inside information. Thus, dealing between two insiders is permitted. Therefore two insiders may trade with one another on inside information, to mutual advantage. As both parties know of the inside advantage, it would appear they will strike an arm's length deal. Therefore the defence would appear fair. See also p 28.

Penalties

Sections 129 and 130 make provision for penalties to be imposed on those who breach s 128. Section 129 concerns criminal penalties. An insider or a tippee is liable to a penalty of $20,000 or five years' imprisonment or both, and a body corporate which contravenes s 128 is liable to a penalty of $50,000.

In addition to these criminal penalties, provision is also made for civil restitution by s 130. An insider or tippee is liable to compensate any other party to the transaction for any loss they sustained. This loss is calculated with reference to the difference between the level at which the shares were traded and the level at which they would have been likely to trade if the relevant information had been generally available. An insider or tippee is also liable to account to the company in whose shares he dealt for any profit made as a result of the dealing. Double penalties may thus be payable by the insider.

Enforcement

In Australia, as in the United States, Japan and England, authorities are becoming much more willing to pursue insider trading prosecutions. The regulatory body in each Australian jurisdiction is taking a more pro-active role in this area, organising random audits of market trading, for example. In Australia, a number of persons have been charged with alleged insider trading offences.

The main step taken has been to focus on arrangements between brokers which are members of the Australian Stock Exchanges. In particular, following the deregulation of brokerage rates and the admission of corporate members to the

Stock Exchange, exchanges have amended their business rules to include rules relating to conflict situations in their member organisations. Amendments to the business rules were allowed which provided for formalised procedures to be adopted by member organisations to deal with conflicts. The Commission monitors the situation through requests for reports from Stock Exchanges on their monitoring of conflict situations from their member organisations.

CHINESE WALLS

Statutory Defences to Insider Trading Charge

Section 128 of the Securities Industry Code is discussed at pp 23–27 above.

Section 128(7)

A 'Chinese Wall' partial defence is provided in s 128(7). Section 128(7) provides that a body corporate is not precluded by s 128(6) from entering into a transaction at any time by reason only of information in the possession of an officer of that body corporate if:

(I)   the decision to enter into the transaction was taken on its behalf by a person other than the officer;

(II)   it had in operation at that time arrangements to ensure that the information was not communicated to that person and that no advice with respect to the transaction was given to him by a person in possession of the information; and

(III)   the information was not so communicated and such advice was not so given.

The stronger a bank's or merchant bank's compliance systems, the more likely that the Chinese Wall will be effective as a defence to liability under s 128. 'Cracks' in the Chinese Wall might arise, for example, from executive staff common to more than one department, or from informal dealings between staff or separate departments.

The onus of proving the existence of a Chinese Wall is on the person seeking to rely upon it as a 'defence' to an allegation of insider trading. That is not clear from s 128(7), but the New South Wales Court of Appeal accepted that this was the position in *Hooker Investments Pty Ltd v Baring Bros Halkerston & Partners Securities Ltd* (1986) 10 ACLR 524.

Thus the defence depends upon there being in operation at the relevant time 'arrangements' to ensure that the information is not communicated. The Chinese Wall defence in s 128(7) is not available to unincorporated bodies.

Chinese Walls in Banks and Financial Advisers

It is not uncommon that a bank or merchant bank or other financial adviser will offer advice to investment clients. This may be a source of difficulty where such advice is offered by the same corporate entity that possesses information within the scope of s 128, even if a Chinese Wall has been established, if the information possessed by an employee on one side of the Chinese Wall is attributed to the company under agency principles.

In these circumstances, it might be said that the bank or other financial institution is under a duty to its client to use all information in its possession in offering investment advice. It might be said that such a duty extends to using any information in the possession of the bank, and that the client should not be prejudiced by the internal arrangements made by the bank. *Black*, p 661 argues that the response to this argument is that even the widest view of a bank's or merchant bank's duty to its investment clients cannot require that the bank or merchant bank breach its obligations under s 128 of the Securities Industry Code, and that therefore there is no breach of the bank's or merchant bank's duty to its client in not revealing inside information.

There appears to be a strong argument that the fiduciary duty owed by a bank or merchant bank to its clients is restricted so that it does not require disclosure of information which is attributed to the company because it is in the possession of one department, where a Chinese Wall prevents disclosure of that information to the department offering investment advice, if the bank or merchant bank has previously advised its clients of the fact that it has a Chinese Wall in place. In principle, it is open to a fiduciary and the beneficiary of a fiduciary duty to restrict the scope of the fiduciary duty obligation by express agreement or by conduct: *Birtchnell v Equity Trustees, Executors and Agency Ltd* (1929) 42 CLR 384 per Dixon J at 408; *New Zealand Netherlands Society v Kuys* [1973] 2 All ER 1222 per Lord Wilberforce at 1225–1226.

That outcome is perhaps less attractive where a bank or merchant bank deals with an unsophisticated investor rather than with a professional or institutional investor. It may be doubted, however, that even the average public investor (to the extent that he or she still exists in the Australian securities markets, given the shift from direct private investment in the stock markets to investment by means of intermediaries) may reasonably expect that a bank or merchant bank, which is known to the investor to perform a number of functions, will use information obtained by one division in performing one function for the purpose of making recommendations by another division where such a use would amount to a contravention of the Securities Industry Code.

The issue of the financial adviser's duties to his client takes on further complexity in Australian law, since s 65A of the Securities Industry Code requires that an investment adviser has, having regard to his knowledge of his client's situation, 'given such consideration to, and conducted such investigation of, the subject matter of the recommendation as is reasonable in all the circumstances'. Again, the better view seems to be that an adviser does not lack a reasonable basis for an investment recommendation merely because a Chinese Wall has prevented certain information coming to his knowledge. In that situation, and assuming that the adviser has properly reviewed the publicly available information, the adviser has no less reasonable a basis for his investment recommendation than would any other adviser who was not possessed of inside information by virtue of a connection with a particular client.

There should be no argument with the proposition that Chinese Walls ought to be accepted as a matter of policy as a reasonable solution to the conflicts facing banks and merchant banks with multiple functions. There can be little doubt that any other result would impose substantial economic costs in requiring divestment of functions by such bodies: *Black*, p 661. However, given the risk of conflict of interest and the possibility of breach of s 128 which arise where banking functions on the one hand and investment advising functions on the other are conducted within a single corporate entity, the separation of corporate functions by shifting financing and investment advisory functions to discrete subsidiaries has substantial attractions. This is particularly the case since, within a single corporate entity, the avoidance of conflicts of interest and of contravention of s 128 will depend upon not merely the existence of a Chinese Wall but upon the continued effective functioning of that Chinese Wall in practice. *Black*, p 662 recognises that:

'Short of divestment, the structure which most fully reduces the risk of failure of the Chinese Wall to prevent the flow of information in a particular case is the separation of corporate and investment advisory functions by shifting one or the other to a discrete subsidiary. If the parent and the subsidiary—at the cost of a loss of synergistic effect— conduct separate operations, then there will be little risk of the possession of inside information from corporate clients impacting upon investment advising functions, or of conflicting duties to corporate and investment clients.'

It remains that the loss of synergistic effect may be a matter that is of substantial concern for a bank or other financial institution, particularly to a smaller merchant bank which is conducting its business in a competitive Australian market and wishes to obtain the maximum advantage from the interaction between its various divisions. In that case, the appropriate commercial choice may be to rely upon the effective functioning of a Chinese Wall so as to preserve the opportunity for cross-fertilisation of divisions in circumstances where no conflict of interest and no breach of s 128 arises.

Defence Under s 128(9)

A further defence to liability for contravention of s 128 is available under s 128(9) of the Securities Industry Code to a licensed dealer in securities where a dealing is in relation to securities listed on the Australian Stock Exchange; the dealing is entered by the dealer under a specific instruction by the client to effect the transaction; the dealer has not given advice to the client in relation to dealing in securities of that class; and the dealer and the client are not associated. It is significant that s 128(9) allows an exemption from the prohibition under s 128 without requiring that a Chinese Wall exists so as to prevent inside information possessed by the broking firm being communicated to the broker who executes the trade: *Black*, pp 659–660.

The defence available under s 128(9) adopts a different approach from that adopted in the United States. Under US law, it appears that a broker would only avoid liability under r 10b–5 where the broker both abstained from advising the client and established a Chinese Wall. This reflects the reluctance of the US courts to accept that a broker which has chosen to place itself in a situation of potential conflict may avoid that conflict while continuing to trade in securities as to which the broker possesses inside information.

Even where s 128(9) does not require a broker to cease to advise its clients where a Chinese Wall is in fact in place, a broker may still choose to establish a 'stop list' procedure in order to avoid 'the difficult situation arising where a broker recommends a purchase of shares on the basis of publicly available information while another division of the firm possesses inside information indicating that the recommendation is ill-advised': *Black*, pp 659–660.

The exemption available to the holder of a dealer's licence under s 128(9) does not assist a dealer which has in fact offered advice to its client, or the holder of an investment adviser's licence under s 45 of the Securities Industry Code. Nor is the operation of s 128(9) without effects upon the market. The fact that a particular dealer ceases to advise its clients as to shares in which it possesses inside information may itself have a significant signalling effect, and be interpreted by observers of the market in the context of existing market knowledge. That signalling effect may also occur where a dealer broker adopts a 'stop list' procedure.

Existence of Chinese Wall in Australia

An exhaustive study in Australia analysed the forms and extent of Chinese Walls, particularly amongst the merchant banks, brokers and solicitors in Australia: Tomasic and Pentony, 'Insider Trader in Australia–Regulation and Law Enforcement' (1988) 71–83. There was an amazing range in the extent to which Chinese Walls are utilised, and in the forms of Chinese Walls. The authors concluded at 83 as follows:

'Whilst it was acknowledged that Chinese Walls may be relatively easy to set up "they are difficult to police". One reason for this lack of confidence in this type of "procedural architecture" is that "the securities industry is very gossipy". The most telling response was provided by another regulator who observed that "Chinese Walls don't exist! I went to see one and couldn't find it".'

The practical difficulties in building effective Chinese Walls were succinctly put by the London panel in 1987, when, in a matter involving a buy out transaction and J Henry Schroder Wagg & Co Ltd, Molins, and Tozer Kemsley & Millbourn (Holdings) plc, the panel did not issue a formal warning but made the following comments about Chinese Walls:

'So the Panel considers that it is inappropriate for a corporate finance organisation or other adviser to seek to resolve problems of conflict of interest simply by isolating information internally.

Confidential documents and other information are supplied to the organisation acting as a corporate finance house and not just to individuals within that organisation. The organisation should respect that confidence by, if necessary, declining to act rather than by the alternative route of adopting internal measures to keep information separate. In any event, there will, in addition to documents, often be informal, internal discussion of situations which may lead to the dissemination of information within an organisation. This emphasises that potential problems cannot be guaranteed to be resolved by the simple isolation of documents or by the assignment of different personnel to act against the party who had previously supplied the information.'

The problem is accentuated in the banking sphere with the increasing use of electronic information. Mere physical separation is not really enough. An essential aspect of the Chinese Wall is access codes and fail-safe systems within a computer.

While Australian courts have not yet grappled in detail with the attribution of knowledge between directors of a corporation, the views of Goodman AJ in *Standard Investments Ltd v The Canadian Imperial Bank of Commerce* 52 OR 473 are important:

'It is my opinion that as a matter of law a corporation may have more than one directing mind operating within the same field of operations but I am of the further view that where such a state of affairs exists a corporation cannot be found in law to have a split personality so that it can rely on the lack of knowledge on the part of one of its directing minds of the acts, intention and knowledge of the other directing mind operating in the same sphere to protect it from the liability for the actions of the first directing mind or the combined activities of both directing minds. At least in civil cases where the element of mens rea is not applicable when there are two or more directing minds operating within the same field assigned to both of them, the knowledge, intention and acts of each become together the total knowledge, intention and acts of the corporation which they represent.'

Notwithstanding s 128(7), it is likely that an Australian court would take a similar approach. This does not, of course, necessarily mean that the bank or the officer would in that situation be guilty of insider trading. The comments by *Black* set out at p 30 are relevant here, and can apply to a bank when acting as a financial intermediary.

2 Austria

Michael Kutschera

BANKER'S DUTY OF CONFIDENTIALITY

Introduction

Austrian law expressly recognises and protects the banks' duty of confidentiality with respect to information received by or relating to its customers. Such duty is primarily governed by ss 23, 23a, 34, and 35a of the Credit System Act ('KWG'). These provisions are supplemented by several provisions of a procedural nature, in particular by the Revenues Penal Code ('FinStrG'). In addition, the Data Protection Act (the provisions of which are not dealt with here) may restrict, among others, the disclosure of data collected by banks.

Sections 23 and 34 of the KWG came into force in early 1979, s 23a was added and s 23 of the KWG amended as of 1 January 1987. Finally, s 35a, a provision of constitutional law, was enacted in July 1988. It has afforded special protection to the provisions of s 23 of the KWG. An amendment of s 23 requires a quorum of at least 50% and a majority of two-thirds of the deputies to the National Counsel (Nationalrat, the more powerful of Austria's two houses of parliament).

During the past ten years, since the codification of the banks' duty of confidentiality in the form of KWG, s 23 (sometimes referred to as 'Bank Secrecy'), a substantial number of legal treatises have been published which, in view of the few cases decided by the courts, are quite controversial on several significant issues. Thus the Austrian law on Bank Secrecy is far from being settled in general.

The Austrian provisions on the banks' duty of confidentiality are of additional significance as Austrian law and banking practice permits the establishment of anonymous accounts in certain cases. In order to avoid the abuse of the Austrian banking system (in particular the possibility of opening and maintaining anonymous accounts) for the purpose of money laundering in connection with criminal offences (primarily illegal drug dealing), the Austrian banks have agreed on the wording of a uniform declaration dated 8 June 1989. By issuing such a declaration, each bank will voluntarily undertake a number of duties to prevent such abuse. The declaration, which is currently in the process of being executed, expands an earlier undertaking of the Austrian banks incurred in 1987 and contains the following main provisions:

(I)   The banks will request disclosure of the identity of owners of bank vaults and continue to request such disclosure for the owners of accounts which serve for money transfer and payment transactions.

(II) The banks will request disclosure of and ascertain beyond doubt the identity and address of any person delivering to them US$ bills in amounts exceeding $50,000. Such person will further be informed that the conversion into account credits of US$ bills in an amount exceeding $5,000 is subject to disclosure requirements under US law and that the Austrian bank in question will disclose the identity of such person in case it receives a request for disclosure from the US collector of the bills.

(III)   The banks will refrain from trading in US$ bills in amounts exceeding $50,000 at the Vienna Stock Exchange.

(IV)   The banks will refrain from or discontinue their doing business with clients if there is a founded suspicion that the origin of moneys involved may be improper.

THE BANK'S DUTY OF CONFIDENCE

Section 23(1) of the KWG reads:

'The banks, their shareholders, organ members, employees, as well as persons otherwise becoming active for the banks, are prohibited from disclosing or exploiting secrets which were entrusted to, or to which access was made available for, them on the basis of the business relationship with clients or on the basis of s 16(2)[1] hereof exclusively (Bank Secrecy). If, in the conduct of their official activities, organs of public authorities or of the Austrian National Bank, receive information which is subject to the Bank Secrecy, they shall maintain the Bank Secrecy as official secret from which they may be released only in one of the cases set forth in s 23(2). The duty of confidentiality applies without limit as to time.'

The views are split on whether the provisions contained in s 23 KWG belong to the fields of private or public administrative law.[2] The expressly stipulated confidentiality obligation on the part of public authorities which gain access to information which is subject to Bank Secrecy, or the supervision of the banks' compliance with the provisions on Bank Secrecy within the frame of the general supervision of banks exercised by the bank regulatory authorities, certainly constitute elements of public administrative law. On the other hand, s 23 KWG also defines the scope of a duty of private law which forms part of every contractual relationship between a bank and its customers. The views are likewise split on whether or not the duties imposed by the statutory Bank Secrecy can be contracted away in whole or in part.[3] If so, such contractual modification cannot expand the scope of the banks' duty to confidentiality in respect of courts and other public authorities. Finally, KWG, s 34 subjects certain breaches of the duty of confidentiality pursuant to KWG s 23, to criminal punishment.

The elements contained in the above s 23(1) of the KWG which are not self-explanatory or the meaning of which is in dispute can be described as follows:

(I)   KWG, s 1(1) defines as a 'bank' whoever is authorised to conduct banking transactions on the basis of the KWG or any other provision of federal law. The views are split on whether the Bank Secrecy also applies to

---

1 Section 16 of the KWG provides that banks have to give certain data on large borrowings to the Austrian National Bank, which collects them and has to pass them on to other banks and to contract insurance businesses upon request. KWG, s 23 applies also to contract insurance businesses in respect of KWG, s 16(2).

2 See Arnold, 'Das Bankgeheimnis', ZGV Service 1/1981, p 20 (following 'Arnold, Bankgeheimnis'); Avancini-Iro-Koziol, Österreichisches Bankvertragsrecht I (1987) p 103 ff (following 'Avancini-Iro-Kozio'); Frotz, 'Die Bankauskunft nach österreichischem Recht' in Hadding-Schneider (Hrsg), *Bankgeheimnis und Bankauskunft in der Bundesrepublik Deutschland und in ausländischen Rechtsordnungen* (1986) p 257 (following 'Frotz'); Jabornegg-Strasser-Floretta, Das Bankgeheimnis, p 31 ff (following 'Jabornegg-Strasser-Floretta'); Laurer 'Das Bankgeheimnis in der Entwicklung von Lehre und Rechtsprechung' (1986) ÖJZ p 385, (following 'Laurer, Bankgeheimnis').

3 See Arnold 'Bankgeheimnis' 20; Arnold 'Zum Bankgeheimnis, Anmerkungen zu einer kontroversiell diskutierten Rechtsthematik—zugleich eine Buchbesprechung' (1986) ÖBA 359 at 360 (following 'Arnold, Zum Bankgeheimnis'); Avancini-Iro-Koziol p 104; for a mandatory nature: Jabornegg-Strasser-Floretta p 34 ff.

institutions which conduct banking transactions without authorisation, i e which have not received the necessary concession.[4] The Austrian National Bank is not subject to the Bank Secrecy provisions of the KWG but to its own provisions. Building and loan associations are also not subject to the KWG provisions on Bank Secrecy with respect to those banking transactions which are characteristic for them (KWG, s 2(2)1).

(II)   It is the prevailing view that the term 'shareholders' as used in s 23 of the KWG means indeed all shareholders of a bank, including shareholders of banks which are publicly traded.[5] 'Organ members' are the holders of offices which are provided for in the applicable corporate law. A trustee in bankruptcy is deemed an organ member of the bank.

'Persons otherwise becoming active for the banks' are physical and other persons which are not integrated into the banks' internal organisation, including their outside counsel but also other banks employed for the accomplishment of banking transactions.[6]

Physical persons may be simultaneously shareholders, organ members, employees of or persons otherwise becoming active for the same bank.

(III)   'Secrets' are facts which are known to a limited group of persons only and to which other interested persons cannot gain access at all or can gain access with difficulty only. Further, an objective interest to keep the facts in question secret is required but regularly presumed on the part of the clients.[7]

(IV)   'Clients' are persons that deal with the banks in the context of banking transactions. It is not necessary that such transactions actually close. If a bank gains access to a secret relating to a client in a manner other than through the business relationship, there is no duty of confidentiality upon the bank pursuant to the Bank Secrecy (exception: KWG, s 16(2), see footnote 1 above). Not clients, and therefore not directly entitled to Bank Secrecy, are third parties with respect to which the banks receive confidential information from clients. The banks are nevertheless obliged towards their clients not to disclose secrets relating to third parties which they learn from clients.[8]

A special issue is whether or not only secrets relating to those transactions defined as banking transactions in s 1 of the KWG may be the subject of the Bank Secrecy, because the renting of bank vaults and trading in coins, medals and bullion are not defined as banking transactions. Contrary to a decree issued by the Federal Minister of Finances, it is the general consensus that secrets relating to such transactions should be treated as bank secrets as well.[9]

---

4   Avancini-Iro-Koziol p 106; Jabornegg-Strasser-Floretta p 55; for banks with concession only: Arnold 'Bankgeheimnis' p 4; Frotz p 257.

5   Arnold 'Bankgeheimnis' p 5; Avancini-Iro-Koziol p 108; Jabornegg-Strasser-Floretta p 56 ff; Kastner 'Kreditwesengesetz und Gesellschaftsrecht' (1980) JBl 62 at 70.

6   Avancini-Iro-Koziol p 110 ff; Jabornegg-Strasser-Floretta p 65 ff.

7   Arnold 'Bankgeheimnis' p 7; Burgstaller 'Der strafrechtliche Schutz wirtschaftlicher Geheimnisse' in Ruppe (Hrsg.) *Geheimnisschutz im Wirtschaftsleben* (1980) 5 at 13; Frotz p 237; Jabornegg-Strasser-Floretta p 37.

8   Arnold 'Bankgeheimnis' p 8; Avancini-Iro-Koziol p 114 ff; Haushofer-Schinnerer-Ulrich 'Die österreichischen Kreditwesengesetze s 23/16 (following: 'Haushofer-Schinnerer-Ulrich'); Jabornegg-Strasser-Floretta p 40 ff.

9   Erlaß Zl FS-130/1-III/9/79; Arnold 'Bankgeheimnis' p 8; Frotz p 239; Jabornegg-Strasser-Floretta p 46.

(V)   'Disclosing' a bank secret generally means making it known (or allowing it to become known by refraining from taking reasonable action to prevent disclosure) to somebody who did not know it before. There is quite a dispute on the scope of those persons to whom bank secrets may be disclosed on the ground that such persons would also be subject to the Bank Secrecy with respect to the relevant information (eg other bank employees etc). One view holds that a bank secret shall only be disclosed to those others within the same organisation (bank) for whom a reasonable ground exists to learn about the secret in question, such ground depending on the relevant internal organisation.[10] There is also the opposite view which advocates that bank secrets may be freely passed on within the same organisation (bank).[11]

(VI)   'Exploiting' a bank secret is generally interpreted as an economic exploitation of a bank secret to the detriment of the bank's client in question.[12] One of the leading commentaries holds that a bank shall be entitled to use clients' secrets for its own business dispositions, provided such use does not adversely affect the clients in question, further for its own dispositions towards the clients even if that would affect them adversely and, finally, for its usual counselling of other clients, provided that the secret is thereby not indirectly disclosed or that the clients in question are not otherwise adversely affected.[13] Only one commentator considered the prohibition against exploiting bank secrets as a possible nucleus or predecessor provision for a regulation of insider trading.[14]

(VII)   Bank secrets disclosed to courts or other public authorities become official secrets and generally must not be disclosed to other courts or public authorities or exploited by the latter as a basis for the initiation of proceedings of any kind. To this extent the (transformed) Bank Secrecy prevails over the general duty of public authorities to mutual assistance.[15] However, the provisions governing criminal proceedings do not address the problem explicitly, further the official secrecy is lifted once a trial has commenced.[16] The provisions on penal administrative law are more specific in that regard (for details see pp 42–44).

CUSTOMER'S REMEDIES FOR BREACH OF CONFIDENCE

Injunction

If a breach of the Bank Secrecy is threatening, whether for the first time or continued, the (possibly) affected client will be entitled to injunctive relief. In rare cases a client may also be entitled to removal ('Beseitigung') of the breach (but in this context not of its consequences), eg by causing a bank to reclaim passed on information which still enjoys the character of a (maybe limited) secret. The

10   Avancini-Iro-Koziol p 125; Jabornegg-Strasser-Floretta p 137 ff.
11   Laurer 'Bankgeheimnis' p 389.
12   Avancini-Iro-Koziol p 125 ff; Haushofer-Schinnerer-Ulrich s 23/7; Jabornegg-Strasser-Floretta p 86; Schinnerer 'Zur Problematik einer gesetzlichen Regelung des börslichen Insider-Geschäftes in Österreich' (1985) ÖBA p 271.
13   Avancini-Iro-Koziol p 126.
14   Roth 'Der Wall Street-Skandal und das österreichische Kapitalmarktrecht' (1987) RdW 219 at 221, 222 (following 'Roth').
15   Avancini-Iro-Koziol p 127; Jabornegg-Strasser-Floretta p 69 ff, p 124 ff.
16   Avancini-Iro-Koziol p 127; Liebscher 'Das Bankgeheimnis im In- und Ausland' (1984) ÖJZ 253 at 255 (following 'Liebscher').

special feature of a client's claim to an injunction or to removal is that no fault (negligence or intent) is required on the part of the person against whom such remedy is sought.[17]

Damages

A client who suffers damage through a violation of the Bank Secrecy is entitled to reimbursement in accordance with the general principles of tort law. In accordance with these principles a client will generally be entitled to reimbursement of the property damages (there is no right to punitive damages or, in this context, to damages for pain and suffering) which have been caused by such violation through a tortfeasor at fault. If the party in breach is a bank (or one of those for whom a bank is liable), property damages will include lost profit; if the tortfeasor is one of the other persons subject to Bank Secrecy, this will often but not always be the case.[18] One commentator advocates that property damages should not be recoverable if constituted by or resulting from fines or prison sentences.[19]

It is the prevailing view that the right to damages may be contracted away in respect of a tortfeasor's lower levels of fault (at least for slight negligence) and that provisions to that effect contained in the bank's general conditions are valid if such conditions have become a part of the contractual relationship between the bank and the client in question.[20] A bank will be liable for all its agents and other personnel, whether employed or not, which afflict damage upon clients through a (faulty) breach of the Bank Secrecy as if the bank itself had committed such breach. On the other hand such agents and other personnel will be protected by the above disclaimer as to lower degrees of negligence as well.[1]

I do not elaborate on the extremely complicated (and unresolved) problem of the liability for breaches of the Bank Secrecy which cause damage to third parties (ie non-clients).

Termination of Business Relationship

A client who is the victim of a violation of the Bank Secrecy by a bank or a tortfeasor whose actions are attributed to such bank, will be entitled to terminate the contractual relationship with the bank for good reason with immediate effect.[2]

Criminal Punishment

A physical person who discloses or exploits facts which are subject to the Bank Secrecy (KWG, s 23) with the malicious intent to enrich himself or a third party or to affect another adversely is subject to criminal punishment (jail of up to one year or fines), but a person who has committed such a crime shall only be prosecuted upon application of such person as was impaired in its interest in confidentiality (KWG, s 34(1) and (3)). Public officials in breach of the Bank Secrecy may be subject to the (even more serious) criminal punishment for the offence constituted by a breach of the official secret.

---

17 Avancini-Iro-Koziol p 163 ff; Jabornegg-Strasser-Floretta p 160 ff.
18 Arnold 'Bankgeheimnis' p 20; Avancini-Iro-Koziol p 164 ff; Jabornegg-Strasser-Floretta p 162 ff.
19 Avancini-Iro-Koziol p 167.
20 Avancini-Iro-Koziol p 165 ff; Frotz p 267 ff; against Jabornegg-Strasser-Floretta p 163.
 1 Avancini-Iro-Koziol p 165 ff.
 2 Avancini-Iro-Koziol p 168; Jabornegg-Strasser-Floretta p 164.

Action by Bank Regulatory Authorities

The bank regulatory authority (the Federal Minister of Finances) has to intervene if breaches of the Bank Secrecy attributable to a bank have led or threaten to lead to a grievance (Mißstand). The most severe consequence could be the withdrawal of the concession.[3]

EXCEPTIONS TO THE GENERAL DUTY OF NON-DISCLOSURE

Section 23(2) of the KWG provides for six exceptions to the Bank Secrecy. It is the general consensus that this catalogue does not constitute a conclusive list of all exceptions to the duties stipulated in s 23, but that there may be others as well.[4] Following is a description of those exceptions set forth in KWG, s 23(2), and those which are based on other provisions or principles of law.

Customer's Consent

There is no Bank Secrecy if the client 'expressly consents in writing' to the disclosure or exploitation of a secret (KWG, s 23(2)3). A valid consent requires a clearly formulated writing signed by the client. If a secret relates to persons who are not clients, the waiver has nevertheless to be issued by the client who passed the secret on to the bank. It is not clear how precisely the waived secrets have to be defined in the declaration of consent and whether a (reasonably defined) waiver can be validly made in advance (eg by accepting the application of a bank's general conditions in writing). But it is the prevailing view that a general waiver of the Bank Secrecy without limit as to time (in particular the future) or scope would not be valid.[5] The general conditions currently used by banks do not provide for such a sweeping waiver of the Bank Secrecy. A waiver of the Bank Secrecy can probably be revoked at any time.[6]

The question of how to qualify a consent obtained pursuant to a foreign court order under the threat of fines or imprisonment (eg a subpoena issued by a US court and served in the US upon the client of an Austrian bank) has never been dealt with by Austrian courts or in Austrian legal treatises. If the consent is deemed to have been obtained by undue force (which is doubtful if the foreign court acts in accordance with the law to be applied by it), it stands nevertheless as given until declared invalid by a court in the course of civil litigation. Such court decisions will not be easily obtainable as the entity which exerted the pressure is not the addressee of the consent. However, the issuer of the consent declaration can revoke it at any time.

Litigation between Bank and Client

There is no Bank Secrecy if the disclosure is 'necessary for the resolution of legal issues arising out of the relationship between banks and clients' (KWG, s 23(2)5). This exception relates to litigation and permits the banks to disclose secrets relating to and learned from the client in a litigation with such client. It is irrelevant whether the bank is plaintiff or defendant.

---

3 Avancini-Iro-Koziol p 170 ff; Jabornegg-Strasser-Floretta p 165 ff.
4 Arnold 'Bankgeheimnis' p 12, p 18 ff; Avancini-Iro-Koziol p 129; Jabornegg-Strasser-Floretta p 93.
5 Arnold 'Bankgeheimnis' p 17; Avancini-Iro-Koziol p 131 ff; Frotz p 244 ff; Jabornegg-Strasser-Floretta p 99 ff.
6 Arnold 'Bankgeheimnis' p 17; Avancini-Iro-Koziol p 139; Frotz p 245; Jabornegg-Strasser-Floretta p 103; against: Laurer 'Bankgeheimnis' 386 FN 19.

General Information on Customer's Economic Situation

There is no Bank Secrecy for 'generally phrased information on the economic situation of a business', as usually given by banks, unless the former expressly objects thereto (KWG, s 23(2)4). This exception permits the banks to inform the public on its clients' economic situation (unless a client objects beforehand). In these cases the bank will have to balance carefully the (frequently conflicting) interests of the clients and those of the recipients of the bank's information. The limit to 'general information' prevents the banks from passing on specific and detailed data. They may only give a general picture of their clients' state of affairs without directly or indirectly disclosing exact data. In order to comply with the above duties of care, the banks normally issue such information by using standard formulations as are commonly employed for such purpose by banks. The banks may rely on the assumption that the recipient understands the meaning of such terminology.[7]

Balancing of Interest

There is probably no Bank Secrecy if, upon a 'balancing of' the client's 'interest' in confidentiality with conflicting interests of the bank or third parties, the bank's or such third parties' interests appear to be significantly overriding.[8] This exception is not set forth in the above generality in a special statutory provision. After all, the expressly codified exceptions to the Bank Secrecy are provisions on special conflicts of interest in which the law stipulates that other interests prevail over the clients' interest in Bank Secrecy. Therefore the balancing of interests in cases not statutorily provided for must result in a clear preponderance of those interests which conflict with the Bank Secrecy.

Typical cases are those in which the bank is asked by persons who actually have posted or are contemplating to post securities for an obligation by a bank's client towards such bank for information on such debtor's financial state.[9] In a recent case which belongs probably also in this category, the Austrian Supreme Court ('OGH') has held that KWG, s 23 did not prevent the issuer of credit cards from disclosing the address of a credit card holder to a business from which the credit card owner had purchased goods employing the credit card, but subsequently requested the issuer of such card not to pay the invoice.[10] The OGH held that the credit card issuer was obliged to disclose such information in that case.

Payment of Another's Debt

There is a further exception to the Bank Secrecy for 'third parties who have paid a client's debt to the bank, for which debt such third parties were personally liable or have posted other security'. Such third parties are assignees of the (bank) creditor's rights by operation of law. Such third parties are further entitled (inter

7 See Arnold 'Bankgeheimnis' p 17 ff; Avancini-Iro-Koziol p 153 ff; Frotz p 242 ff; Jabornegg-Strasser-Floretta p 105 ff.
8 See Arnold 'Bankgeheimnis' p 19; Avancini 'Der Auskunftsanspruch des Bürgen gegenüber dem Gläubiger—Zugleich ein Beitrag zum Bankgeheimnis' (1985) JBl p 193 at p 204 ff (following 'Avancini, Auskunftsanspruch'); Avancini-Iro-Koziol p 161 ff; Frotz p 254 ff; Jabornegg-Strasser-Floretta p 142 ff; Steiner 'Zur Aufklärungspflicht der Kreditunternehmung bei Wechseldiskontge-schäften' (1983) JBl p 189 (following 'Steiner').
9 See Avancini 'Auskunftsanspruch' p 193 ff; Steiner p 189 ff.
10 OGH 8.3.1988, (1989) ÖJZ 1.

alia) to delivery of all other security posted for the debt in question and of such other documents or information as are necessary for the payors to pursue their right to recourse against the debtor and against others who have posted security for such debt (s 1358 of the Civil Code ('ABGB')).

The OGH has held twice that s 1358 of the ABGB prevails over s 23 of the KWG.[11] In the older case, the OGH held that a surety who had paid the secured debt was entitled to receive the underlying credit agreements, other suretyship agreements, drafts, and the correspondence executed by the other sureties or the debtor and relating to the debtor's credit account (but not the internal memoranda and correspondence signed by the bank). In the more recent case the OGH held that a mortgagor's rights under s 1358 of the ABGB prevailed over s 23 of the KWG as well.[12]

It is not settled whether or not the above exception belongs to one of those categories set forth already above and, if so, to which one. Therefore it is dealt with separately here.

Inventorisation of Estates by the Probate Court

There is no Bank Secrecy 'towards the probate court' and its aids 'in connection with the inventorisation or other determination of the assets and obligations which belong to the estate of a deceased person' (KWG, s 23(2)2). A request for information made by the probate court requires the revelation of concrete indications of the assets or liabilities forming part of the estate. The exception pursuant to s 23(2)2 applies only to requests for information by Austrian probate courts in Austrian probate proceedings. There is no exception to the Bank Secrecy for requests by foreign probate courts, whether made directly or through letters rogatory.[13]

Criminal Proceedings

There is no Bank Secrecy 'towards Austrian penal courts in connection with initiated judicial criminal proceedings and towards Austrian fiscal penal authorities (Finanzstrafbehörden) in connection with initiated penal proceedings because of intentional fiscal offences (vorsätzliche Finanzvergehen) except for fiscal irregularities (Finanzordnungswidrigkeiten). The above provision, which is contained in KWG, s 23(2)1, forms the core of the exceptions to the Bank Secrecy by virtue of compulsion of law.

Criminal proceedings are proceedings with respect to such crimes or offences (including certain crimes and offences of a fiscal nature) as shall be conducted by the regular court system. Fiscal offences are certain offences provided for in the Revenues Penal Act (e g tax fraud and smuggling) and other fiscal offences defined as such in other statutes. Fiscal offences are only offences against the federal tax system; they may be subject to judicial criminal punishment or to administrative (fiscal) penal punishment. Fiscal irregularities are fiscal offences of a lesser degree. Fiscal penal authorities are administrative agencies. Decisions of the fiscal penal authorities may generally be appealed to the Administrative Court or the Constitutional Court.

11 OGH 2.2.1984, SZ 57/29; OGH 29.4.1986, (1986) JBl p 511.
12 See OGH in SZ 57/29 and (1986) JBl p 511; Avancini-Iro-Koziol p 157; Frotz p 252 ff; Jabornegg-Strasser-Floretta p 151 ff.
13 Arnold 'Bankgeheimnis' p 15 ff; Avancini 'Auskünfte über Sparbücher im Verlassenschaftsverfahren' (1985) NZ p 21; Avancini-Iro-Koziol p 150 ff; Frotz p 251 ff; Jabornegg-Strasser-Floretta p 126 ff.

Whether or not courts or fiscal penal authorities may request the disclosure of bank secrets depends on two main issues, namely, whether or not a relevant proceeding is deemed 'initiated' and whether or not there is (sufficient) 'connection' between the proceeding and the requested disclosure. A resolution of these issues must take the generally advocated principle into consideration that the exception to the Bank Secrecy in connection with criminal and certain administrative penal proceedings shall not enable the prosecution to gather indicia for potential crimes or offences ('fishing expeditions') but only to corroborate (or dispel) well-founded and reasonably defined suspicions of such crimes or offences.[14]

'Initiated' Criminal Proceedings

Under Austrian law, a criminal proceeding is normally conducted in three stages. The initial stage is the preliminary inquiry (Vorerhebung) conducted under the guidance of the public prosecution, which in turn employs police or courts for the actual inquiry. The next phase is the preliminary investigation (Voruntersuchung) in which a judge is in charge. This is followed by the trial as the last stage. A preliminary investigation can be directed against one or more identified persons only, whereas a preliminary inquiry may also be directed against unknown perpetrators.

The issue of whether a criminal proceeding should be deemed initiated upon the commencement of preliminary inquiries or only upon the opening of a formal preliminary investigation was the subject of a considerable scholarly dispute.[15] The question has probably been resolved by a recent (unpublished) decision of the OGH,[16] which held that the taking of any measures against known or unknown perpetrators in the course of criminal proceedings, including the stage of preliminary inquiries, constituted the initiation of criminal proceedings.

There is still a dispute on whether or not a court which is in charge of investigations or entrusted with inquiries may employ the police for the opening of bank secrets.[17] Although the above question has not been the subject of a court decision, it is the prevailing (and uncontested) practice that the courts do have the actual investigation conducted by the police.

The above is somehow modified and limited for criminal proceedings conducted by the small claims courts (Bezirksgerichte) on which I do not elaborate here.

'Initiated' Fiscal Penal Proceedings

Fiscal penal proceedings are formally initiated by an appealable decree pursuant to FinStrG, ss 82, 83. The suspect must receive notice of such initiation. A fiscal penal proceeding is to be initiated if there is suspicion of a fiscal offence unless the offence can probably not be proven, suspected facts do not constitute a fiscal offence, or the suspect has not committed the offence or cannot be prosecuted or punished for it.

---

14 Arnold 'Entscheidungsanmerkung' (1986) AnwBl p 417; Avancini-Iro-Koziol p 141; see also Jabornegg-Strasser-Floretta p 110 ff.
15 Jabornegg-Strasser-Floretta p 109; Avancini 'Neueste gesetzliche Regelungen zum Bankgeheimnis' (1986) RdW 294 at 296 ff (following 'Avancini, Bankgeheimnis'); see also Arnold 'Bankgeheimnis' p 13.
16 OGH 18.1.1989, 14 Os 170–173/88–6.
17 For this possibility: Avancini-Iro-Koziol p 142; against: Jabornegg-Strasser-Floretta p 118.

Sufficient 'Connection'

There is a sufficient connection between proceeding and bank secret if there is an objectively ascertainable relevance of the requested information to the proceeding in question. As this is a question of degree and there are no court decisions in point, I do not report the various attempts to define the necessary degree in the abstract. It is, however, the prevailing view that such relevance may also exist for the bank secrets of one party in relation to a crime or fiscal offence of a third party in which the former did not participate.[18]

Search and Seizure

The scope of the court and fiscal penal authorities' right to obtain bank secrets by way of search and seizure and to use bank secrets obtained in such manner is of particular significance because an obligation of disclosure is only relevant to the extent it can be actually enforced. It ought to be mentioned that there is (theoretically) also the possibility of enforcing disclosure indirectly by fining a bank (or its shareholders etc) that refuses to disclose a bank secret upon a request issued by a fiscal penal authority.

The reason why I commence with the fiscal penal authorities' (and not the courts') right to search and seizure follows.

After the KWG's coming into force in March 1979, the fiscal penal authorities continued their former practice. They conducted searches and seizures with banks because of particular fiscal offences, but seized as well any means of evidence which indicated the commission of intentional fiscal offences (including offences totally unrelated to those in respect of which the actual searches had been ordered) by other bank clients which had nothing to do with the subject matter of the original search order.[19]

In 1986 the Constitutional Court (in another context) struck down several provisions of the Revenues Penal Code, holding that a legally acknowledged right to refuse testimony because of the privilege of self-incrimination could not be thwarted by obtaining the denied evidence through search and seizure or other undue means (eg indirect pressure such as assessments based on estimates).[20] Based on this ruling, the legislation amended the provisions on the right to search and seizure as contained in the Revenues Penal Code. Although the provisions on search and seizure pursuant to the Criminal Procedure Code ('StPO') were not changed, their interpretation will henceforth have to take the principles underlying the amendment of the Revenues Penal Code into consideration, the latter in particular in view of a statement made by the Constitutional Court which indicates in its decisions that its holding on the struck-down provisions of the Revenues Penal Code should apply somehow to the comparable provisions of the Criminal Procedure Code as well.[1]

The new s 89(4) of the FinStrG addresses the issues which arise if evidence of

---

18 Avancini-Iro-Koziol p 141, p 144; Jabornegg-Strasser-Floretta p 108 ff; Liebscher p 254; against a lifting of the Bank Secrecy: Arnold p 13.

19 W Doralt 'Das Bankgeheimnis im Abgabeverfahren' (1981) ÖJZ p 652; W Doralt 'Entscheidungs-anmerkung' (1984) RdW p 128.

20 VfGH 3.12.1984, AnwBl 1985, p 43; see Arnold 'Die Finanzstrafgesetznovelle 1985' (1986) ZGV p 5 (following 'Arnold, Finanzstrafgesetznovelle'); Arnold 'Aktuelles zum Bankgeheimnis' (1985) ÖBA p 19; Beiser 'Entscheidungsanmerkung' (1985) ÖStZ p 24; Avancini 'Bankgeheimnis' p 298 ff; Avancini-Iro-Koziol p 145.

 1 Arnold 'Finanzstrafgesetznovelle' p 9; Avancini 'Bankgeheimnis' p 298 ff; Avancini-Iro-Koziol p 145, 147.

breaches of the law other than those which form the basis of the initial (lawful) search order are accidentally found by the searching authorities. It provides that such evidence which is in the custody of banks and which concerns secrets within the meaning of s 23(1) of the KWG may only be seized if it is 'directly connected' with the intentional fiscal offence(s) (not just fiscal irregularities) for which the Bank Secrecy is (already) lifted pursuant to KWG, s 23(1)1.

That means that the accidentally found evidence can only be seized to the extent that it relates to a fiscal offence (not to a crime, another fiscal offence or other contraventions of the law) which is not just a fiscal irregularity and which is directly connected with the fiscal offence(s) for which the search was originally conducted.

This limitation applies not only for the benefit of the party whose suspected fiscal offence formed the basis of the initial search order, but in particular for the benefit of third parties. The direct connection between the originally suspected fiscal offence and one on the part of such third party which comes into the open in the course of a search and seizure, is probably only present if it turns out that the third party is a direct accessory to the original suspect's fiscal offence. A closely related but formally separate fiscal offence will probably, a crime or other contravention of law certainly, not suffice.[2]

If the bank formally alleges that information was seized in violation of the Bank Secrecy (ie the requirements of s 23(2)1 of the KWG or those of FinStrG, s 89(4) were not fulfilled), such information must be sealed and a formal decision on the legality of the seizure must be issued. Such decision can be appealed.

Finally, s 98(4) of the FinStrG provides that evidence seized in violation of the above must not be used for the rendering of the decision (punishment order) to the detriment of the accused or of an accessory. This provision is interpreted to mean (in addition) that the fiscal authorities must not use such evidence in an initiated proceeding and no court or other public authority may use it to commence proceedings whatsoever against those involved.[3]

There is probably one exception to the above: the fiscal authorities which receive such privileged information may use it for an assessment (or reassessment) of the original suspect's taxes (but not for any measures of penal character).[4]

I do not deal separately with (additional) prerequisites for a search order because a bank will probably hand over the requested information and request its sealing and the rendering of a formal and appealable ruling as set forth above, rather than have the fiscal penal authorities go through its files.

The corollary to s 89(4) of the FinStrG is StPO, s 144, which, as indicated above, does not contain a comparable limitation but rather provides broadly that objects shall be seized if they are found during a search and indicate the commission of other crimes which shall be prosecuted ex officio. It is the prevailing view[5] that a limitation as contained in s 89(4) of the FinStrG has to be read into StPO, s 144, in view of the Constitutional Court's above ruling. If that is the case, a seizure of objects beyond such limitation will be illegal and a (criminal) judgment rendered on the basis of such evidence could be appealed as

---

2 Arnold 'Finanzstrafgesetznovelle' p 7; Avancini-Iro-Koziol p 146.
3 Arnold 'Finanzstrafgesetznovelle' p 9; Avancini 'Bankgeheimnis' p 299; Avancini-Iro-Koziol p 146.
4 Avancini 'Bankgeheimnis' p 299; Avancini-Iro-Koziol p 147.
5 Arnold 'Finanzstrafgesetznovelle' p 9; Avancini 'Bankgeheimnis' p 299; Avancini-Iro-Koziol p 147.

void. Section 145(2) of the StPO affords the person from whom objects were seized (eg the bank) the right to request a sealing of the seized objects (eg information). In such a case, a panel of three judges resolves on the legality of the seizure. Their ruling cannot be appealed. It is quite hard to predict whether or not and, if so, to what extent the courts will follow the above line of thought. According to information informally received by the author, the courts do not apply the principles of s 89(4) of the FinStrG to StPO, s 144 at present. Consequently, there is no limit to the use of crime-related information accidentally gathered in the course of an official and legal search conducted in the course of criminal proceedings.

Bank Secrecy and Foreign Legal Proceedings

There is no exception to the Bank Secrecy if foreign courts or other public authorities themselves approach a bank directly, whether in a civil or criminal matter. It is, however, the prevailing view[6] that there may be exceptions to the Bank Secrecy if foreign courts (and other public authorities) request the assistance of Austrian courts or other Austrian public authorities in criminal proceedings by way of letters rogatory.

Letters Rogatory

In the absence of applicable treaties, the Act on Extradition and Legal Assistance in Matters of Criminal Law ('ARHG') of December 1979 governs the grant of legal assistance to foreign authorities. Pursuant to ARHG, s 50, legal assistance may be granted by or through Austrian courts to foreign courts, foreign public prosecutors and foreign prison authorities, provided there is reciprocity. Legal assistance shall not be granted if (inter alia):

(I)   the offence on which the request for legal assistance is based is:
    (A)   not subject to judicial criminal punishment under Austrian law,
    (B)   of political nature,
    (C)   of military nature, or
    (D)   'a violation of revenues, monopolies, or customs laws', or a breach of exchange control, rationing, import or export control laws;
(II)   the request is made by a country the criminal procedure and enforcement system of which does not meet certain human rights standards;
(III)   the special requirements under Austrian law for certain measures (in particular seizure and opening of mail, or wire-tapping) are not met;
(IV)   'the legal assistance would lead to a breach of Austrian law providing for duties of confidentiality which shall be maintained in regard to penal courts as well'; or
(V)   'the compliance with the request for legal assistance would be contrary to the public policy or other essential interests of the Republic of Austria.'

I have placed in quotes the exceptions most relevant in connection with the Bank Secrecy.

    Whereas one view holds[7] that legal assistance, if it required a lifting of the Bank

---

6 Avancini-Iro-Koziol p 149; Jabornegg-Strasser-Floretta p 156; Laurer 'Bankgeheimnis' p 393; sceptical: Arnold 'Bankgeheimnis' p 15; Binder 'Österreichs Bankgeheimnis im internationalen Steuerrecht' (1985/13) SWK p 9.
7 Beiser 'Das österreichische Bankgeheimnis (s 23 KWG) im Verhältnis zum Ausland, insbesonders zur Bundesrepublik Deutschland' (1985) ÖJZ p 178 (following 'Beiser, Bankgeheimnis').

Secrecy, should only be granted in 'classical criminal' matters, and after a balancing, in every individual case, of the Austrian interests in respecting the Bank Secrecy against the Austrian interests in the (worldwide) prosecution of crimes, it is the majority view[8] that such legal assistance shall be granted on the basis of the ARHG if its conditions are met *and* the special requirements and limits under which the Bank Secrecy may be lifted in purely domestic proceedings are fulfilled (ie initiated criminal proceedings, sufficient connection, and safeguard against the use of accidentally gathered evidence which is not directly related to the offence which formed the basis of the request for legal assistance—the latter under the assumption that this principle applies to judicial criminal proceedings as well, see pp 42–44 above. According to information informally received by the author, the Austrian authorities do not request safeguard against undue use of accidentally gathered evidence by foreign courts at present.).

Austria is further a party to the European Convention on Mutual Assistance in Criminal Matters of 20 April 1959. The main requirements for and exceptions to Austria's duty to render legal assistance under this treaty (in its original version and to the extent relevant for the Bank Secrecy) are the following:

(I)   Legal assistance will only be granted for offences which are subject to judicial criminal punishment in the requesting country *and* in Austria (art 1(1) and Austrian Reservation thereto).

(II)   Legal assistance will not be granted in respect of political or *fiscal* offences (Austrian Reservation to art 2a).

(III)   Legal assistance will not be granted if it impaired Austria's sovereignty, security, ordre public or other essential interests (art 2b; Austria has made a Reservation to art 2b declaring that it understood as 'other essential interests', in particular, respecting the duties of confidentiality provided for by Austrian law).

(IV)   'Austria will only comply with requests for search or seizure if such search or seizure is in accordance with Austrian law' (Austrian Reservation to art 5(1)).

In 1983, Austria ratified the Additional Protocol to the European Convention on Mutual Assistance in Criminal Matters (BGB1 296/1983), in which it waived the exception as to fiscal offences (see art 2a above) for violations of revenues, tax and customs laws. Upon the ratification of the above Protocol, Austria made a declaration in which it stated that it would grant legal assistance in criminal proceedings relating to revenues, tax and customs laws only subject to the condition that, in accordance with the duties of confidentiality provided for by Austrian law, information and evidence received by way of legal assistance will only be used in the criminal proceeding for which legal assistance was requested and in revenues, tax, or customs proceedings directly connected to such proceeding.

In an additional, unilateral Declaration (BGB1 203/1983) Austria withdrew the Reservation it made to art 2a (see above) with respect to those parties to the Convention which had not become parties to the above Additional Protocol, and announced that it would henceforth apply art 2a of the Convention in accordance with domestic law, ie the ARHG. Indeed, ss 14 and 15 of the ARHG (providing

---

8 Avancini-Iro-Koziol p 149; Jabornegg-Strasser-Floretta p 156; Laurer 'Bankgeheimnis' p 393.

for the above set forth exceptions (I)(B), (I)(C) and (I)(D)) are quoted verbatim in this Declaration.[9]

If this unilateral Declaration is valid (which is somehow doubtful under principles of international law), there are two groups of members to the Convention now, those who are parties to the Additional Protocol and to whom legal assistance will be granted in criminal proceedings of a fiscal nature as well, and those who are not parties to such Protocol and who will not receive such assistance (in the absence of further bilateral treaties, see below). I believe that the above-mentioned special requirements and limits under which the Bank Secrecy may be lifted in purely domestic proceedings will apply likewise to the grant of legal assistance under the Convention (to either group), this in view of the above Reservation to art 2b and the declaration on duties of confidentiality made in connection with the ratification of the Additional Protocol.[10]

Austria has in addition entered into a number of bilateral treaties, some of which are supplementing the above described Convention. One of the latter (and a good example of some relevance) is the Treaty between Austria and the Federal Republic of Germany Supplementing the European Convention for Mutual Assistance in Criminal Matters and Facilitating its Application, dated 31 January 1972 (BGB1 36/1977). The Federal Republic of Germany has not ratified the above Additional Protocol.

This treaty expanded the scope of the original Convention (which continues to apply in general) considerably. In particular, the covered offences include proceedings for violations of revenues, tax, customs and monopolies laws. Further the police authorities of either country shall render and may request mutual assistance as well.

Indeed, the Administrative Court has held that s 23 of the KWG did not prevent an Austrian administrative agency from granting legal assistance to a German authority in fiscal matters.[11] Upon compliance with such requests, the Austrian authorities had to act in accordance with Austrian law and thus had the same rights as if they were themselves the investigating authorities in a purely domestic proceeding. This decision was severely criticised by one author[12] who believed that the lifting of the Bank Secrecy in fiscal matters violated an essential interest of Austria as set forth in art 2b of the Convention, this in particular in view of the Reservation made to art 2b and to the Declaration referred to above. Therefore, Austria should deny legal assistance in all fiscal matters if such assistance led to a revelation of bank secrets. However, most other[13] commentators agreed with the court's ruling on the legality of such legal assistance and emphasised that care should be taken that the requirements for the limits to the disclosure and use of bank secrets were indeed fulfilled and respected upon the rendering of legal assistance involving bank secrets.

Summary

Austrian authorities will not render legal assistance to foreign authorities in civil matters if such assistance is contrary to the Bank Secrecy. Austria will render legal assistance in criminal matters in accordance with applicable treaties or the

---

9 For a detailed description of the above see Laurer 'Bankgeheimnis' p 391 ff.
10 Avancini-Iro-Koziol p 149.
11 VwGH 21.10.1983, (1984) ÖStZB p 189.
12 Beiser 'Entscheidungsanmerkung' (1984) RdW p 192; Beiser 'Bankgeheimnis' p 178; see also Arnold 'Entscheidungsanmerkung' (1984) AnwBl p 172.
13 Avancini-Iro-Koziol p 150; Jabornegg-Strasser-Floretta p 156; Laurer 'Bankgeheimnis' p 393.

ARHG even if that requires a lifting of the Bank Secrecy, provided the requirements for and the limits to a lifting of the Bank Secrecy in a purely domestic situation are fulfilled and respected. If provided for in applicable treaties, such (foreign) criminal matters may include fiscal offences and both requesting authorities and authorities rendering legal assistance may be administrative agencies as well.

Tax Liabilities of Deceased Persons

There is no Bank Secrecy in respect of the banks' duty to 'give notice to the fiscal authorities of assets belonging to or deposited with them for the disposition of a deceased person' (i e assets which were held in deposit or administered for the deceased in the course of the banks' business) within one month from the death becoming known to the banks (Estate Tax Act, s 25).

Enforcement Proceedings

There is no Bank Secrecy with respect to requests for information on a person's claims against banks which were attached in enforcement proceedings.[14]

Assessment of the Banks' Taxes

There is no Bank Secrecy to the extent a disclosure of bank secrets is necessary for the assessment of taxes to be paid by the banks themselves (KWG, s 23(3)). Certainly, bank secrets obtained by the (fiscal) authorities in such manner are subject to the official secrecy, must not be passed on to other public authorities and must not be used in whatever manner in regard to third parties to which such bank secrets relate.

Exchange Control, Income Tax and Bank Regulatory Authorities, Audit Office, Trustee in Bankruptcy

There is further no Bank Secrecy with respect to the Austrian National Bank's right to certain information in matters of exchange control, with respect to certain notice requirements under the Income Tax Act or other revenue laws, in regard of the bank regulatory authority's and the Audit Office's (Rechnungshof) right to information and towards the trustee in bankruptcy in bankruptcy or reorganisation proceedings. Naturally, bank secrets disclosed to the Austrian National Bank, the bank regulatory authorities or the Audit Office are subject to the official secrecy and must not be passed on to other authorities.[15]

If a bank secret is disclosed pursuant to the terms immediately above or below, and illegally used as a basis for the initiation of other proceedings, it is probable that the same principles on the use of such evidence will apply as outlined on pp 42–44 above for illegally seized evidence.

Foreign Bank Regulatory Authorities

Pursuant to KWG, s 23a the Federal Minister of Finances may give official information to foreign bank regulatory authorities provided:

(I)   the ordre public, other essential interests of the Republic of Austria and the Bank Secrecy are not violated thereby;

---

14 Arnold 'Bankgeheimnis' p 22; Avancini-Iro-Koziol p 158; Jabornegg-Strasser-Floretta p 153 ff.
15 Avancini-Iro-Koziol pp 159, 160; Jabornegg-Strasser-Floretta p 129 ff.

(II)   there is reciprocity; and

(III) a similar request for information made by the Federal Minister of Finances
       would be in accordance with the purposes of the KWG.

The above does not apply if applicable treaties provide to the contrary. At present,
however, there is no such treaty.

FIDUCIARY DUTIES AND CONFLICTS OF INTEREST

The contractual relationship between the banks and their clients entails certain
mutual fiduciary duties and duties of care (Schutz- und Sorgfaltspflichten) as a
matter of contract law.[16] In addition, the introduction to the General Conditions
for the Austrian Credit Institutions commences with the statement that the
business relationship between client and credit institution is a relationship of
trust (Vertrauensverhältnis). I therefore believe that the banks are under an
obligation towards clients to avoid situations which would expose them to a
conflict of interests between clients to the extent possible. In the absence of cases
and scholarly comment on this issue, it is impossible to set any guidelines for the
scope of such duty or to elaborate on (actually available and effective) remedies
within the scope of this contribution.

INSIDER TRADING AND CHINESE WALLS

As indicated on p 36 above, s 23 of the KWG prevents the exploitation of bank
secrets. Whereas the majority view[17] holds that the exploitation of a bank secret as
defined in KWG, s 23 means only the use of a bank secret to the client's
detriment, there is also the view that ss 23 and 34 of the KWG cover insider
trading as well.[18] In addition ss 121 and 122 of the Austrian Penal Code sanction
certain offences involving professional, trade and business secrets. However, I
am not aware of any instance in which any of these provisions has ever been
employed by a court in relation to alleged insider trading (in fact I am not aware
of a single Austrian case involving insider trading). In addition, the protection
which KWG, s 23 may afford against insider trading would be of a limited value
only. In insider trading cases, the party suffering damages is normally not the one
whose information was used for insider trading. However, (probably) only the
latter (the bank's client) is protected by the KWG in its interest in maintenance of
the Bank Secrecy (including the duty to refrain from an exploitation of bank
secrets). Thus, those who suffer damages from insider trading will probably not
be entitled to recover them and those who are injured in their right to Bank
Secrecy do not suffer damages.[19]

   In order to address the problem of insider trading, the Vienna Stock Exchange
issued Guidelines for the Prevention of Insider Trading in 1987 (the
'Guidelines'). This relatively late action can be explained by the fact that the
Vienna Stock Exchange began to become really active again only a few years ago

---

16 Avancini-Iro-Koziol pp 42, 43.
17 Avancini-Iro-Koziol p 126; Jabornegg-Strasser-Floretta p 86; Schinnerer 'Zur Problematik einer
   gesetzlichen Regelung des börslichen Insider-Geschäftes in Österreich' (1985) ÖBA p 271
   (following: 'Schinnerer, Insider-Geschäft'); Schinnerer 'Fragen zum Bankgeheimnis nach s 23
   and s 34 KWG' in Barfuß-Torggler-Hauer-Wiltschek-Kucsko *Wirtschaftsrecht in Theorie und Praxis*
   (Gedenkschrift für Fritz Schönherr) p 267.
18 Roth pp 221, 222.
19 Roth p 222.

after decades of relatively modest activity, and that to date no cases of insider trading have received public attention.

The Guidelines request all members of the Vienna Stock Exchange and all issuers of securities to promise compliance with the Guidelines. Pursuant to the Guidelines they are further obliged to cause the following parties to commit themselves to compliance with the Guidelines to the extent possible (s 6):

(I)   such Insiders as are active within their business (the term 'Insiders' is defined in s 1, see below);
(II)   their shareholders and holders of other participations (to the extent a participation in the issuer's nominal capital is not just de minimis) and such Insiders (s 1) as are active within such shareholders' or other participation holders' business, provided such Insiders are not obliged themselves to submit the Guidelines;
(III) those banks and independent brokers admitted to the Vienna Stock Exchange which are in a specific business relationship with them and such Insiders (s 1) as are active in such banks' or independent brokers' business, provided such insiders are not obliged themselves to submit to the Guidelines.

A list of all legal and physical persons which have submitted to the Guidelines is maintained at the Vienna Stock Exchange and published regularly.

Section 1 of the Guidelines defines as 'Insider' a party which has information known to him alone or to him and a few others only. An Insider receives this information through its position with or its direct or indirect relationship to the issuers of securities listed at the Stock Exchange. Such persons include among others:

(I)   persons having a right to representation by virtue of law and members of supervisory boards of issuers of securities (s 1(1)a);
(II)   other persons to the extent they are in a position to obtain insider information in the course of their professional activities performed for the issuer; persons which professionally deal with the procurement of information (s 1(1)b);
(III) shareholders and holders of other participations of issuers of securities and their representatives and employees referred to above (s 1(1)a,b), to the extent their participation in the issuer's nominal capital is not just de minimis (s 1(1)c);
(IV)   banks doing business in Austria and independent brokers admitted to the Vienna Stock Exchange and their representatives and employees referred to above (s 1(1)a,b), provided the bank or the independent broker is in a specific business relationship with the issuer of the securities (s 1(1)d).

Section 2 of the Guidelines defines as 'Insider Information' such information as relates to unpublished facts which, if they became known, are likely to affect the development of prices for securities traded and officially listed at the Vienna Stock Exchange.

Section 3 of the Guidelines provides that 'Insiders which are in the possession of Insider Information shall refrain from':

(I)   the 'purchase or sale of securities' to which the Insider Information relates, whether for their own account or for the account of third parties (s 3(1)a);
(II)   the 'passing on of Insider Information' to certain third parties with the intent to procure for such third parties an economic advantage or to inflict an economic disadvantage upon them (s 3(1)b).

Exempt from the above prohibitions are securities transactions of banks and independent brokers upon clients' orders or within the frame of their otherwise usual securities business (the latter being the case if the securities business is conducted separately from the administration of participations and of loans within the same enterprise) (s 3(2)a).

Further exempt are the transactions set forth in s 3(1)a if effected by shareholders or holders of other participations in the issuer on the basis of their own business planning and if such actions are within the corporate powers and not performed with the purpose of inflicting damage upon third parties (s 3(2)b).

Exempt are, finally, the transactions set forth in s 3(1)a if made pursuant to orders with which the recipient must comply (the latter exemption does not affect the responsibility of the issuer of the order).

Section 4 of the Guidelines governs the investigation of insider transactions. Basically, the Council of the Vienna Stock Exchange monitors securities prices. If there is an irregular price development and a well founded suspicion of a prohibited insider transaction, a special commission for the investigation of insider transactions established by the Council of the Vienna Stock Exchange has to investigate such transactions. If there is the founded suspicion of a violation of s 3 of the Guidelines, the Insider in question has to disclose to the commission all transactions in the security in question during the period in which he was presumably in the possession of Insider Information. The Insider is further obliged to waive the Bank Secrecy pursuant to s 23 of the KWG towards those banks which effected the securities transactions for the Insider.

An Insider is obliged to remit to the Council of the Vienna Stock Exchange as *liquidated damages* any economic advantage he may have gained through a violation of the rules established by the Guidelines or which a third party has gained through the Insider's passing on of Insider Information (s 5(1)). The Stock Exchange shall use any amounts of liquidated damages received as a security for potential claims to damages because of insider transactions. The liability of the Insider towards those having incurred damages because of the insider transaction is not affected thereby (s 5(3)).

The Council of the Vienna Stock Exchange has to keep such amounts until a final decision (whether in court or otherwise) on the claims for such damages is made. If third parties are awarded or become otherwise entitled to damages, they will receive such funds from the Council of the Vienna Stock Exchange out of the deposit (s 5(4)).

If no claims to damages are raised in court within seven years from payment of the above liquidated damages and no judgment or settlement has been rendered or made, the Council of the Vienna Stock Exchange has to transfer such amounts to a charity (s 5(4)).

Special rules of procedure govern the constitution and proceedings of the investigating commission, including certain time limits. Probably of interest is the provision that a decision in which the commission has found a violation of the Guidelines shall be published. So far no proceedings have been initiated by the commission because of alleged insider trading.

Most Insiders employed by major banks have indeed obliged themselves to compliance with the above Guidelines upon request by their employers, who have themselves committed themselves to such compliance.

Chinese Walls (ie organisational separations of the securities business from other bank departments to limit the flow of potential Insider Information) have gradually developed to a certain extent, this within the frame of practically existing limits to the internal flows of information due to and along the lines of the banks' internal organisation (see p 36 above).

Finally, this chapter addresses a word as to the Austrian Bank Secrecy in regard to requests for legal assistance from foreign authorities because of illegal insider trading. Such requests will have to be examined in accordance with the principles set forth on pp 44–47 above, and will in all likelihood fail because most cases of insider trading are probably not subject to criminal punishment in Austria (see p 37 above). Further, in view of the requirement of an express and written consent to disclosure (see p 38 above), there is probably no room for the assumption that an insider trader who entrusts an Austrian bank with securities transactions abroad has waived the Bank Secrecy by conduct.[20]

POST SCRIPTUM

As of 1 December 1989, a new Stock Exchange Act (BörseG, BGBl 555/1989) has come into effect in Austria, ss 26 and 82 of which contain the following provisions on insider trading:

s 26(1): 'The trading at stock exchanges shall take place in accordance with just rules following the principle of equal treatment of all market participants. In particular, no sham transactions or transactions for the purpose of inflicting damages upon third parties shall be made. The Council of the Stock Exchange shall issue such rules providing for the equal treatment of the market participants as are necessary in the interest of investors' protection and for the safeguarding of the Austrian Stock Exchanges' reputation. Such rules shall correspond to the provisions of ss 82(5) and (6) hereof if issued for securities exchanges.'

s 82(5): 'No issuer may, during the time securities issued by such issuer are either officially listed or traded on the regulated over-the-counter market, enter into securities transactions in which such issuer takes advantage of the knowledge of unpublished facts and which transactions may inflict damages upon other investors because of the price development of such securities being affected by the unpublished fact or the transaction connected thereto. All members of the issuer's managing and supervisory board shall submit to an agreement with the Council of the Stock Exchange providing for liquidated damages. The liquidated damages shall secure the claims of investors having suffered damages and shall be kept in deposit by the Stock Exchange for seven years. Amounts not claimed for the intended use shall be forfeited for the benefit of the Republic of Austria after the expiration of such time period.'

s 82(6): 'The agreement providing for liquidated damages may further provide that the employment by the issuer of persons shall be deemed contrary to the provisions of such agreement if such persons can obtain insider information (s 82(5)) because of their position with the issuer but refuse to enter into the agreement for liquidated damages in spite of their being requested to do so by the Stock Exchange.'

To date the Council of the Vienna Stock Exchange has not yet issued the regulations pursuant to the foregoing provisions. It is expected to do so in mid-1990. Until then the status quo will persist. As of now it is very likely that the new regulations will not materially differ from the Guidelines.

---

20 Schinnerer, Insider-Geschäft p 273.

3 Belgium

Chris Sunt and Jacques Richelle

INTRODUCTION

As in many other legal systems, the bankers' duty of confidentiality is a long-established concept in Belgian law. This duty is based largely on tradition. Unlike in other European countries, it was never embodied in any statutory provision in Belgium. Furthermore courts have rarely had the opportunity to apply the concept and, therefore, have not been of much help in determining the nature and the scope of the duty, the remedies available to the customer or the exceptions to the rule of confidentiality. This area of the law has been developed primarily by legal doctrine.

The specificity of Belgian law with regard to the banker's duty of confidentiality lies more in the exceptions to the rule than in the duty itself. The duty, in its principle and its scope, is similar to its counterpart in other European countries. Most of the exceptions, however, are derived from specific procedural rules in various areas of the law.

With regard to terminology, it seems more correct to use the expressions 'duty of confidentiality' or 'duty of discretion' (as used by the Cour de Cassation, see below) than 'bank secrecy' ('secret bancaire', 'bankgeheim') as it is usually referred to in Belgium. Article 458 of the Criminal Code (see below), which uses the term 'professional secrecy', applies to physicians, lawyers and others, but not to bankers. Secondly, a duty which suffers so many exceptions of disclosure can hardly be called one of 'secrecy'.

It should be noted that a new statute that came into effect on 16 September 1989 makes insider trading a criminal offence in Belgium. The parliamentary report clearly mentions bankers as potential insiders. This law is based on the same principles as the proposition of an EC directive and other similar national legislations.

NATURE OF THE DUTY OF CONFIDENTIALITY

The Breach of the Duty of Confidentiality does not Constitute a Criminal Offence

By its decision of 25 October 1978, the Belgian Cour de Cassation (Supreme Court) clearly determined that the breach of the bankers' duty of confidentiality is not a criminal offence. The issue before the Court was whether bankers were to fall under art 458 of the Criminal Code, which provides that physicians, surgeons, health officers, pharmacists and all other persons who, because of their status or profession, are confided secrets will be, subject to certain exceptions, fined and/or imprisoned if they reveal these secrets.

The court held that this article does not apply to bankers because they are merely held to a duty of 'discretion'. The court added that neither the nature of their duties nor any statutory provision makes them subject to art 458 of the Criminal Code.

The judgment of 1978 is very short. Hints as to the court's reasoning can be found in previous decisions and in the comments of legal authors:

(I)   bankers do not have any legal monopoly as is the case with the professions mentioned in art 458;

(II) entering into a relationship with a banker does not necessarily involve confiding him secrets; at least, it is not the banker's primary function; and

(III) it is not deemed as socially important for a banker to keep the secrets he is told than for a lawyer or a physician; the latter have a much more intimate relationship with their clients, whose trust is essential to their function.

These arguments have been the object of controversy among legal authors. But whatever the underlying reasoning, the rule of law is clear: bankers are not criminally liable for revealing secrets confided to them by their clients.

The Duty of Confidentiality as a Common Civil Law Concept

The banker may be liable in damages to his clients if he breaches his duty of confidentiality. The nature of the duty and its resulting liability depend on the circumstances.

When the banker and his client reach an agreement, the duty arises out of the contract, itself. Whether expressly provided for in the agreement or, as in most cases, merely implied, the duty is undoubtedly contractual.

The nature of the duty is not so clear, however, in the absence of a contract, e g during the negotiation process or when a person cashes a blank cheque as a one-time operation. Authors have put forward many legal grounds on which to enforce the banker's duty in such circumstances:

(I)   in torts, on art 1382 of the Civil Code;
(II)   on an implied precontractual agreement;
(III) on a sui generis contract;
(IV)   on the culpa in contrahendo doctrine;
(V)   etc . . .

It seems that, in most cases, liability could be based on an implied agreement of confidentiality, independent from any later formal contract. If evidence of such an agreement cannot be shown, however, art 1382 of the Civil Code is always applicable.

CLIENT'S REMEDIES

If the duty of confidentiality is contractual, the client may claim damages for breach of contract (arts 1142 and 1145 of the Civil Code).

As far as tortious liability is concerned, pursuant to art 1382 of the Civil Code, the client will have to establish that there has been a fault, a damage and a causal link between the two.

SCOPE OF THE DUTY OF CONFIDENTIALITY

As in other countries, the scope of the banker's duty of confidentiality is very broad. It may be approached from three different angles.

Type of Operations

The duty applies to banking operations in the broad sense: deposit taking, credit, transfer of funds, foreign exchange, financial advice, safe rental, letter of credit etc. It would not apply to activities unrelated to banking, such as operating a travel agency.

Origin of the Information

The duty extends to all facts the banker comes across in the course of his business relationship with his client. This includes information released directly by the client himself as well as that known by the banker from any other source (eg banker's own investigation, 'blacklists' of clients—see later in this chapter). Mere hints or facts suspected by the banker are also included.

Some authors have suggested that (i) facts known by the banker in another capacity (eg as a friend), and (ii) facts discovered by the banker by a mere coincidence, are not included in the scope of the duty because they do not come to the banker's attention 'in the course of his business relationship with the client'. Such fine line drawing must be handled very cautiously.

Type of Information

The following are included within the confidentiality duty:

(I) facts about the customer himself, eg financial situation, commercial practices or strategy etc;

(II) types of banking operations, eg opening of an account, of a line of credit, transfer of funds, reception of funds etc; and

(III) amounts involved, account balances etc.

It must be added that the mere disclosure of the existence of a business relationship does not seem to constitute a breach of the banker's duty of confidentiality under Belgian law.

EXCEPTIONS TO THE DUTY OF CONFIDENTIALITY

Introduction

'Higher social interests' may sometimes override the need for banker's discretion, thus creating numerous exceptions to the banker's duty of confidentiality. In all of these situations, however, it must be kept in mind that confidentiality remains the rule and disclosure the exception. Therefore, the banker's duty of disclosure is strictly limited to the protection of these higher interests. This limit has to be carefully appraised by the banker, as any unnecessary disclosure can lead to liability to the client.

As a general rule, banker's duty of disclosure, when applicable, is limited to material facts. It does not include confidences, projects, suspicions etc.

Client's Consent

The client can relieve the banker from his duty of confidentiality, either expressly or implicitly. The underlying reasoning in this rule is that the banker's duty only protects his client's private material interests, not any larger public interest.

Interest of the Bank

A banker is allowed to release information about his client when his own material interest is at stake. Whether or not such disclosure is limited to judicial proceedings to which the banker is a party is the object of controversy among authors.

Criminal Proceedings

A banker can be compelled to disclose information about his client's operations at various stages of criminal proceedings, eg during the investigation process and by the court at the trial hearings. In these cases, his duty of confidentiality is irrelevant: the banker must testify or accept a search, just like any other person.

The same rules apply if the banker is himself under investigation or on trial. In that case, however, his fundamental right of defence to remain silent supersedes any duty of disclosure. Therefore, he cannot be forced to testify.

Investigation Stage

The judge leading the investigation ('juge d'instruction') has the power:

(I) To compel the banker, as any other person, to appear before him and to testify as witness by disclosing confidential information about his client (art 71 ff of the Code of Criminal Procedure—'Code d'Instruction Criminelle'—hereinafter referred to as 'CIC').

The judge may delegate this power to the public prosecutor ('procureur du roi' and his 'substituts') or to the judicial police ('police judiciaire'). If the banker refuses to testify, he can be fined and forced to appear (CIC, art 80).

At this stage, a false testimony is not a criminal offence. The witness can modify it up until the closing of the trial. This traditional rule, however, is now called into question by some authors and courts.

(II) To order a search ('perquisition') at the bank (CIC, art 87). This is the judge's most effective alternative since the banker may not oppose the search. The banker may, however, write down comments on the official minutes of the search. He will do so when:

(A) a procedural rule has been violated, eg if the judge lacks territorial jurisdiction; or

(B) the search is unrelated to the charges held against the person under investigation.

This may lead the trial court eventually to reject as evidence material found during the search.

It is important for the banker to distinguish the official, formal investigation just described from an unofficial one ('enquête officieuse' or 'information') led by the public prosecutor. In the latter case, as there is no legal obligation for the banker to answer any questions, his duty of confidentiality should keep him from disclosing any confidential information.

Trial Stage

At the trial hearings, the trial court may order a banker, as any other person, to testify (CIC, arts 153, 190 and 315). A refusal to testify then leads to the same consequences as at the investigation stage (CIC, arts 157, 189 and 355).

Spontaneous Disclosure

Article 30 of the CIC provides that anybody who witnesses an attempt to commit a crime against the 'public safety' or the life or property of an individual must advise the public prosecutor. Faced with such situation, the banker would not be liable to the client for disclosing information evidencing the attempted crime.

Subpoenas from Foreign Jurisdictions

Belgium is a party to the European Convention on Judicial Assistance in Criminal Matters signed in Strasbourg on 4 April 1959 and to various other bilateral and multilateral treaties. Under the European Convention, a subpoena from a signatory state must be executed by the judicial authorities of the other in accordance with the latter's own procedural rules. Therefore, once the subpoena is accepted by the Belgian authorities, the banker finds himself in the same situation as when faced with a subpoena from a Belgian judge.

In the absence of an international treaty, the foreign subpoena must be authorised by the Belgian Minister of Justice (art 873 of the Judicial Code).

A specific procedure for foreign subpoenas ordering searches or the production of documents is set forth in art 11 of the 1874 Law on Extraditions.

Conclusion—Banker's Attitude

The banker's room for manoeuvre when faced with criminal proceeding is very limited. In most cases, he will have no other option in order to avoid criminal sanctions but to disclose information about his client or suffer a search.

In these circumstances, the banker will not be liable to his client for breach of the duty of confidentiality, provided that he stays within the general limits of disclosure (see p 54). This would require him, for instance, to limit his answers to the precise questions asked during the testimony and to mention any procedural illegalities related to the search that he would be aware of.

The banker will never be liable to his customer if the latter is eventually convicted of the charges pending at the time of the investigation or of the trial.

Civil Proceedings

Bankers' Testimonies and Production of Documents

Principles

The rules relating to evidence in Belgian civil procedure are based on two principles:

(I)   litigants and third parties must co-operate in the search for the truth; and
(II) the court may force them to do so.

The court may compel litigants (arts 871 and 877 of the Judicial Code—'Code Judiciaire'—hereinafter referred to as 'CJ') and third parties (CJ, arts 877–878) to produce documents. If they fail to comply with the court's order, they may have to pay damages to the party to whom their attitude causes a prejudice (CJ, art 882). Similar rules apply to testimonies (CJ, arts 915–916). Besides possible damages, a refusal to testify may also lead to criminal penalties, including imprisonment (art 495 bis of the Criminal Code, see also art 495).

This broad duty of disclosure is, however, qualified by two sets of rules:

(I)   the Court's subpoena must be valid; and
(II) the subpoena may be opposed for a 'legitimate reason'.

As in criminal proceedings, the banker, despite his duty of confidentiality, is bound by the same rules of disclosure as any other person.

The Subpoena must be Valid

The tests are laid down in arts 877 (production of documents), 915 (testimony at the request of the litigant) and 916 (testimony at the request of the court) of the Judicial Code. They can be summarised as follows, the first test applying to both testimony and presentation of documents, the other two to the latter only:

(I)   it must present the evidence of a relevant and precise fact: requests which are too broad (eg 'all documents in your possession') or too vague (eg 'any relevant document available') do not meet this test;

(II)   there must be precise and serious presumptions that the document is in the hands of the person requested to produce it: a mere suspicion of the possession of the document is therefore not enough; and

(III) the document must exist at the time of the request: a demand to establish a new document will be rejected.

Opposition to the Subpoena for a Legitimate Reason

Article 929 of the Judicial Code provides that:

(I)   witnesses may ask the court to be relieved from their duty to testify because of a legitimate reason ('motif légitime');

(II)   professional secrecy, among others, is to be deemed a legitimate reason; and

(III) the court must hear the witness and the (other) parties before reaching a decision as to this request.

By its terms, this provision only applies to testimonies. It is, however, widely accepted that the same rules apply to the production of documents (see CJ, arts 878 and 882 and the Van Reepinghen Report, on which the 1967 enactment of the Code Judiciaire was based).

The banker's duty of confidentiality is not generally deemed a duty of professional secrecy within the meaning of art 929. In specific circumstances, however, it can constitute a legitimate reason for not testifying or producing documents. Therefore, the judge would have to take the banker's request into consideration and balance his duty of confidentiality with the requirements of the search for the truth. Authors generally believe that such request by a banker is not likely to succeed, as courts would construe the 'legitimate reason' concept narrowly.

Subpoenas from Foreign Jurisdictions

As for criminal matters, Belgium adheres to many bilateral or multilateral treaties, including the International Convention on Civil Procedure, signed in The Hague on 1 March 1954. The same general principle of execution of the subpoena following the requested party's own procedural rules applies (see p 56).

Article 873 of the Judicial Code is applicable in the absence of an international treaty (see p 56).

Conclusion—Banker's attitude

As in criminal proceedings, the banker does not have many options when requested to testify or produce documents about his clients. He will not be liable to his client for breach of his duty of confidentiality, provided he has verified the validity of the subpoena, has raised any available legitimate reason to oppose disclosure and has stayed within the general limits of his duty of disclosure (see p 54).

'Garnishee Orders' ('Saisies-arrêts')

Notion

A creditor of the banker's client may have the banker 'garnished' as a third party owing money or property to the client-debtor. The order may be either a mere sequestration pending the outcome of litigation ('saisie-arrêt conservatoire'), or a step in the execution of a judgment ('saisie-arrêt exécution'). The procedures are strictly regulated by art 1386 ff of the Judicial Code.

This procedure obviously entails disclosure of information by the garnishee, ie by the bank.

The Banker must be the Client's Debtor—Specific problems

The fundamental test to be met in order for the 'procedure' to be valid is that the banker must be the client's debtor for the particular amount of money or property, object of the order. Questions arise as to what is a debt in a banker–client relationship:

Safe: If the client leaves property to be kept by the banker in the bank's safe, the banker owes him a duty of delivering it back to him, at his request. The banker is thus the client's debtor. If the client rents a private safe at the bank, however, the banker is a mere lessor and is not a debtor as to any of the property contained therein.

Line of Credit: The issue is not yet settled in Belgian law. The Van Reepinghen Report and a recent decision by the attachment judge ('juge des saisies') of Brussels have declared valid the application of the procedure to a line of credit, but some authors disagree. The practical significance of this is, however, limited, as the banker can revoke the line of credit for loss of confidence vis-à-vis his client at the time he receives the notice.

Pending Operations: The debt is equal to the credit balance of the account at the time notice of the order is given to the banker. Some operations prior to that date but affecting the balance at a later stage must also be taken into account. Such is the case for cheques signed by the account holder but not yet presented for payment at the bank. Such is not the case, however, for transfers of funds ordered prior to the garnishee order but not yet executed by the bank.

Operations taking place after the notice is given do not affect the amount of the debt subject to the order.

Banker's duty to disclose

Upon receipt of a notice of a 'saisie-arrêt' related to one of his clients, the banker must disclose to the creditor (with copy to the client), within a 15-day period, the following information (arts 1452–1456 of the Judicial Code):

(I)   In case he is currently the client's debtor:
        (A) origin of the debt, ie type of account or other banking operation the debt derives from;
        (B) amount of the debt;
        (C) terms of payment, if any; and
        (D) particular conditions of the debt, if any.
(II)   In case he has never been the client's debtor, the banker may simply declare so; or
(III) in case he is no longer a debtor, he must state when and how the debt was paid off and produce any relevant document evidencing such fact.

The banker must also disclose prior orders of which he received notice. It is not clear whether he must inform the creditor about accounts with a credit balance. The banker may always turn to the attachment judge to know the extent of the required disclosure.

Failure to issue such statement within the 15-day period or any misrepresentation of facts may result in the banker being held liable for part or all of his client's debts. The Van Reepinghen Report mentions fraud, bad faith or negligence as possible grounds for such measure, but it is left entirely up to the attachment judge whether and to what extent such penalty will be imposed. For instance, a short delay due to technical reasons or harmless to the client's creditor will normally not be sanctioned by the attachment judge.

Conclusion—Banker's Attitude

Given the penalty at stake, the banker must be careful to meet strictly the requirements of the 'saisie-arrêt'. His role is not to protect his client, who has at his disposal various means of opposing wrongful or abusive proceedings by his creditors. The banker is not expected, for instance, to oppose an order relating to amounts much greater than the client's debt. Many bankers seem, however, to have the habit of disclosing and blocking any increase of the account's credit balance after notice of the 'saisie-arrêt' is given, until the credit equals the client's debt to his creditor. Such practice is overly cautious and lacks any legal ground.

Communication of Information among Bankers

The Credit Risks Centre ('Centrale des Risques de Crédit')

Bankers are compelled to notify the National Bank ('Banque Nationale de Belgique') and the Banking Commission ('Commission Bancaire') of any grant of a credit or a loan of an amount superior to BF 1 million. Both institutions may ask the bank for further details, such as the level of withdrawals.

The National Bank gathers this information to constitute the Credit Risks Centre. It is accessible to banks, provided they have granted, or are negotiating, a credit or a loan greater than BF 1 million. The information disclosed includes the total amount of the client's credits from all banks in Belgium and the amount actually drawn, without any reference to specific banks or operations. The Credit Risks Centre is 'positive', i e it discloses all credit information, whether or not the client defaulted.

The Central Consumer Credit Office ('Centrale de Crédits à la Consommation')

The 1957 Law on Sales with Instalments Plans and their Financing provided the possibility for a central office for the registration of all such sales to be established. This Central Consumer Credit Office has operated since 1985 as part of the National Bank.

As far as banks are concerned, the following contracts need to be registered:

(I)   sales of movable property or loans with instalment plans falling under the 1957 statute;
(II)   the amount involved being between BF 10,000 and BF 1 million; and
(III)   there being a default on at least three of the instalments.

The information registered includes the type of contract involved, the identity of the parties to the contract and details on the way the credit has evolved.

The registered materials are available for consultation to:

(I)   individuals to a registered contract, but for that particular contract only;

(II)   individuals and companies authorised under the 1957 Law to operate sales or their financing with instalment plans;
(III) banks;
(IV)   the Banking Commission.

It is in fact compulsory for these categories to check the registration list prior to entering into any contract subject to the 1957 statute. Failure to disclose the required information or any misrepresentation thereof may lead to the withdrawal of the above-mentioned authorisation. This Central Consumer Credit Office is 'negative', as it is limited to the disclosure of clients' defaults.

Private 'Blacklists'

Private organisations have also set-up data systems to gather information for their members about their clients, especially in case of defaults or frauds. They include:

(I)   the 'Secrétariat Eurochèque';
(II)   the 'Union Professionnelle du Crédit' and its 'Mutuelle d'Information sur le Risque'; and
(III) the Belgian Association of Bankers and its 'Mutuelle d'Information pour favoriser la sécurité des opérations bancaires'.

Authors seem to agree that such private blacklists are legal, whether they are positive or merely negative. This exception to the banker's duty of confidentiality is accepted on the following grounds:

(I)   disclosure is made to other bankers: their duty of discretion prevents information from leaking to the general public;
(II)   such disclosure is justified by a higher social and economic interest: a safer and healthier credit for the public as a whole; and
(III) the system only affects 'bad' clients ie the ones who do not faithfully disclose the existence of other credits to their bankers and the ones who have defaulted on previous credits.

Information to the Tax Authorities

Registration Tax

Various types of operations, such as the sale of real estate, are subject to registration and payment of a tax to the Registration Administration ('Administration de l'Enregistrement et des Domaines'). Bankers may be compelled by this administration to disclose any information and document deemed relevant to determine the exact tax to be paid, when the bank or one of its clients is subject to such taxation (art 183 of the Registration Tax Code—'Code des Droits d'Enregistrement').

Inheritance Tax

The following rules of disclosure only apply when the deceased is a Belgian resident. (Non-residents are not subject to Belgian inheritance taxes, except in the case of real estate.)

Bankers' Passive Duty of Disclosure

Bankers have a similar passive duty of disclosure as the one related to registration taxes: the Registration Administration (which is also in charge of the collection of the inheritance taxes) may ask bankers for information relating to any operation of the deceased, his or her spouse, the heir, or any third party, that took place before or after the death and that may affect the taxation of the inheritance (art 100 of the Inheritance Tax Code—'Code des Droits de Succession').

Bankers' Active Duty of Disclosure

Bankers must keep records of all clients depositing sealed envelopes or boxes or renting safes, along with the identity of their spouses. They also keep a list of signatures of all client's mandatees or co-lessees asking to have access to the envelope, box or safe. These records are transmitted to the Registration Tax Administration (art 102–1 of the Inheritance Tax Code). The following disclosures occur in the event of death of a client or his or her spouse:

(I)   The banker must transmit to the Administration a list of all of the client's funds, securities or other properties in the bank's possession, before paying or delivering it back to the estate (art 97 of the Inheritance Tax Code).

(II) If the banker is in possession of sealed envelopes or boxes or if the client has rented a safe, he must:
  (A) notify the administration of the intended opening of the envelope, box or safe, at least 5 days in advance, and
  (B) transmit a list of the content of the envelope, box or safe at the time it is opened. The Registration Tax Administration may send one of its agents to witness the opening (arts 98 and 101 of the Inheritance Tax Code).

Value Added Tax ('Taxe sur la Valeur Ajoutée')

Bankers, like any other person subject to VAT, must list all operations with clients which are themselves subject to VAT. Bankers also owe a passive duty of disclosure: they must, if requested, transmit any relevant information and document enabling the VAT Administration to establish a correct taxation (art 61, para 2 of the VAT Code).

Revenue Taxes

Taxation Stage

The Revenue Tax Administration ('Administration des Contributions Directes') may request from any individual, corporation or other, information and relevant material necessary to determine the taxation of that party or of any third party (arts 221, 222, 223, 228 ff of the Revenue Tax Code—'Code des Impôts sur les Revenus' hereinafter referred to as CIR). As far as bankers are concerned, this broad duty of disclosure is qualified by CIR, art 224, 1, which provides that the Revenue Tax Administration may not check banks' books or records in order to determine their clients' taxations.

However, if in the course of an inquiry related to the banker's òwn tax situation, the Administration discovers relevant information leading to the presumption of the existence of a mechanism by which the banker and its customer are trying illegally to avoid the taxation of the latter's revenues, the Administration is allowed to investigate into the banker's records in order to determine the client's taxation (CIR, art 224, 2). If the Banking Commission, whose role is to supervise bankers, discovers such a mechanism, it must advise the Revenue Tax Administration, thus extending the latter's power of investigation to the same extent (CIR, art 235, para 5).

Articles 242 and 243 of the CIR provide that information discovered by one tax administration may be used by another to determine another category of tax. It seems, however, that the Revenue Tax Administration may not use this provision as a basis for requesting other tax administrations to get from a bank the information it needs about one of its clients. Such construction of the statute would render meaningless the limits to the Revenue Tax Administration's power of investigation. Article 224 was enacted in 1980, over 40 years later than arts 242 and 243 and it should be understood as limiting the rule of co-operation among the various tax administrations.

Complaint Stage

When the taxpayer contests the taxation of his revenue, the Revenue Tax Administration may require information from his banker, to investigate the validity of the complaint (CIR, art 275). It is accepted, however, that the taxpayer may forbid his banker from disclosing any information, even though such attitude will obviously greatly undermine his chances of succeeding with his complaint. Bankers often spontaneously refuse to release information that could reveal the identity of other clients.

Information to Regulatory Authorities

Banking Commission

The Banking Commission supervises bankers through auditors. Neither auditors nor members of the Banking Commission may reveal any information they come across in the course of their supervision activities, subject to certain exceptions such as judicial proceedings.

A breach of this rule leads to the criminal sanctions provided for in art 458 of the Criminal Code (see p 52) (arts 40 and 45 of the Royal Decree No 185 of 9 July 1935).

The banker's duty of disclosure to the Banking Commission and the National Bank as to credits and loans superior to BF 1 million has been mentioned above (see p 59).

Foreign Exchange Control

Various types of operations must be disclosed by banks to the 'Institut Belgo-Luxembourgeois du Change' ('Arrêté-loi' of 6 October 1944 and the various application statutes and regulations).

Information to Persons in the Sphere of Confidentiality

Certain persons may require information from the banker because of their special relationship with the client if they are associated with, or have taken over, the management of the client's assets and are, therefore, included in the sphere of confidentiality. These situations should not be considered as real exceptions, but rather as flexible applications of the rule of confidentiality.

The following categories can be identified:

(I)   persons representing the client, including the representative of the legally incapable, the client's agents (e g the directors of a corporation), the administrator of a bankrupt company, the company's liquidator etc;

(II)   persons continuing the client's legal status after his death, e g the legal heir or the heir by will having accepted the estate as a whole ('légataire universel');

(III) persons having the same right as the client on the assets in the banker's possession, eg the spouse under certain circumstances. The banker must advise the client's spouse of any opening of an account or renting of a safe (art 218 of the Civil Code). The spouse may request information from the banker as to the client's assets, provided he or she shows evidence that such money or property belongs to the couple's common property.

CONCLUSION

This description of the banker's duty of confidentiality has put much more emphasis on the exceptions to the rule, more specific to Belgian law, than on the duty itself. In many circumstances, the banker will not be allowed to raise his duty of discretion to oppose requests of disclosure.

It must be remembered, however, that the rule of confidentiality, in its principle and scope, and the potential liability in case of breach are clearly established in Belgium. Therefore, the banker, if required to disclose information about his client's operations to public authorities or private persons, must not depart from his traditional cautious attitude: he will ensure that procedural rules have not been violated and limit the release of information or documents to the required minimum.

4 Canada

David W Drinkwater and James E Fordyce*

INTRODUCTION

This chapter examines Canadian legal aspects of the relationship between a bank and its customers. The analysis has become more complicated and the implications potentially more significant as a result of the desire and newfound ability of Canadian banks to diversify into new areas of financial services. These factors have also been affected by the apparent willingness of Canadian courts to impose responsibilities and obligations upon banks which reflect their new powers and activities and which go beyond those which banks have traditionally assumed.

The relationship between a bank and its customers has always been multi-faceted but, in the past, relatively straightforward. It is one of debtor and creditor as regards the money in the customer's account but better characterised as one of agent and principal with respect to the bank's obligations to pay the customer's cheques. The nature and extent of the obligations which flow from these relationships are generally understood and accepted by the banks. More recently, however, Canadian courts have held, under the appropriate circumstances, that a bank may be held to be a fiduciary in relation to its customer.[1] In addition to judicial development, there are statutory responsibilities, some expanded by recent legislative initiatives, that apply in new areas of activities for Canadian banks, such as securities dealing and investment banking. These developments may also pose some new and quite significant obligations on banks as they attempt to provide a broader range of financial services. These new judicial and legislative responses have developed from the changing nature of contemporary banking in Canada. Although these changes are partly due to domestic developments, they are also partly a response to various international trends and initiatives which are part of the evolution of modern banking in the context of the general trend of business toward globalisation.

Changes are particularly noticeable in the competitive arena of corporate banking where the entry of Canadian banks into the securities field is part of a general movement towards universal or 'one-stop' financial shopping. This has brought with it not only many opportunities but some potential problems in areas such as conflicts of interest and disclosure.

Until recently, the financial sector in Canada had a Glass-Steagall style separation of functions, referred to as the 'four pillars'. These pillars represented banking, insurance, trust operations and the securities industry, with separation between the four sectors strictly maintained. In the last few years legislation has been introduced to break down these distinctions and banks are now permitted

---

* With assistance from Rosemary Schmidt.
1 D Waters 'Banks, Fiduciary Obligations and Unconscionable Transactions' [1986] 65 Can BR 37.

to operate in the securities industry, albeit primarily through separate subsidiaries. As a result, all but one of the major Canadian banks have each acquired a major Canadian securities firm.

These developments and the ongoing administration and regulation of these activities are complicated in Canada by the constitutional structure which is a federal system that places banks under the overlapping jurisdictions of the federal and provincial governments. While banking is a federal matter governed by the federal Bank Act,[2] other financial transactions in which banks or their subsidiaries are involved, such as securities matters, are primarily under provincial jurisdiction. Moreover, to the extent not specifically dealt with by federal banking legislation, matters such as contract law and agency, are governed by the laws (common law and statutory) of each province.[3]

The developments have led to new challenges involving balancing the banks' desire to expand their scope of operation and the customer's need for secrecy and the banks' duty of confidentiality and the conflict of interests that may arise. The implications are not confined to the domestic context but also have an international dimension.

THE BANK'S DUTY OF CONFIDENTIALITY

Confidentiality is fundamental to the relationship between a bank and its customers. In Canada the bank's legal duty of confidentiality is founded in the common law and consists of an implied contractual duty not to divulge information about its customer's accounts to third parties without the consent of the customer as laid down in the leading English case of *Tournier v National Provincial and Union Bank of England*.[4] Although the principle is easy to state, its ultimate scope continues to evolve such that the potential breadth always remains somewhat unclear. The duty is not absolute, however, and a number of exceptions exist. These exceptions, as discussed below, have been further refined in the courts, but the main spur to development of the law in this area has come from statutory enactments that delimit the bank's obligations of secrecy and clarify the circumstances under which a bank is entitled or even bound to disclose what would otherwise be confidential information.

---

2 RSC 1985, c B-1. Although banks in Canada are governed by federal law and may (and normally do) carry on business through branches in one or more provinces, ss 211 and 212 of the Bank Act provide in essence for a 'branch of account' for each deposit account of a customer, which is the situs of the debt owing by the bank to the customer in respect of that account and also provide that notices of process or assignment and the like relating to an account only bind the bank if served on the branch of account. Apart from providing relief to banks with many branches in different provinces (up to a thousand or more) these provisions codify and refine the common law as to situs of the contract of confidentiality between a bank and its customer and hence the governing law of such contract.

It should also be noted that the Bank Act applies to foreign banks carrying on the business of banking in Canada. These banks may only do so by way of subsidiaries and not by way of branches (although a foreign bank subsidiary may have more than one branch in Canada).

3 While there may be some variation between the laws of the Canadian common law provinces, mainly as a result of statutory provisions, it may in general be said that laws applicable to commercial operations are similar in each of those provinces. In addition, the laws in the Province of Quebec are based on the French civil law system, which although often similar in result to that found in the common law provinces, nevertheless further complicate the regulatory system. For purposes of this paper, federal and Ontario laws are discussed.

4 [1924] 1 KB 461.

Limitations on Duty of Confidentiality

The *Tournier* case outlines four exceptions to the bank's duty of confidentiality:

(I)   the bank may disclose information when the customer consents to the disclosure expressly or by necessary implication;

(II)   disclosure may be made when it is necessary to the bank's interests;

(III)   the bank must disclose confidential customer information when it is so compelled by law; and

(IV)   disclosure is permitted where there is a public duty to do so.

These exceptions are discussed in light of relevant developments in Canadian law.

Express/Implied Consent of the Customer

As a general principle, no disclosure is authorised beyond what is necessary by implication in order to carry out the customer's instructions. Thus, as indicated in *Tournier*, it is clearly permissible to disclose customer account information when the bank has been asked to give a credit reference. However, consent is not to be implied simply because the banker believes disclosure to be in the customer's best interest, particularly if it is possible to contact the customer to ascertain directly whether permission would be given. In addition, the information which may be disclosed in a credit reference without express consent is limited.[5]

In the Bank's Own Interest

In *Tournier* this exception was discussed as referring to cases where a bank brings an action against its customer for payment of a debt owed. It is necessary under such circumstances to disclose the amount owed even though this would otherwise be in breach of the bank's duty of confidentiality. This exception does not apply, however, to cases where the bank is a third party to a proceeding.

Banks may wish to exchange information for a variety of reasons. In some cases the exchange is supported by a statutory provision. For example, the federal

---

5   For instance, *Tournier* stated that the bank would be justified in disclosing that a cheque could not be honoured due to lack of sufficient funds, but to disclose the extent of the insufficiency would be more information than was strictly necessary to enable the bank to perform its duties. Although the precise extent to which customer consent to disclosure can be implied is unclear, in the Ontario case of *Hull v Childs & Huron and Erie Mortgage Corp* [1951] OWN 116 (HCJ), where the customer had signed a series of blank cheques, the financial institution was held liable for breach of its duty of secrecy because it disclosed to the bearer of the cheques the total amount of money in the account so as to enable him to withdraw it all. The court held that it was unwarranted for the bank to infer that the customer intended all of his funds to be withdrawn by virtue of his having given someone blank cheques.

It should also be noted that there is provincial consumer reporting legislation, such as the Consumer Reporting Act in Ontario RSO 1980, C 89, which govern the operations of credit bureaus. The legislation does not require explicit consent before a credit reference can be given by a bank or other credit granting agency. It does, however, differentiate between 'credit' information and 'personal' information. If personal information is to be supplied or if a report is to be requested from a credit bureau regarding a customer, the customer must be notified in a prescribed manner prior to making a request for a credit report or providing such personal information. As a matter of routine, however, this notification is incorporated into standard forms, such as applications for loans, used by banks and credit reports are routinely given and obtained by Canadian banks on their customers through independent credit reporting agencies as well as by way of direct reports to other banks. Normally a bank will not knowingly give a credit report other than to another financial institution or a bona fide credit reporting agency.

Competition Act[6] contains express provisions setting out conditions under which banks are permitted to have agreements or arrangements with one another which might otherwise be considered as anticompetitive. Among the permitted arrangements are those for the exchange of credit information.

Compulsion of Law

The bank's duty to disclose confidential information under compulsion of law is expressed primarily in the ever-increasing web of statutory provisions.

Legislation Relating to Evidence

There are federal and provincial statutes which generally provide that a bank must disclose records in its possession where they could serve as evidence in the course of civil, criminal or arbitral proceedings not involving the bank. However, a court order is usually required before the bank can be compelled either to appear as a witness or to produce a customer's records.[7]

Tax Legislation

Under the Income Tax Act,[8] Revenue Canada may examine a third party's records if they relate to a taxpayer and the third party must answer any relevant questions. Therefore, a bank may be required to provide for inspection to Revenue Canada a customer's bank records and respond to inquiries on the customer's transactions. These provisions have been interpreted to mean that a bank can be required to disclose records of transactions even if the result would mean disclosing private information of the bank's customers who are not themselves under investigation.[9]

Securities and Corporate Law

The provincial securities Acts provide broad powers of investigation, search and seizure which Securities Commission staff utilise in investigating securities law matters. These are frequently used to investigate a wide range of securities-related activities such as allegations or suspicions of insider trading or other misuse of confidential information.[10]

Criminal Law

The federal Criminal Code also contains typical powers of search and seizure in connection with the commission of a crime.[11] More recently, tracing the proceeds of crime has become an increasing concern in Canada, as it has in other jurisdictions.

---

6 RSC 1985, c C-34, as amended, s 49.
7 For example, see the Canada Evidence Act RSC 1985, c C-5. The provisions in the Evidence Act ensure that bank records are not seized every time one of its customers is in litigation, and they take precedence over the Criminal Code provision RSC 1985, c C-46, which permits seizure of records where there are reasonable grounds to believe the records will afford evidence of the commission of an offence. *R v Mowat, ex parte Toronto Dominion Bank* (1967) 1 OR 179 (Ont HCJ). In general terms, these provisions are not dissimilar to those of the Bankers' Books Evidence Act (1879 (UK)) which has been widely adopted in British Commonwealth jurisdictions.
8 RSC 1985 Supplement.
9 *Canadian Bank of Commerce v A-G of Canada* (1962) 35 DLR (2nd) 49 (SCC).
10 For example see the Ontario Securities Act, RSO 1980, c 466, s 11. There are also powers that can be granted to inspectors under the corporate law statutes. See, for instance, the Ontario Business Corporations Act, SO 1982, c 4, Part XIII. In the Canadian context these latter powers are used less frequently than in some other jurisdictions given the broad powers and responsibilities of securities regulators. Investigations under the powers of the corporate statutes tend to focus on internal matters involving the corporation and its directors or holders of its securities.
11 RSC 1985, c C-46.

In response to this concern, the federal government has recently enacted 'money laundering' legislation[12] in the form of amendments to the Criminal Code, the Food and Drugs Act[13] and the Narcotic Control Act[14] which affects banks in two primary ways. First, there is created an indictable offence of knowingly dealing with the proceeds of selected drug related and 'enterprise crime' offences, such as bribery, fraud and bookmaking. Second, the statute establishes that there will be no civil or criminal liability in disclosing to the authorities facts upon which a person suspects that certain property may be the proceeds of crime. Thus, while a bank can be held liable for knowingly dealing with such funds and cannot be liable for disclosing a reasonable suspicion, there is no affirmative duty on the bank to make such disclosure if it only suspects the money to have come from illegal sources but has no definitive knowledge thereof. Nevertheless, the legislation creates an incentive for the bank to report what it regards as suspicious financial activity. The bank will want to ensure that in any potential prosecutions it does not find itself in the position of having to assert that, though it suspected, it did not know, that certain funds were proceeds of crime. This can be contrasted with the legislation in other jurisdictions under which it would be an offence for the bank not to report such suspicions.

These new duties of disclosure under Canadian legislation are still less intrusive compared to those of certain other common law jurisdictions. For example, in addition to there being no obligation to report suspicions, as noted above, there is no legislation requiring the disclosure of specified cash transactions as in the United States and Australia. Neither is it an offence under these federal provisions for the bank to inform its customers under certain circumstances that it has been required to disclose information as it is in the United States and England. On the other hand, under securities legislation it would be an offence to inform a customer of a requirement to disclose information in the context of a securities investigation.[15]

Other Legislation

In addition to the foregoing, there are many other statutes in Canada, ranging from bankruptcy to public inquiries which can also apply as exceptions to the duty of confidentiality.[16]

Public Duty to Disclose

This rarely-used exception was referred to in *Tournier* in the context of preventing acts that might present a danger to the state and the decision seemed to imply that there would be a wide range of circumstances in which this exception might apply.

---

12 SC 1988, c 51.
13 RCS 1985, c F-27.
14 RCS 1985, c N-1.
15 See for example the Ontario Securities Act, above n 10, s 14.
16 Bankruptcy Act RSC 1985, c B-3. The Bankruptcy Act imposes on the Bank an affirmative duty to inform the Trustee in Bankruptcy if the bank discovers that its customer is an undischarged bankrupt. In addition, banks may be ordered by the court to produce the records or accounts of a company winding-up under the provisions of the Winding-Up Act, RSC 1985, c W-10.

 Inquiries Act RSC 1985, c I-13. Banks can also be subject to the Inquiries Act which provides that in the course of an inquiry any person can be subpoenaed to appear, testify and produce any documents in his possession which relate to the subject matter of the inquiry. This provision is particularly far-reaching since there are at least 47 federal statutes which confer powers of inquiry by reference to the Inquiries Act and hence any of these statutes could be used to impose a duty of disclosure. See R Regan 'You don't say' (1982) 89 *Canadian Banker* 32 at 34.

In a sense the primary 'public duty' obligations come under specific legislation such as the traditional evidence legislation or the new 'money laundering' provisions. The legislated duty relieves the bank of having to decide whether a sufficiently high public good would be served by disclosure so as to supersede the private duty to maintain confidentiality. This difficult judgment, combined with the ever broadening legislative requirements, may explain why this has been a little used exception.[17]

International Aspects

Provisions to Restrict Demands for Information

The banks have always operated on an international basis and the nature and scope of these activities have gradually been developing and expanding along with the general trend to globalisation. This has been combined with an increasing degree of legislative and judicial activity in, or affecting, many jurisdictions in a manner and to an extent which did not happen in the past. The interaction of rules of two jurisdictions can result in conflict of legislative goals and therefore courts and legislators have attempted to deal with banks or others caught between conflicting rules.

For example, when Canadian banks are subpoenaed by foreign courts to provide information regarding customer accounts, they may be protected from having to breach their customers' confidence by virtue of the blocking legislation in the Foreign Extraterritorial Measures Act.[18] This statute provides that the Attorney General of Canada can block the production, disclosure or identification of any records in the possession or control of a Canadian citizen or a person resident in Canada if he believes that significant Canadian interests in international trade will be adversely affected. Such an order can be made in response to an order by a foreign tribunal, a foreign court judgment or measures taken by a foreign state. The term 'records' is defined very broadly so as to include virtually any stored or recorded information. If the Attorney General makes such an order and believes that it may not be complied with, he may apply to a superior court to seize the records in question for safekeeping. Contravention of a blocking order by the Attorney General is an indictable offence even if it is committed outside Canada and is punishable by a fine of up to C$10,000 or a prison term of up to five years. There are, however, no reported cases where this legislation has been used to prevent disclosure of confidential customer records by a Canadian bank.

The Competition Act may also be used to block the implementation of foreign judgments, decrees, orders or other processes in Canada if the Competition Tribunal finds that their effect would be detrimental to competition, trade or industry in Canada without providing compensating advantages.

---

17 An interesting interpretation was placed on the public duty exception in *Canada Deposit Insurance Corporation v Canadian Commercial Bank* [1989] AJ No 44, No 8503–23319, (Alta QB). There the plaintiff deposit insurance corporation (an agency of the federal government) brought an action against a bank which had gone into receivership, in order to obtain access to the bank's records directly rather than by way of discovery. Such access would enable it to more effectively seek recovery of funds it had paid out to the bank's depositors. The court held that this case fell under *Tournier*'s public duty exception, and that the public interest required that disclosure be made in this more efficient way.

18 RSC 1985, c F-29.

Procedures for Agreed Exchange of Information

Although Canadian legislators have attempted to ensure there would not be inappropriate compulsion of information by foreign tribunals, they have also co-operated to facilitate exchange in appropriate circumstances. Perhaps the best recent example is the memorandum of understanding ('MOU') executed in January 1988 between several Canadian provincial securities regulators and the United States Securities and Exchange Commission. These MOUs provide for broad exchange of information in the interests of regulating securities markets which are increasingly international in scope. When combined with the broad powers of search and seizure provided to provincial securities regulators, the MOUs increase the potential for confidential information being distributed to an even wider group.

Domestic Proceedings to Obtain Information from Foreign Banks or Branches

Although there is Canadian legislation to block information going abroad in circumstances where it would be contrary to Canadian policy, the same can occur in reverse where a Canadian court attempts to overcome restrictions on disclosure in a foreign jurisdiction. The conditions under which Canadian courts will insist on disclosure of records from a foreign bank have been explored in *Frischke et al v Royal Bank of Canada et al*[19] and *Re Spencer and the Queen.*[20]

Frischke involved an appeal from a court order requiring Royal Bank employees in Panama to give evidence about certain customers' accounts in breach of Panamanian law. The court, in allowing the appeal, refused to use its jurisdiction over the Royal Bank to order it to compel its Panamanian employees to break their own country's laws.

Frischke was distinguished in *Re Spencer*, however. There the Crown sought to call an employee of the Royal Bank as a witness on charges against a customer of the bank under the Income Tax Act. While a subpoena of this kind would present no problems in the normal case, the employee was at the material time manager of the Royal Bank's Bahamian branch, and was being asked to give evidence regarding transactions which had been made in the Bahamas, contrary to bank confidentiality provisions of Bahamian law. The Ontario Court of Appeal held that compellability of a witness was a matter for the *lex fori* and that in Canada, this witness was compellable. He was not being forced to give any evidence in contravention of Canadian laws even though he might be exposed to liability in another jurisdiction.

On appeal to the Supreme Court of Canada, the Court of Appeal decision was upheld on the grounds that even if the giving of evidence in Canada constituted a crime in the Bahamas, the courts and the public have a right to the evidence. To permit a witness to refuse to testify would be to permit a foreign country to frustrate the administration of justice in Canada with regard to a Canadian citizen. It was suggested by Estey J, however, that comity would require that the witness be allowed to make an application to that foreign jurisdiction to permit disclosure before the court compels him to do so.

FIDUCIARY RELATIONSHIP

As noted above, although the traditional bank/customer relationship is normally one of debtor and creditor or principal and agent, under the appropriate

19 (1977) 80 DLR (3d) 393.
20 (1983) 145 DLR (3d) 344 (Ont CA), affd (1985) 21 DLR (4th) 756 (SCC).

circumstances it can become a fiduciary relationship. Such a relationship goes beyond confidentiality and may impose additional duties upon a bank. In Canada, a fiduciary relationship has been considered to arise when a bank steps outside its conventional relationship and gives advice to a customer, upon which the customer relies (to the bank's knowledge) and from which the bank stands to receive a benefit or alternatively when the bank misuses information obtained from a customer. Although it is possible that such a relationship can arise in circumstances where a bank is confining itself to more traditional banking activities, the circumstances in which it may be created are being expanded as the banks move into the securities dealing and investment banking fields and take a broader and more active role in areas such as trading, investment management, takeovers and mergers and acquisitions.

The leading Canadian case dealing with a bank's fiduciary duties towards its customers is *Standard Investments Ltd et al v Canadian Imperial Bank of Commerce*.[21] In this case the plaintiffs attempted to acquire control of a publicly quoted trust company. They sought the advice and assistance of the bank's president, who agreed to help them. Unbeknownst to the president, however, the bank's chairman had already decided to have the bank purchase for its own account just under 10% of the shares of the trust company in order to thwart an anticipated takeover attempt, which some speculated was to be made by the plaintiffs. An outside director of the bank was also a director of the trust company and controlled or influenced significant shareholdings in the trust company. Both this director and the trust company were important customers of the bank. In addition, when it became clear there was a fight for control, the bank subsequently assisted another of its customers in the purchase of a 44% interest in the trust company which, together with the bank's 10% interest (which it subsequently sold to that other customer) effectively prevented the plaintiffs' takeover from being successful.

It was held at the Court of Appeal that a fiduciary relationship had been created. The plaintiffs had 'bared their souls' to the bank by providing it with confidential information regarding their takeover plans. In addition, the plaintiffs relied on the advice and assistance of the bank in their endeavour and the bank was aware of that reliance. Finally, the bank itself had obtained a benefit through the increased business that resulted from the plaintiffs' relationship with the bank as a result of their previously transferring accounts to the bank. Thus, all the criteria for the establishment of a fiduciary relationship were satisfied. As a result, the court held that the bank had a duty to disclose its conflict of interest.

It might be noted that there were actually two conflicts at play in this case. First, there was a conflict between the bank's interests and those of its customers, the plaintiffs. Second, there was the conflict between the interests of plaintiffs and those of the bank's other customers who, to the knowledge of the bank, wanted to prevent the takeover from occurring. The Court of Appeal acknowledged that the bank probably had a legal obligation not to disclose the second conflict. However, the court said that if the bank was either unwilling or unable to disclose the nature of the conflicts, it should have said that it was unable to advise the plaintiffs due to existing conflicts of interest. Alternatively, if the bank was unwilling or felt unable to disclose to a customer that a conflict existed, the bank should simply have refused to advise the plaintiffs on the matter. In fact, the court found the bank did neither of these things but rather allowed the plaintiffs to believe, over the course

---

21 (1985) 52 OR (2d) 473 (CA).

of seven years, that their takeover bid had a chance of success. The bank was, therefore, held to be in breach of its duties to them. Damages were assessed at the amount of the plaintiffs' purchase price of the trust company shares, plus the interest lost from what would have been safe investments, minus the amount received in dividends and ultimate proceeds from the sale of the shares, which fell substantially in value when the third party was able to acquire control.

Although the courts have been careful to point out that the question of whether a fiduciary relationship will be found to exist depends on all of the circumstances of a given case, there appear to be some common threads. For example, where the bank goes further than to simply explain the nature and effect of a transaction, and advises on its merit, it may be held to have 'crossed the line' from a normal debtor/creditor relationship into one involving fiduciary duties.[22]

It would appear, however, that in order for a fiduciary relationship to be established, there must also be an element of special reliance or confidence placed in the branch by the customer, either by virtue of communication of particular knowledge or by reason of ignorance or infirmity of the customer. In either case, the bank must either know, or be in circumstances where it ought to know, of the reliance being placed upon it. Once that reliance is found, then a fiduciary relationship may be said to exist and the breach thereof by misuse of information provided or by permitting the bank's own interests to conflict with those of the customer, is actionable.

Standard Investments provides an illustration of a finding of reliance by reason of the customer having provided particular information, notwithstanding that the customer's principals were experienced businessmen. An example of reliance found by reason of the circumstances of the customer (a more common situation) is *Hayward v Bank of Nova Scotia*[23] where the trial judge found a fiduciary relationship to exist where a highly respected small-town bank manager undertook to advise a farm widow in modest circumstances on investments in exotic cattle for which she was proposing to borrow from the bank against the security of the family farm. Through dealings with the promoter of the investment (who was also heavily indebted to the bank and behind in his obligations in respect of that debt) the bank manager had gained considerable knowledge of the exotic cow business. His enthusiasm for the business was not shared to the same extent by his superiors although their doubts were not fully communicated to the bank manager.

At trial, the case turned on the naivety of the customer and the faulty advice provided by the bank manager coupled with the inequality of bargaining position. Little, if anything, was said about where the proceeds of the investment were to go. Presumably, they went to pay down the promoter's loans, which would, of course, be of advantage to the bank since he was behind in his payments. The Court of Appeal reluctantly affirmed the trial decision disapproving however, the trial judge's reliance on the inequality of bargaining position as being relevant to the breach of fiduciary duty as opposed to the creation of the fiduciary relationship. However, the Court again made no clear reference to what appeared to be a direct conflict between the bank's interest in having support for the cow business and its obligation to provide appropriate advice to the widow. In both judgments, the courts appeared to rely upon the decision of the English

22 Waters 58.
23 (1984) 45 OR (2d) 542 (HC), affd 510 OR (2d) 193 (CA).

Court of Appeal in *Lloyds Bank Ltd v Bundy*.[24] The reasons of the Court of Appeal in *Hayward*, however, also referred to the later decision of the House of Lords in *National Westminster Bank plc v Morgan*[25] quoting from Lord Scarman's speech,[26] to the effect that the presumption of undue influence cannot arise from the evidence of the relationship of the parties without also evidence that the transaction itself is wrongful in that it constitutes an advantage taken of the party subjected to the influence. Thus, the notion that a fiduciary relationship can be established by reason of inequality of bargaining power alone was rejected.

Standard Investments and cases such as *Hayward*, which were decided in the early and mid-1980s, represented perhaps the culmination of a series of cases where it appeared that the courts were becoming more than willing to find the existence of a fiduciary relationship. More recent cases give some indication that the courts are again becoming less inclined to superimpose a fiduciary relationship on the dealings between a bank and its customers, particularly if the plaintiffs are themselves knowledgeable business people.[27] It remains to be seen, however, whether these more recent cases will really assist the bank in circumstances such as contested takeovers where the parties do have a significant degree of investment experience and sophistication. The principle is, however, clearly established and one which Canadian banks will have to bear in mind as they develop their entry into an ever-increasing breadth of financial services.

CONFLICTS OF INTEREST

As mentioned in the preceding discussion, banks have duties of confidentiality in the normal course of a banking relationship. Such a relationship can be expanded to a fiduciary one and, in these circumstances, a bank may have an affirmative duty to disclose or at least not to act in a transaction if to do so would result in a conflict of interest. As the range of activities in which banks and their affiliates are engaged has increased, so has the potential for such conflicts.

Perhaps the most straightforward conflict is the situation where a director or officer of the bank is considered to have an interest in a transaction to which the bank is a party. The Bank Act adopts a conventional corporate law approach and provides that except under specified circumstances, a director may not attend or vote at a board or committee meeting at which the bank is considering whether to advance funds to him, to a firm of which he is a member or a corporation of which he is a director. In addition, the Bank Act sets out certain restrictions on loans to officers, employees and directors of a bank and to entities in which officers or directors of a bank have interests.[28] The fact that there is in Canada a relatively small number of banks which are large in size and that these banks tend to have large boards of directors, when combined with a significant, and increasing, concentration of ownership in Canadian business make these potentially more significant provisions than may first appear.

A more frequent and increasing occurrence is that of conflicts of interest between customers. In the field of hostile takeovers, the interaction of the concentration of ownership of Canadian business and the relatively small

24 [1974] 3 All ER 757.
25 [1985] All ER 821.
26 Ibid at 827.
27 For example, see *Continental Bank of Canada v Hunter*, Alta CA 6 November 1986; and *Sugar et al v Peat Marwick Limited et al* (1989) 66 OR (2d) 766.
28 Bank Act, above no 2, ss 52 and 174.

number of large Canadian banks can make such conflicts particularly problematic. As in the United States, most Canadian bids are financed with a significant amount of debt. It is not uncommon in a major takeover bid in Canada to have most of the major Canadian banks holding significant amounts of debt of the target. As a result, in order to preclude any claim of conflict, the acquiror may seek, to finance the acquisition debt completely from non-Canadian bank sources.

Conflicts can also arise between the interests of the bank and those of its customers as exemplified in *Standard Investments* where the bank purchased shares in the target trust company for its own account while simultaneously 'assisting' the plaintiff customers in their takeover bid and also keeping the plaintiffs' important banking business. As noted, the court held that the bank could have resolved the conflict by either disclosing to the customers the nature of the conflict or by simply refusing to advise them on their takeover plans.

The potential of conflict may now also arise between the banks' lending activities and the underwriting and selling activities of their new securities affiliates. When it was agreed that banks could enter the securities business, the securities regulators expressed concern about the potential for conflict if a securities firm was underwriting and distributing debt or equity securities of a third party issuer in circumstances when that issuer was significantly indebted to, or otherwise connected in a material way with, the securities dealer's bank affiliate. Accordingly, a complex set of regulations is now in place to attempt to meet these concerns.[29]

The bank's securities affiliate must prepare a statement of policies outlining how it will deal with the securities of connected issuers and must send the policy to the regulators and to customers. If a third party issuer is considered 'connected' to the bank then any prospectus of the issuer in which the securities affiliate is an underwriter must disclose the existence and nature of the relationship in bold print on the cover of the prospectus with a more detailed description in the body of the prospectus. The interpretation and application of these provisions is made difficult by the subjective nature of their application. An issuer is considered 'connected' to a bank when

(I)   the level of indebtedness or other relationship is such as to lead a potential purchaser of securities to question the independence of the issuer from the bank, or

(II) when there is a reasonable likelihood such investor would consider such indebtedness or other relationship important in his investment decision.

In addition to the disclosure requirements there are certain prohibitions. The securities affiliate is not permitted to underwrite securities of any connected issuer, or those of its bank affiliate, unless an independent dealer underwrites at least the same proportion as the bank's securities affiliate.

The concern about conflicts between banks and their securities affiliates has also been noted by the federal banking regulators. The federal authorities recently released revised guidelines for the procedures for federally-regulated financial institutions, such as banks, obtaining approval for the acquisition of more than a 10% interest in a Canadian corporation, such as a securities firm.[30] The guidelines require the applicant to outline specifically their policies and

---

29 See Part XII of the regulations to the Ontario Securities Act, above no 10.

30 Guideline 18, Re Shareholdings by Federally Regulated Financial Institutions in Securities Dealers. Published by the office of the Superintendent of Financial Institutions of Canada, 27 July 1989.

procedures 'for effective handling of any conflicts of interest that may arise between [the bank] and the [securities firm]'.

MISUSE OF CONFIDENTIAL INFORMATION

The recent changes to the Canadian regulatory framework referred to above permitting banks to undertake securities activities have also increased the potential for misuse of confidential information. In the context of the new multi-service approach of contemporary Canadian banking, this problem can arise more often as a result of the bank's obligations to different clients in its various areas of business. For example, problems could arise if confidential information moved between a bank's commercial lending services and its new securities sales, trading or related activities. Information held by one department or affiliate could materially affect the decisions made in the other if that information were available to it.

To date, the methods which have been utilised to deal with these potential concerns have evolved, or been derived, primarily from the North American securities experience and practice. The principal approach is to rely on concepts such as Chinese Walls, or other systems which are intended to provide for segregation of information within separate areas and departments so as to allow financial institutions to conduct activities in all areas of the financial services sector without improper use of information.

As discussed further below, most banks and other financial instititions active in a range of financial services have now instituted procedures to avoid potential conflicts of interest by preventing the transmission of information among departments or to subsidiaries. In addition to Chinese Walls, restricted securities lists such as so-called 'grey' or 'watch' lists which prevent or restrict trading by employees or departments in specified securities are now commonly employed.[31]

The additional responsibilities, and the steps taken to deal with them, have not arisen solely by virtue of expanding the banks' areas of permitted activity. At the same time as the restrictions on the activities of banks and other financial institutions have been reduced, securities legislators have also been introducing expanded rules relating to insider trading or other misuse of confidential information.

Regulation of insider trading is considered within the legislative competence of both levels of government. The federal government (through the Bank Act and the Canada Business Corporations Act)[32] and the provinces (through securities statutes) have enacted legislation dealing with insider trading. The legislation typically precludes trading on the knowledge of a material fact or a material change concerning a public company which has not been generally disclosed.[33] It also precludes informing, or 'tipping', anyone about such information, except in

---

31 A 'grey' list refers to a list of companies for which a dealer has been retained on a matter which represents, or makes the dealer otherwise aware of, material undisclosed information in respect of a public company. As the information is not public, only certain senior officers of the dealer would be aware of the companies on the grey list and would be responsible to ensure the dealer undertook no trading or other improper activity. A 'restricted' list is broadly circulated within the dealer and used for companies for which the dealer will not trade due to the activities of the dealer or the issuer. At this stage the activities have been released publicly but the restriction on trading continues.

32 See the Bank Act, above no 2, Part IV, Division H and regulations; the Canada Business Corporations Act RSC 1985 c C-44 Part XI; and the Ontario Securities Act above no 10, s 75.

33 Ontario Securities Act, above no 10, s 75.

the necessary course of business. In either case in order for the trading or tipping to be an offence the party in question must be in a 'special relationship' with the public company. The term special relationship is broadly defined, however, and includes any party that engages or proposes to engage in a business or professional activity on behalf of a party such as a prospective bidder. As a result a bank which proposes to fund or advise a bidder is in a special relationship and subject to the legislation and can only disclose material information to the extent it can conclude it is in the necessary course of business to do so.

In certain provinces insider trading legislation has become increasingly stringent both in scope of application and potential fines. For example, previously it was possible to defend a charge of insider trading by showing that, although the vendor or purchaser of securities was aware of material undisclosed information, it did not make use of it in making the trade. Therefore, if material undisclosed information was known by persons in different departments in a financial group it did not preclude trading so long as the party did not make use of the information in trading. The regulators became increasingly concerned that it would be difficult to prove whether or not a party made use of the information and accordingly the regulators have removed the exception. The vendor or purchaser must now show that persons who participated in the decision to implement the trade did not have access to the information.

This change could have an impact on the methods by which certain financial institutions conduct their activities. For instance, in the past, it would not have been unusual for one or more members of senior management of a bank to have knowledge of the major activities of, or developments in, more than one department. They could have had knowledge of undisclosed negative information about an issuer emanating from the corporate lending department, and at the same time been aware of principal trading, research or underwriting in securities of the issuer in other departments. Under the previous test mere knowledge alone was not a sufficient base for a case of improper trading, the issue was whether the bank made use of such information in any securities dealings. Under the new and more restricted exception, the information must now be kept separate from all persons who may be considered to participate in trading decisions.

At the same time as they narrowed the exception, securities regulators have introduced provisions which provide that the existence and maintenance of policies relating to confidential information will be a factor in discharging the burden of proof in any action for breach of the rules.[34] Some other jurisdictions have questioned whether segregating or compartmentalising information, through Chinese Walls or otherwise, can ever solve these concerns. In the new provisions, however, the Canadian securities regulators have specifically endorsed the concept of Chinese Walls. In fact they have gone further and implemented a policy to serve as a guideline for establishing a Chinese Wall.[35]

The provisions acknowledge that the particular procedures that are appropriate for a given company or industry will vary and require that parties dealing with confidential market-sensitive information must set out their policies in writing. The policy outlines suggested procedures in the areas of employee education, containment of information, restriction of transactions and compliance. The policy is drafted primarily for dealers in securities, but also

---

34 Ibid, regulations s 156d.
35 OSC Policy 10.2, Guidelines for the Establishment of Procedures in relation to Confidential Information (1989), 12 OSCB 2387.

states that financial institutions in general should consider how they might implement procedures to protect themselves from allegations of insider trading. In fact the policy has found the support of the Canadian Bankers Association.[36]

It is reasonable to conclude that in determining an appropriate standard, whether in litigation or in order to prevent it, the guidelines prescribed by the securities regulators, and the steps taken by others to attempt to follow them, are likely to be a standard against which activity will be tested.

Although the regulators have endorsed the concept of Chinese Walls, there may be some question as to how the Canadian courts will react. In addition to the issue of fiduciary duties, the *Standard Investments* case discussed above also considered the problem of the bank's responsibility for the conflicting acts and intentions of two or more responsible officers, in that case the president and chairman. The court's solution was to extend a doctrine of 'identification' for corporate responsibility in criminal actions previously enunciated by the Supreme Court of Canada[37] and apply it to civil actions regarding corporate breaches of fiduciary duties.[38]

The court in *Standard Investments* held that it is possible for a corporation to have more than one directing mind in the same field of operations and that one person's lack of knowledge about the actions of the other will not serve to protect the corporation from liability for the actions of either or the combined effect of both. It commented that:

'In civil cases, where the element of *mens rea* is not applicable, when there are two or more directing minds operating within the same field assigned to both of them, the knowledge, intention and acts of each becomes together the total knowledge, intention and acts of the corporation which they represent.'[39]

One can argue that the court was, in effect, implying that a company could not in some way keep separate the knowledge it has within separate departments. Although this case can be distinguished on its unusual facts, and although there has been legislative action by the securities regulators supporting Chinese Walls, these judicial comments may be used to question the appropriateness and effectiveness of Chinese Walls from a judicial perspective.

CONCLUSION

In the last several years the Canadian financial industry has undergone unprecedented change as a result of factors both from within Canada and from abroad. The broader powers Canadian banks now possess, many as a result of their own requests, have unquestionably opened up new opportunities for them. It is clear, however, that the Canadian courts and regulators are prepared to impress these new powers with new duties and responsibilities and, in order to operate successfully in this new regime, the banks must be mindful of this potential for expanded duties and responsibilities. It remains to be seen, however, after banks, regulators and courts have had further experience with integration of the 'four pillars' of the financial industry, whether the regulatory and judicial approaches to governing the financial sector will become increasingly activist or evolve into a more 'laissez-faire' mode.

36 Regulations to the Ontario Securities Act subsection 156d (3).
37 *Canadian Dredge and Dock Company Ltd et al v The Queen* [1985] 19 DLR (4th) 314 (SCC).
38 The test for establishing that an employee's actions can be atttributed to the corporation involves showing that the action: (a) was within the field of operation assigned to him; (b) was not totally in fraud of the company; and (c) was by design or result partly for the benefit of the company.
39 Above no 21 at 494.

5 Denmark

Per Overbeck

INTRODUCTION

A reflective Danish writer, C E Soya, once said that money can do two things: it can make people independent and it can also make them dependent. It can be put in different ways, but there is no doubt that the fundamental role played by money for the people or business enterprises who have it, or who owe it to others, is the basis for the demands made on the banks. We demand of the bank where we deposit our money, or borrow our money, that the information we give to the bank is kept confidential. We demand that no bank employee may use knowledge concerning a particular customer for his own personal gain. We demand that the bank's organisation and work is planned so that conflicts of interest do not arise in relation to a customer, either in relations with the bank or with other customers.

Most people would agree on the general level that this is how it should be, but it can quickly become difficult in the multitude of situations arising in our practical lives. Should a bank inform the police that a heroin dealer is laundering his money through the bank? What if it is 'only' a case of tax fraud? If a bank employee needs money for a new car, may he then not be allowed to sell his shareholding in Sermitsiak Ltd, inherited from his grandfather, if he happens to have special knowledge of the shares' net asset value through his work in the bank? What about the banks' internal conflicts of interest: the credit manager has lunch with the securities manager and tells him that the bank's exposure with Sermitsiak Ltd is in jeopardy. Should the securities manager then refuse to assist Sermitsiak Ltd with a new share issue? Should the securities manager refuse to sell Sermitsiak shares to customers wishing to buy? Cannot the bank on the contrary be reproached for not professionally amalgamating or combining all knowledge throughout the bank, without operating with Chinese Walls?

No legal systems exist in which these issues have been considered clearly and exhaustively via legal provisions or judicial practice. This is hardly possible and the best advice to banks and their employees is to endeavour to steer clear of problems of this nature, not only by following the legal provisions prevailing at any time, but also by applying moral and ethical standards.

This is not to say that the legal regulation of these circumstances is unimportant. On the contrary, legal regulation is extremely important. Legal regulation is necessary, but it is not sufficient. In respect of Danish law the perhaps rather provocative contention can be put forward that the legislature has either given up or gone too far. This may also be true for other countries. Under the Danish Banking Act there is a criminal clause concerning breach of certain forms of obligatory discretion, but not of bank secrecy as such. There are no legal provisions (i e by Act of Parliament) which with certainty comprise bank secrecy itself, even though it might be useful to know where the line for punishment is drawn. The Stock Exchange Act goes to the other extreme with a prohibition on insider trading with a wording which is so far-reaching that any lawyer would be obliged to advise dealers to avoid getting out of bed in the morning. This is simply too dangerous. However, Danish law does not yet include building regulations concerning Chinese Walls in banks.

THE BANK'S DUTY OF CONFIDENCE

For the first time in 1974, reference to a discretion obligation was added to the Danish Banking Act. No position is taken on the concept of bank secrecy as such, but the following rule can be found in Ch 13, s 54 (sub-s 2) of the Act, concerning penalty clauses:

'Members of board of directors . . . auditors . . . general managers and other employees who without authority disclose matters of which they have gained knowledge during the course of their duties can be made subject to a penalty of a fine where a more rigid penalty is not merited according to the Criminal Act.'

Like an equivalent provision s 160 (sub-s 1), of the Danish Companies Act, the provision is directed at business and trade secrets. It cannot be stated exactly what circumstances this secrecy obligation comprises, but its primary purpose is undoubtedly to protect the business secrets of the relevant company, in this case the bank, and not those of customers.

The reason for the addition of this rule to the Banking Act 1974, despite the fact that banks as limited liability companies were already covered by the Danish Companies Act, was solely to extend the provision also to include savings banks (also comprised by the Danish Banking Act), since savings banks as independent institutions do not fall under the Danish Companies Act.

Since then, in 1985, this secrecy obligation has been extended to comprise 'other employees' as well, and this is a significant extension of the scope of the rule compared to the Danish Companies Act, which solely comprises managements.

A related rule, where the concept 'industrial secrets' is expressly stated, can be found in s 9 of the Danish Marketing Act. According to this rule, a person in the service of or who co-operates with an enterprise, or who holds an office for an enterprise, may not 'by improper means' obtain 'industrial secrets' or 'without authority' use or pass on such secrets.

The penalty-incurring secrecy obligation in the Banking Act does feature some elasticity. The words 'without authority' and 'disclose' are of a nature which can only be more closely decided on in judicial practice (ie by court decisions). However, the interpretation will not be pursued further here, where the main topic is actual bank secrecy concerning customers and not the bank's own business secrets.

Basis for the Bank's Duty of Confidence

Although the wording of s 54 (sub-s 2) of the Banking Act is wide enough to cover information relating to bank customers, the most important legal source for the obligation to respect secrecy concerning customers' circumstances in Denmark has so far been 'customary law'.

Customary law is rarely invoked as a legal source in Danish law. Danish lawyers usually base their arguments on Acts of Parliament, contracts or court decisions. Customary law as a legal source demands that a custom not only exists but also that the custom arises in an area otherwise subject to regulation, so that the relevant course of action is considered to be legally binding.

In addition to a long-standing custom of respect for bank secrecy, this principle has many years of support in judicial practice of the courts and the practice of the administrative authorities. In varying forms, the principle has existed for as long as banks have existed.

By bank secrecy is simply meant the obligation of the banks, including management and employees, to observe secrecy concerning matters which the banks' customers have confided to the bank. This is fundamental for customers but it is also fundamental for the banks. As we know, banks base their activity on confidence, and confidence means that customers can give details of their personal, business and financial circumstances to the bank without running the risk that such information is passed on by the bank to other persons or business enterprises, or to public authorities.

This form of bank secrecy, however, is now to a larger degree than previously covered by the wording of s 54 of the Danish Banking Act. Two new provisions of the Banking Act 1989 are directly relevant. In s 54 (sub-s 2) there has been inserted an access clause to pass on 'customary information on customer relations . . . which are subject to secrecy . . . provided this is substantiated for business reasons' to 'companies within the same group'. This rule aims to comply with the requirements of, for example, a bank and a stock-broking company owned by such bank or within a large financial group to exchange customary information. The relevant employees of the group's individual companies will be subject to secrecy upon receipt by them of such information.

The new s 54 (sub-s 2) lays down that 'information on purely private matters may only be passed on subject to the customer's consent'. This exception stems from a general principle in Danish legislation which stipulates that business considerations can substantiate a certain exchange of information while purely private information is subject to a more strict protection. Without the legislative authorities having given this matter much consideration, the explicit insertion in s 54 (sub-s 2) of a distinction between business information and private information means that the provision to a larger extent than previously prevailed can be said to cover the traditional bank secrecy. Previously s 54 (sub-s 2) largely comprised the banks' own business secrets and only to a limited extent those of the customers, but the new provision now also directly covers the customers' 'purely private matters'.

Remedies for Breach of Confidence

When examining the consequences of infringements of the bank secrecy, a distinction must be made between the consequences for the bank itself and for the employee who has infringed the secrecy obligation. A distinction must also be made between criminal liability, compensation liability, the sanctions of contract law between the bank and the customer, and disciplinary sanctions towards employees of the bank.

Criminal Liability

Criminal liability can only exist if imposed by an Act of Parliament. This could result from s 54 (sub-s 2) of the Danish Banking Act, but is more likely to result from the Criminal Act itself. Infringement of bank secrecy is not an independent crime as defined by the Criminal Act but, according to the circumstances, can be included in other criminal actions covered by the Criminal Act. Infringement of bank secrecy can thus be envisaged to be included in, for example, certain instances of breach of privacy or libel and certain unlawful gain offences. If, however, infringement of bank secrecy falls under neither s 54 (sub-s 2) of the

Danish Banking Act, nor a criminal action described in the Criminal Act, it is not likely to warrant criminal penalty under Danish law.

Compensation Liability

Compensation liability can arise where infringement of bank secrecy, either intentionally or by negligence, and in a foreseeable way, involves damage which in turn results in financial loss. However, the scope of this form of sanction has its limitations, since often it can be particularly difficult for the injured bank customer to prove that a financial loss has been suffered.

Contract Law

In the contractual relationship between bank and customer, breach of bank secrecy might result in a fundamental breach of confidence creating a substantial breach of contract. The customer will thus be able to terminate the agreement and/or—if financial loss can be proved—demand compensation.

Disciplinary Sanctions

However, the most significant sanction to protect bank secrecy is arguably to be found in the salaried employee law or disciplinary area. Breach of bank secrecy will have consequences for the general manager or employee who has passed on details of customers' circumstances to third parties. In serious cases breach of bank secrecy can undoubtedly result in immediate dismissal. Other sanctions can include dismissal with normal notice or degradation.

Exceptions to the General Duty of Bank Secrecy

Since bank secrecy rests on customary law or—so far more exceptionally—a provision of law, i e s 54 (sub-s 2) of the Banking Act, exceptions from the bank secrecy will assume authority in law. This will most often be a direct or indirect legal authority, exceptionally the source of law which we call the nature of the circumstances. The following will provide a review of the exceptions from bank secrecy in Danish law. It will perhaps be useful to try to divide them into three groups:

(I)   exceptions by consent of the customer;
(II)   exceptions in the interest of the bank or of third parties; and
(III) where the banks are statutorily bound to report details of customers' circumstances to the public authorities.

Disclosure by the Express or Implied Consent of the Customer

(I)   Cases where the customer expressly asks the bank to pass on information. Typical examples are information to the customer's trade creditors, providers of loans, or credit card companies, concerning customers' creditworthiness.
(II)   General credit information concerning commercial enterprises, who are aware that this practice exists and have not expressly forbidden the bank to provide other enterprises with the usual credit details on request.
(III) Cases where the customer otherwise has accepted that the information is passed on by the bank. In case there may be any doubt whether a legal and sufficient acceptance is available in each individual case, the bank should

request instructions from the customer. If no contact can be made with the customer, the bank secrecy should be maintained in cases of doubt.

It is not always the case that the customer's request or acceptance is sufficient, since bank secrecy can also be based on consideration of other customers or the bank itself.

Disclosure in the Interests of the Bank or of Third Parties

(I) Cases where the customer sues the bank or the bank sues the customer, for example to collect a debt, and where the bank submits details of customer circumstances to protect its own interests.

(II) Cases where a court rules that a bank employee must give evidence regardless of bank secrecy, but possibly at a court hearing held in camera. This can take place in civil suits as well as in criminal cases, cfs 168, 170 (sub-s 3) and 173 (sub-s 2) of the Danish Administration of Justice Act.

Where, in connection with a court case in another country, the need arises for examination in court of a Danish bank employee, there are a number of procedures which could be applicable. Denmark has acceded to several international conventions relevant in this area, including the Hague Conventions, other multilateral conventions and bilateral treaties and agreements. The approach to the witness will often take place by forwarding the subpoena via official channels, i e the Danish Ministry of Foreign Affairs or the Danish Ministry of Justice. The procedure to be followed may depend on whether the Danish witness is to be examined in a Danish court or foreign court. The EEC Convention on courts' local competence in civil law suits and the close legal co-operation between Denmark and the other Nordic countries may also be relevant to cases involving relations with EEC countries or the Nordic countries.

It is possible in some cases to obtain a court order for the submission of the bank's documents or for a search or confiscation. A court order is necessary since the police alone cannot request that bank secrecy be broken.

Where foreign countries are involved, such a court order will typically be obtained in collaboration with the Danish police. The examination of an employee of a Danish bank or of a branch in Denmark of a foreign bank in a Danish court—on the precondition of acceptance by the judge—may concern all information possessed by the relevant person or by the relevant bank or branch in Denmark. The fact that knowledge may possibly be connected to circumstances which in another country is protected by bank secrecy, in principle does not prevent a Danish court from deciding that a bank employee of Denmark shall be put on the stand, if necessary in camera.

Banks and savings banks operate a cheque abuse register which is a special warning system regulating customers who have overdrawn their accounts by issuing cheques. In respect of a number of conditions the system has been approved by the Danish Data Surveillance Authority pursuant to the Private Data Register Act.

In connection with the opening of a current account with cheques, the account holder is made familiar with the special rules concerning cheque abuse registration and accepts these rules. According to s 3 (sub-s 6) of the Private Data Register Act, the prior permission of the Data Surveillance Authority is required for the establishment of warning registers. According to the grounds for the Act, on the drawing up of this provision the banks' cheque abuse register was considered in particular and the exception from bank secrecy which the establishment of the relevant register implies is thus upheld in legislation on data registers.

Disclosure by Compulsion of Law to Report to Public Authorities

The Danish Supervisory Authority of Financial Institutions

According to s 50 of the Danish Banking Act, banks must provide the Supervisory Authority of Financial Institutions with the information required for the Authority's activities. In its capacity as supervisory authority sanctioned by the Banking Act, the Supervisory Authority has access to all necessary information. According to a special rule in s 50 (sub-s 3) of the Banking Act, which refers to the Criminal Act, employees of the Supervisory Authorities are obliged under criminal sanction 'to keep secret all knowledge obtained during the course of their activities'. According to s 152 of the Criminal Act, the penalty is up to two years' imprisonment.

Section 50 (sub-s 4) of the Danish Banking Act stipulates that the professional secrecy which rests with the employees of the Danish Supervisory Authority does not prevent this authority from passing on information to other supervisory authorities if the information, on its receipt, is subject to similar professional secrecy. Information which the Danish Supervisory Authority receives from the supervisory authorities with the indication of being confidential is also subject to professional secrecy. This provision applies to the co-operation between the Danish Supervisory Authority of Financial Institutions and other supervisory authorities, both in Denmark and abroad.

Danmarks Nationalbank

Pursuant to the Danish Ministry of Industry's Executive Order on Foreign-Exchange Regulations of August 1988, Danmarks Nationalbank (the central bank of Denmark) may request a number of details related to the foreign-exchange transactions of physical and legal entities resident in Denmark. Reports must thus be filed with Danmarks Nationalbank concerning payments between such persons, and physical and legal entities not resident in Denmark.

As Denmark's central bank, the Nationalbank is subject to a special secrecy obligation. The Nationalbank is an independent institution whose activities are based on an Act passed in 1936.

Tax Authorities

The Danish Tax Control Act stipulates rules for the bank's obligation to report customer circumstances to the Danish tax authorities. The legislation is worded so as to provide for automatic reporting of a number of circumstances, as well as for tax authorities, as an element of tax control, to require specific details of specific circumstances. The following provisions are relevant:

(I)   Section 8 H on the reporting obligation concerning customers' deposits and accrued interest thereon;

(II)   Section 8 P concerning loans to customers and interest thereon, as well as the reporting obligation for use in the tax authorities' calculation of interest tax;

(III)   Section 10 concerning details of share dividends disbursed;

(IV)   Sections 10 A and B concerning bonds: Market value, purchases and sales and interest accrued;

(V)   Section 8 F concerning details of deposits etc in respect of certain pension schemes;

(VI)   Section 8 Q with its rules concerning details of mortgage deeds held in safekeeping for administration;

(VII)   Section 8 G of the Act, giving the tax authorities access on request to details of customer deposits, loans etc from the banks if such information is of substantial significance for tax assessment;

(VIII) Section 8 A, under which, at the request of the tax authorities, banks trading in public securities must provide details of sales and purchases of securities; and

(IX)   Section 8 D, which gives the tax authorities wide-ranging powers to collect information for use in tax assessment, also from the banks.

When residents hold deposits on accounts with foreign banks or have deposited securities with foreign banks, a condition pursuant to the Executive Order on Foreign Exchange Regulations is that the resident reaches agreement with the relevant foreign bank on reporting to the Danish tax authorities, according to more detailed rules, of the size of deposits, securities deposited, addition of interest etc.

Naturally Danish legislation cannot amend bank secrecy rules abroad but the technique is to include a contractual acceptance and obligation for both parties in the civil law contractual agreement between the Danish customer and the foreign bank.

The tax authorities are subject to special rules concerning secrecy under s 4 of the State Income Tax Act, which under criminal liability, cf the Criminal Act, requires 'unconditional secrecy concerning details of taxpayers' income and assets'. According to s 87 of the Tax At Source Act, the secrecy obligation also concerns other financial circumstances and commercial and private matters. According to s 152 of the Criminal Act, the penalty is up to two years' imprisonment.

The Social Security Authorities

Legislation on social security provides no authority to request details of bank exposures without customers' consent.

In December 1985, Denmark passed the Open File Act. As a starting point the Act allows any individual access to documents received or created by an administrative authority. However, there are a number of exceptions and the right to file access does not include details of individuals' private, including financial, circumstances, nor does the right to file access cover commercial or business matters of which the secrecy is of considerable financial importance. This Act does not warrant any breach of bank secrecy.

INSIDER TRADING

Under the Copenhagen Stock Exchange Act of June 1986, for the first time in Danish law, a rule on insider trading was introduced. Section 39 now provides:

'Purchase or sale of stock-exchange listed securities may not be conducted by any person who holds knowledge of not yet published information concerning the relevant issuer, if such information can be assumed to be of significance for the securities' price fixing.'

Section 53 (sub-s 2) of the Danish Companies Act contains a prohibition on the performance of or participation in speculative deals concerning shares in the company or in companies inside the same group by members of boards of directors and managements. Section 19 (sub-s 4) of the Danish Banking Act also provides that managers and employees of a bank may not perform or participate in speculative deals on their own account.

Legislation does not define what is meant by speculation, but according to usual interpretation one typical characteristic of a speculative deal will be that the purchase or sale of a security or other asset is made with the intention of rapid sale or purchase of the same asset to achieve a quick gain. Purchase of assets for capital accumulation, ie as long-term investment, will normally not fall under the speculation concept. A fundamental problem in the legal evaluation of concrete instances is that an opinion must be formed of the subjective intentions of the relevant person at the time of the first transaction, purchase or sale, while the subjective intention at the time of the second transaction, sale or purchase, must also be evaluated. The concept of speculation in the Danish Banking Act and the Danish Companies Act is not necessarily the same as the concept of speculation in other parts of the legislation, e g in tax legislation.

No judicial practice at present exists to illustrate the extent of s 39 of the Stock Exchange Act. However, it clearly applies not only to employees of the company whose shares are being traded, but also to external consultants and other persons who have gained knowledge of unpublished information. The latter will often comprise banks and their employees when they undertake tasks in relation to customers who are limited liability companies.

The word 'knowledge' should probably be read to mean that concrete knowledge of specific facts is required, while assumptions or estimates are not sufficient to fall under the legal provision. It is not a condition that the relevant party actively has gained knowledge, since also knowledge obtained passively or accidentally leads to insight. The words 'can be assumed to be of significance' are remarkably far-reaching. Thus, it is not necessary to be comprised by this provision that the relevant person's insight in actual fact is of importance seeing that it is sufficient that it may be of significance. Furthermore, there is no mention of substantial significance but merely of significance in general.

Section 39 of the Stock Exchange Act prohibits direct use of inside knowledge to own advantage, but to a certain degree also indirect use in the form of the passing of information to third parties if the purpose is to enable them to benefit therefrom.

The adoption of the EEC directive proposal concerning insider trading put forward by the Commission can be expected to imply more concise formulations of the scope of these rules and of the passing of information to third parties. It would appear useful, as attempted in art 6 of the directive proposal, to endeavour to go a little further towards clarifying what is meant by 'inside knowledge'. As art 6 is currently drafted, internal knowledge is considered to be 'knowledge of an exact nature which is not accessible or available to the public and which concerns one or several issuers of securities and which, if it were published, would significantly influence the price of the relevant security(ies)'.

CONFLICTS OF INTEREST AND CHINESE WALLS

The concept of the 'Chinese Wall', as known in English and US law in particular, can briefly be said to be an expression for the rules concerning the internal circulation of information in banks and other financial institutions, designed to prevent or at least restrict the risk of the amalgamation of confidential information. The intention is to avoid conflicts of interest and abuse thereof. A Chinese Wall should thus not be understood as something physical but as a description of what in Danish are called 'watertight hatches' between those sections of, for example, a bank's organisation involved in different and perhaps mutually conflicting interests. It is a matter of course that those employees of a bank responsible for portfolio management must look after their customers' interests. These interests can be in conflict with the interests which other employees, e g in the bank's capital market division, securities division or credit division are responsible for handling on behalf of other customers or in other contexts.

Danish law has no special rules on Chinese Walls of this nature. They may not be necessary and perhaps not even appropriate. The rules of Danish law referred to above, i e the bank secrecy requirement and the far-reaching prohibition in Danish law against insider trading and speculation in themselves constitute very significant protection of the considerations for which a Chinese Wall is designed. Furthermore, according to the general rules of Danish law concerning authority to act on behalf of other parties, a bank which undertakes to carry out a customer order must carry out this order in the customer's interests and in the best professional way. It is a matter of course that employees of a bank must loyally look after customers' interests and not those of others when acting on behalf of the customer, just as the requirement of professionalism is also a matter of course. Exaggerated division of a bank's organisation into small employee groups which are not permitted to communicate with each other can in fact be an impediment to professionalism and efficiency.

It should also be remembered that when a customer approaches a bank he enters a contractual relationship with the bank as legal entity and not with the employee responsible for his dossier. In the final analysis the bank's management is responsible for the planning and organisation of work so that the interests of each customer are handled loyally and professionally.

If a bank is approached by a company that requests the bank's assistance in an attempt of a hostile take-over of another company, which is also a customer of the bank, conflicts of interest can naturally arise. Which customer the bank wishes to serve is a political choice, and should it not be possible to undertake both customers' interests both loyally and professionally, the bank may have to recommend that one of the two customers seek another bank.

Danish banking does not have the same tradition as in the UK and the USA for a distinction between commercial banks and investment (or merchant) banks, since Danish banks typically are active in both business areas. In Denmark, banks have started to build up financial groups which carry out stockbroking activities, or possibly insurance, in addition to these categories of banking. According to legislation, however, these activities must be placed in different limited liability companies, i e different legal entities. The bank must be an independent company, the stockbroking company must be an independent company and the insurance company must be an independent company. These companies can be owned by the same holding company, however, so that Danish law does have de facto 'Chinese Walls', since there are special professional secrecy rules in the Banking Act, the Stockbroking Act and the Insurance Act, respectively. However, the new wording of s 54 (sub-s 2) of the Danish Banking Act reduced these walls within certain areas, as described in more detail above. The secrecy requirement etc in stockbroking companies corresponds to that for the banks, whereas rules in the insurance area are not quite so stringent.

Despite the fine motives behind provisions for Chinese Walls in financial institutions, the concept has to be treated with care. The multiplicity, complexity and the rapid development of financial institutions and financial markets make divisions with thick concrete and cement walls an unrealistic proposition.

Considering the Chinese Wall metaphor positively, it is not about rigid primitive regulation, but on the contrary regulative flexibility and adaptability. The genius of the Chinese Wall is that it can pass through all kinds of terrain and is adapted to ever-changing conditions. It is flexible rather than rigid and clumsy.

With a wall there is a risk of the blurring of protection rules which are already efficient, in Danish law at any rate. Efficiency and professionalism will be jeopardised, to the detriment of the customers the walls are intended to protect. A false sense of security can be feared. Notwithstanding how many rules are introduced some people will break them and in the final analysis it is the management's overall responsibility to organise a company so that full account is taken of both legal and ethical norms.

We are thus back at what was mentioned in the introduction, which is that certain legal rules are necessary but that legal rules can never be sufficient in areas such as these, where moral and ethical norms are also of such great significance.

6 England

Richard Grandison

INTRODUCTION

English law recognises a duty of confidence owed by a bank to its customer. The right of confidentiality belongs to the customer, not to the bank. It is by no means easy, because of the relative lack of authority on the extent of the bank's duty of confidence and the way in which exceptions to the general rule have been established, either to arrive at a safe general summary of the applicable principles or to provide guidance in particular difficult cases. As will be seen later there are considerable inroads being made into the bank/customer relationship as a result of the introduction of both civil and criminal statutory provisions permitting or compelling disclosure of confidential information by banks. In January 1987 HM Treasury, in association with the Bank of England, set up an independent Review of Banking Services law. Its purpose was to examine the statute and common law and practice relating to the provision of banking services within the United Kingdom to personal and business customers. Under the chairmanship of Professor RB Jack, the Committee examined (inter alia) bank/customer relations, devoting a whole chapter to the specific duty of confidentiality owed by a banker to its customer. The Jack Report, containing the Committee's recommendations to which reference will be made throughout the course of this chapter, was published in February 1989.

THE BANK'S DUTY OF CONFIDENCE

It is a general rule of English law that the contract between a bank and its customer is governed by the laws of the place where the account is kept, in the absence of agreement to the contrary. The duty of a bank under English law to keep its customer's affairs confidential is an implied term of the contract between bank and customer, no more and no less. The duty is subject to certain, fairly obvious exceptions discussed below, but is otherwise a very strict one. It extends to all information which the bank has about its customer. *Tournier v National Provincial and Union Bank of England* [1924] IKB 461, is the leading case in this area of the law, and recently in *Lipkin Gorman v Karpnale Ltd* [1989] 1 WLR, May LJ stated 'the correctness of the principles of law stated by the majority in *Tournier*'s case has not been doubted since the case was decided'. Atkin LJ in *Tournier*'s case described the extent of the duty thus:

'It [the obligation of secrecy] clearly goes beyond that state of the account, that is, whether there is a debit or a credit balance, and the amount of the balance. It must extend at least to all the transactions that go through the account, and to the securities, if any, given in respect of the account; and in respect of such matters it must, I think, extend beyond the period when the account is closed, or ceases to be an active account . . . I further think that the obligation extends to information obtained from other sources than the customer's actual account, if the occasion upon which the information was obtained arose out of the banking relations of the bank and its customers—for example, with a view to assisting the bank in coming to decisions as to its treatment of its customers . . . In this case, however, I should not extend the obligation to information as to the customer obtained after he had ceased to be a customer.'

As implied in this passage, the only information not covered by the obligation of confidence might be information obtained by the bank in some manner which is clearly independent of the bank/customer relationship, for example information about the customer supplied by a third party, other than in the course of banking relations between the bank and its customer. However, a bank should be very careful before relying on this exception, for several reasons. First it is derived by reasoning from general principles and there is no conclusive authority in its support. Second, there is the difficulty of distinguishing between information obtained in consequence of the bank/customer relationship and other information, and the likelihood that the other information is obtained in circumstances which, if not giving rise to a duty of confidence to the customer, nevertheless give rise to a duty of confidence to a third party. Third, there is the risk of an action for defamation.

As the bank's duty of confidence is merely an implied contractual obligation, Parliament can override the duty by statute and impose an obligation to disclose, and Parliament frequently has. Examples are given below. In broad terms, it can be said that English law, both statutory law and the common law, recognises the principle that the right of confidentiality is the customer's, not the bank's. Thus, generally speaking, one can assume that in any case where the customer can be compelled to disclose his secrets, his bank can also be compelled to disclose them.

CUSTOMER'S REMEDIES FOR BREACH OF CONFIDENCE

The customer has two remedies for breach of confidence; he may sue for damages after disclosure, or for an injunction to restrain disclosure or a repetition of a previous disclosure.

Damages

Damages will clearly in many cases be a thoroughly inadequate remedy—once disclosure has taken place, the damage is done and, indeed, it is difficult to see how, in many cases, the customer's loss can be measured in monetary terms. Exemplary or punitive damages would not, except possibly in extreme circumstances, be awarded.

Injunction

Accordingly, the main protection for the customer is his ability to obtain an injunction. This is an order of the court restraining the bank from making disclosure; failure to comply with such an order would in most circumstances constitute a contempt of court. However, the court will not grant an injunction without some evidence that a disclosure is threatened. Prima facie, therefore, the customer has a dilemma, because disclosure can very easily take place before he knows about it.

An injunction can be obtained speedily by means of ex parte proceedings. The term 'ex parte' means that the application is made to the court without notification to the bank and only the applicant's legal advisers appear before the court. Otherwise, if time allows then the application can be made 'inter partes' when both the customer and the bank will be represented. In both cases, the application is supported by affidavit evidence and the court must be satisfied that an unauthorised disclosure is threatened. If the injunction is granted the applicant is required to give a cross-undertaking in damages in the event that the injunction is subsequently discharged either before or at trial and the bank has suffered damage as a result of the imposition of the injunction.

BASIS FOR THE BANK'S DUTY OF CONFIDENCE

It was stated at the outset that the bank's duty of confidence was an implied term of the contract between the bank and its customer. Before going on to examine *Tournier*'s case in detail, it should be noted that the English courts have shown themselves willing to imply obligations of confidence into commercial relationships. In *Argyll v Argyll* [1967] Ch 302, a case in which a husband had been restrained from disclosing his wife's secrets learned during the marriage, the court held that a contract or obligation or confidence need not be expressed but can be implied, and a breach of contract or trust could arise independently of any rights of property or contract, and the court in the exercise of its equitable jurisdiction would restrain the breach of confidence independently of any rights at law. This principle was relied on by the Lord Chief Justice in *Attorney General v Jonathan Cape Ltd and Others* [1975] 3 All ER 484. While refusing the injunctive relief sought, he unequivocally decided that a duty of confidence could be enforced independently of any rights of property or contract.

As the court can in its discretion grant equitable relief to enforce obligations of confidence, it follows that at present one has to say that one cannot forecast where the English courts will place the limits. Perhaps the correct approach is not to ask about the custom and practice of bankers, but simply to ask what seems fair, just or right.

It is appropriate to consider *Tournier*'s case in more detail, while bearing in mind that the common law is, and always will be, an evolving system of law.

TOURNIER v NATIONAL PROVINCIAL AND UNION BANK OF ENGLAND [1924] 1 KB 461

The facts were as follows. Tournier was a customer of the defendant bank. A cheque was drawn by another customer of the defendant in favour of Tournier who, instead of paying it into his own account, endorsed it to a third person who had an account at another bank. On the return of the cheque to the defendant, its manager inquired of the other bank to whom it had been endorsed and was told it was a bookmaker. The defendant disclosed that information to third persons.

Tournier brought an action for slander (which need not be considered here) and for breach of an implied contract that the defendant would not disclose to third persons the state of his account or any transactions relating thereto. The judge's question to the jury was: 'Was the communication with regard to the Plaintiff's account at the Bank made on a reasonable and proper occasion?'

Tournier appealed on the ground that the jury should have been given directions as to the circumstances in which the occasion would be reasonable or proper. On this particular point Bankes LJ said:

'A direction to the jury in a case such as the present must inform the jury of the nature and limits and qualifications of the duty of the Bank as a matter of law, leaving to them only questions for the purpose of ascertaining their view whether the communication complained of was or was not made, and whether it did or did not come within any of the protected occasions to which I have called attention.'

The Court of Appeal thus moved firmly away from the practice in the previous cases of asking the jury to decide upon the existence or the scope of the duty of confidence.

As one can see from the passage of Atkin LJ's judgment, *Tournier*'s case gives only limited guidance about the scope of the duty or about the information which is subject to the duty of confidence.

Bankes LJ summarised the position thus:

'The duty is a legal one arising out of contract . . . it is not absolute but qualified. It is not possible to frame any exhaustive definition of the duty. The most that can be done is to classify the qualifications and to indicate its limits.'

The qualifications can be classified under four heads:

(I)   where the disclosure is made with the express or implied consent of the customer;

(II) where the interests of the bank require disclosure;

(III) where disclosure is under compulsion by law; and

(IV) where there is a duty to the public to disclose.

THE FOUR EXCEPTIONS TO THE GENERAL DUTY OF NON-DISCLOSURE LAID DOWN IN *TOURNIER*'S CASE

Where the Disclosure is By the Express or Implied Consent of the Customer

One of the qualifications to the bank's duty of confidence is the situation where disclosure is by the express or implied consent of the customer. Therefore, if the bank were to notify each of its customers and state clearly what it proposed to do and why, and actually received consent (preferably in writing) from a customer, there would be no breach of duty if that customer's documents and/or information were disclosed pursuant to that consent. However, under English law, if notice were given to a customer by the bank and the customer did not reply, the bank would not be entitled to assume that the customer had impliedly consented.

Consent Directives

An important recent development in the context of implied consent is the United States practice of consent directives. These are documents whereby a customer or former customer of the bank authorises or directs the bank to disclose certain information concerning his dealings with the bank to the US authorities. The consent is signed pursuant to a court order under the threat of fines or imprisonment for failure to sign.

The issue whether or not a person can be compelled to sign a consent directive was considered in the case of *John Doe v The United States* [June 22, 1988], in which the US Supreme Court held that a person could be compelled by court order to sign such directives, that failure to do so was contempt of court and would be punishable by fines and imprisonment, and that such a process does not violate an individual's Fifth Amendment rights against self-incrimination under the US Constitution.

The treatment of such consent directives by banks in foreign jurisdictions is a matter of considerable general concern to banks as it is far from clear that a consent directive amounts to real consent such as is sufficient to justify the bank disclosing the information in circumstances where, as in England, the duty of confidentiality imposed on banking institutions is an implied contractual duty. However, the practical consequence of a bank not complying with the consent directive may be to expose its customer to the possibility of fines or imprisonment.

Following Staughton J's judgment in *Libyan Arab Foreign Bank v Bankers' Trust Co* [1988] 1 LLR 259, it is a general rule of English law that the contract between a bank and its customer is governed by the laws of the place where that account is kept, in the absence of agreement to the contrary. This will result in the situation where a foreign customer of a foreign bank whose account is kept at a London branch will find that English law will govern the nature of the confidential relationship between itself and the bank. Nationality of the customer and the bank will be irrelevant.

The question therefore arises as to the validity or non-validity of consent directives under English law. At present there does not appear to be any English authority on the point, although it is interesting to note the attitude of the English court towards other orders from foreign jurisdictions purporting to have extra-territorial effect. In *XAG and others v A Bank* [1983] 2 All ER 464, the English High Court granted an injunction restraining the London branch of a US bank whose customer was under investigation by the US Department of Justice, from complying with a subpoena issued by the New York Court and served on the bank's New York office requiring the production in the US of documents relating to the operation of that customer's London account. The conflict between the attempt by a Court in one jurisdiction to assert extra-territorial jurisdiction on the one hand, and the duty of confidentiality owed by a bank in another jurisdiction to its customers on the other, is something which has yet to be resolved satisfactorily.

A Cayman Islands decision, *In the matter of ABC Ltd* [1985] FLR 159, is a case which considered the question of 'consents' given under the order of a foreign court and their effect on a bank's duty of confidentiality towards its client. The applicant bank applied to the Grand Court, Cayman Islands, for a direction as to whether it would be entitled under the Cayman Islands Confidential Relationships (Preservation) Law 1976, as amended, to disclose confidential information relating to the client pursuant to a 'consent' signed by the client in compliance with an order of a US court.

The court held that the applicant bank would not be entitled to disclose confidential information relating to a client's affairs in such circumstances. A consent signed by a client in compliance with the order of a foreign court would not amount to 'consent' for the purposes of s 3(2)(b)(i) of the Act, and would create no obligations on the bank's part, nor any enforceable rights on the part of foreign law enforcement agencies, as it would not be given voluntarily and freely in the exercise of an independent and uncoerced judgment, but under pain of criminal penalty. Further, a foreign court could not be permitted by means of a consent directive (which is in reality a direction by it rather than the client to the bank to disclose confidential information) to undermine the Cayman Islands' statutory provisions. The following passage from Summerfield CJ's judgment is worth noting:

'The applicant's obligation and duty is to its client. The applicant might just as well be liable in damages to its client for not giving effect to a client's lawful instructions as for wrongly giving effect to them or for any other misfeasance.

So far as the terms of the consent directive . . . are concerned, the applicant would be under no obligation to the United States Department of Justice or any attorney thereof. Such a consent directive would give rise to no legal or other relationship so as to create any such obligation on the part of the applicant. Neither would such a consent directive give rise to any rights in the United States Department of Justice or any attorney thereof as against the applicant. The client would retain authority over the disposition of the confidential information relating to him.

The purported irrevocability of the consent directive is inoperative. The client could always revoke the instructions in it before effect had been given to them.

The main point . . . is whether consent given pursuant to an order by a foreign court under pain of criminal penalties amounts to consent for the purpose of s 3(2)(b)(i) of the Confidential Relationships (Preservation) Law 1976, as amended. It must be stressed that the only alternative to signing the consent directive ordered by the court is punishment by way of fine or imprisonment. It is signed under compulsion backed by criminal sanctions.

I am of the view that such a consent directive does not amount to consent as contemplated by s 3(2)(b)(i) and that it is ineffective for the purposes of that provision. In saying this I am not unmindful of the fact that this court has itself ordered directions in substantially similar terms for the purpose of enforcing an order for premature discovery and the preservation of property. Those directions were aimed at banks within the jurisdiction . . . The position may have to be reviewed in the event of a similar application coming before the court.

In our law where consent is a material element giving rise to a legal consequence, it must be voluntarily and freely given in the exercise of an independent and uncoerced judgment. This is a well-established principle in every sphere of our law, civil and criminal, and there is no reason to give any different meaning to the expression "consent" in s 3(2)(b)(i). To make any other view would result in allowing a foreign court to undermine and circumvent the provisions of the Confidential Relationships (Preservation) Law. This is not only important to this country where that law exists but would be equally important in many other common law countries which respect the principle in *Tournier* . . . governing the duty of a bank to maintain secrecy . . .

Although in form the consent directive purports to be a consent and direction given by the client of the bank it is in substance a direction given by the foreign court. It is not real consent at all. In reality it is the foreign court directing the bank to disclose confidential information. In my view the Confidential Relationships (Preservation) Law does not contemplate that situation . . . In short, consent given under compulsion is merely submission to force and is not consent for the purposes of s 3(2)(b)(i).'

In the absence of other authority in England, this decision, which applies the principle in *Tournier*, may assist in considering the position under English law. It seems arguable that 'consent' under this *Tournier* exception is consent 'voluntarily and freely given in the exercise of an independent and uncoerced judgment'. This exception is dependent on the customer's consent being maintained at the time the bank makes disclosure. A practical solution may be to require a letter from the customer giving his express consent to the disclosure of the relevant information. Conversely, if the customer withdraws his consent prior to the bank making disclosure, the bank would probably be breaching its duty of confidentiality if it complied with the consent directive.

Data Protection Act 1984

This Act is designed to allow the United Kingdom to ratify the Council of Europe's 'Convention for the Protection of Individuals with regard to Automatic Processing of Personal Data'. In a policy statement published on 3 December 1986 by the Data Protection Registrar, concerning the implementation of the Act, he described the objectives of the Convention as being first to protect individuals in circumstances where information about them is processed automatically and, secondly, to facilitate a common international standard of protection for individuals, such that the free flow of information across international boundaries can proceed properly.

The Act gives an individual to whom information processed by computer (personal data) relates, the right to have access to that data, challenge the data and claim compensation for damage and any associated distress arising from the loss, inaccuracy or unauthorised destruction or disclosure of that data.

The obligations on data users to follow proper practices in relation to their use of the data is laid down in eight Data Protection Principles contained in Sch 1 to the Act. Of concern here is Principle 1: 'the information to be contained in personal data should be obtained and personal data shall be processed, fairly and lawfully'. In determining whether the information was obtained fairly, the Act (Part 2, Sch 1) provides that 'regard should be had to the method by which it was obtained, including in particular whether any person from whom it was obtained was deceived or misled as to the purposes for which it is to be held, used or disclosed'.

It would appear that in order not to breach confidentiality rules, banks will have to ensure that a customer is made aware at the start of the relationship what uses and disclosures will be made of information obtained about him.

The Act provides an exception to the above requirement by providing that information shall be deemed fairly obtained if it is obtained from a person 'authorised under any enactment to supply it' or who is so required by any enactment, convention or other instrument imposing an international obligation on the United Kingdom.

Another point of interest to the banks is s 5 of the Act. On the assumption that the bank will have been obliged to register under the Act, s 5 prohibits disclosures of information held by a 'data user' relating to 'data subjects' to third parties other than those set out in the data user's entry on this register. This has obvious repercussions for the transfer of data between the different offices of a banking group. The Data Protection Registrar has recently published his responses to various queries concerning the working of the Act, including how the Act will affect transfers of personal data between a data user and an office overseas, for example between the branch of a foreign bank in England and its head office abroad. ('Data' in this context means information in data form and not for example in the form of a computer print-out or other printed material derived from data). In his reply, the Data Protection Registrar pointed out that, under s 5(2)(e) of the Act, it is an offence to transfer data outside the UK except to a country described in the data user's registered entry. It may be that in submitting an entry for registration, the bank had already declared its intention of making such disclosures. It would however be necessary to look at the bank's entry to determine the position. Subject to this registration requirement however, transfers of personal data may continue to be made unless, for some reason, the powers to issue a transfer prohibition notice conferred on the Registrar by s 12 of the Act are exercised.

In addition, there is an exception in s 34(5) to the general prohibition set out in s 5 whereby disclosures required by 'order of the court' or 'for the purposes of or in the course of legal proceedings' are exempt from the non-disclosure provisions. The Act does not specify whether 'a court' and 'legal proceedings' include foreign courts and foreign proceedings and there is, as yet, no authority on the point. It is probable that the references are to English enactments, laws and courts so that the exceptions may not apply to the case of an obligation imposed overseas. The use of the letters rogatory procedure under the Evidence (Proceedings in Foreign Jurisdictions) Act 1975 and any Order made thereunder would thus have the further advantage of giving the bank protection under s 34(5) of the Data Protection Act.

The consequence of an unauthorised disclosure, from a customer's viewpoint, is that he or she could claim compensation from the bank for any resulting loss. However, that unauthorised disclosure is also an offence under s 5(5). Conviction on indictment would make the bank liable to a fine up to an unspecified amount and on summary conviction to a fine not exceeding £2,000.

When the Interests of the Bank Require Disclosure

This exception was illustrated in *Tournier*'s case by an example given by Bankes LJ of a bank issuing a writ claiming payment of an overdraft, stating on the face of it the amount of the overdraft.

Another example arose in *Sunderland v Barclays Bank Ltd* [1938] The *Times* 25 November. The facts were that the bank dishonoured the plaintiff's cheque because there were insufficient funds in her account. The real reason, however, was the bank's knowledge that she was betting. The plaintiff complained to her husband, and on his advice telephoned the bank. The husband interrupted the conversation to take up his wife's case, and was informed that most cheques passing through the wife's account were in favour of bookmakers. Du Parcq LJ thought that in the circumstances, the interests of the bank required disclosure since it was being forced to give a reason for the policy it adopted. However, it was also noted by the judge that since the husband joined the conversation, the bank had the customer's implied consent to disclose the information to him.

More recently, the interpretation of this exception has been considered in the cases of *XAG v A Bank* [1983] 2 All ER 464—a decision of the High Court in London and *FDC & Co Ltd v The Chase Manhattan Bank NA* (Civil Appeal No 65 1984)—a decision of the Hong Kong Court of Appeal. In both cases, customers of the respective banks obtained interlocutory injunctions to restrain the banks from disclosing documents/information in order to comply with subpoenas of Courts in the United States. The banks argued that it was in their interest to disclose, because otherwise they would be in contempt of court in the United States. These arguments were rejected on the ground that the banks' 'interest' in disclosure was of a different character from that contemplated in *Tournier*.

Where disclosure is made under this exception, it must be limited strictly to information necessary to protect the bank's interest. Disclosure will be necessary and permissible under this exception whenever there is litigation between the bank and its customer; likewise if the bank brings an action against a guarantor.

Since *Tournier*'s case, there have arisen two major areas of concern (considered by the Jack Report) relating to this exception.

Disclosure within the Banking Group

First, there is a growing feeling amongst banks that they are entitled to release confidential information about their customers without their consent to other companies within the banking group, some of which may be non-banking subsidiaries. They maintain that their customers have given their implied consent to such disclosure, although this has not been tested in the courts. However, the recent decision in *Bank of Tokyo Ltd v Karoon* [1987] AC 45 held that, for confidentiality purposes, each corporate entity within the banking group must be viewed as a separate entity.

The Jack Report has recommended that for practical purposes, in order to enable a banking group to be run in a cost effective way, the law should allow confidential information to be passed between the holding company, being a bank, and such of its subsidiaries as are banks without the need for a customer's consent, provided it is for a strictly defined purpose. However, a customer's consent should still be required for transmission of such information to non-banking subsidiaries.

Credit Reference Agencies

The second area of concern falling within this exception relates to the growth of credit reference agencies. This was dealt with at some length by the Jack Report. There is some doubt as to which exception is applicable (if any). Some authors consider it in the context of 'consent of the customer', others within the 'duty to the public' exception. The Jack Committee chose to consider it under the 'interests of the bank' exception, 'partly because it does not have overtones of crime or national security, and partly because from a customer's standpoint, the question has close affinities with that of disclosure within a banking group'.

Credit reference agencies collect information on the creditworthiness of particular persons from various public sources and providers of credit who are willing to contribute. They then sell it to subscribers, who are normally potential lenders who need to have a reliable source of information about the creditworthiness of potential customers. All such agencies have to be licensed by ther Director General of Fair Trading under s 25 of the Consumer Credit Act 1974. Licences may be revoked (inter alia) for participating in business practices appearing to the Director General to be deceitful or oppressive, or otherwise unfair or improper (whether unlawful or not).

Banks have until recently been able to use information by such agencies, but not contribute information to them. However, the government has increasingly put pressure on them to contribute such information themselves. An agreement was reached in May 1988 between the banks and the credit reference agencies under which, for a trial period of one year, the banks would make available information about customers who are in default. It is said there is a clear trend in Britain towards banks making more information available to credit reference agencies. In a lecture given to the Chartered Institute of Bankers (29 November 1988) the Governor of the Bank of England said:

'I hope that, even if it has to await a change in the law, the banks and all other lenders will consider very carefully whether they cannot provide more data, subject of course to proper safeguards about its confidentiality. That, it seems to me, will be an essential step towards insuring that the consumer credit industry operates in the interests of lenders, of borrowers, and thus of the community as a whole.'

The Governor was talking not only about information regarding customers in default ('black' information) but also information about customers who are not ('white' information). It is unclear whether those in favour of disclosing 'white' information to agencies without the customer's express consent would seek to justify it under one of the exceptions to *Tournier*. It is also as yet unclear what view the courts would take. It is clear, however, that expansion of this area will constitute a very large inroad into any of the original *Tournier* exceptions.

Where Disclosure is by Compulsion of Law

This exception can be dealt with in two broad categories, following which we can consider the question in relation to foreign law. These two categories are:

(I)   compulsion by order of a court, and
(II) compulsion by statute.

Compulsion by Order of Court

An order of the court will usually take the form of a subpoena duces tecum, which, when served on a bank official, orders him to attend court and to bring with him books, documents or letters relating to a customer's affairs specified in the subpoena. Films and tape recordings are regarded as 'documents' for these purposes and would include computer records.

Bankers' Books Evidence Act 1879

Alternatively, an order can be made under s 7 of the Bankers' Books Evidence Act 1879 which states: 'on the application of any party to a legal proceeding a court or judge may order that such party be at liberty to inspect and take copies of any entries in a banker's book for any of the purposes of such proceedings'. The Act defines 'legal proceedings' to mean 'any civil or criminal proceedings or enquiry in which evidence is or may be given, and includes an arbitration'; and 'banker's books' are defined to include 'ledgers, day books, cash books, account books, and all other books used in the ordinary business of the bank'.

The purpose of the act was primarily to relieve banks and their officials from the obligation to appear in court personally to give evidence. Section 3 provides that 'a copy of any entry in a banker's book shall in all legal proceedings be received as prima facie evidence of such entry, and of the matters transactions and accounts therein recorded'. The Act was an early attempt to mitigate the rigours of the hearsay rule of evidence and save banks time, but also to provide some protection to banks so that a bank was not compellable to produce any books unless so ordered by a judge with special cause (s 6). The Act therefore follows the principle described earlier, in that if a customer is involved in civil or criminal proceedings, he thereby subjects himself to the necessity of disclosure of all relevant facts of such proceedings and this will apply equally to his bank.

It is important, however, to distinguish between civil and criminal proceedings in applying s 7 of the Act. In criminal proceedings, the position is as stated by Lord Widgery LJ in *Williams v Summerfield* [1972] 3 WLR 131:

'. . . in criminal proceedings, justices should warn themselves of the importance of the step which they are taking in making an order under s 7; should always recognise the care with which the jurisdiction should be exercised; should take into account among other things whether there is other evidence in the possession of the prosecution to support the charge . . .'

In particular he warned justices not to allow 'fishing expeditions' such as when 'a police officer seeking to make investigations of a suspect bank account started legal proceedings for that purpose and no other'. Justices should therefore 'limit the period of the disclosure of the bank account to a period which is strictly relevant to the charge before them'.

In respect of civil proceedings, the rule which has been laid down is that the statutory power to order inspection should not be inconsistent with, and not overreach the general law of discovery. (See *Parnell v Wood* [1892] P 137; *South Staffordshire Tramways Co v Ebbsmith* [1895] 2 QB 669; *Pollock v Garle* [1898] 1 Ch 1; *Waterhouse v Barker* [1924] 2 KB 759). Bankers' books relating to an account of the party to litigation will be ordered to be disclosed under s 7 if they are relevant to the issues in the litigation and not privileged from production.

The Court of Appeal, in *Bankers Trust Co v Shapira* [1980] 3 All ER 353, extended the circumstances in which an order for discovery could be used to coerce banks to reveal details of its customers' accounts. The court held that the court's power to order discovery of information at the earliest stages of an action to give effect to a defrauded plaintiff's equitable right to trace and recover property of which he claimed to have been wrongfully or fraudulently deprived, may be used to order a bank to disclose documents and correspondence relating to the account of a customer who is prima facie guilty of fraud, even though such material would normally be subject to the banker/customer obligation of confidentiality. The evidence of fraud against the customer had to be very strong, but, where it was, the customer was not entitled to rely on the confidential relationship between him and his bank to prevent the discovery.

Of particular interest is the stance taken by the English courts in relation to foreign banks having branches in England. Under the Act, the definition of 'banker' for some time was such that most foreign banks having branches in England were not 'bankers' within the meaning of the Act. This has now been changed by the Banking Act 1979.

In the criminal case of *R v Grossman* [1981] 73 Cr App Rep 302, the Court of Appeal refused an order under s 7 which would have required disclosure in England and Wales of a bank's books held in the Isle of Man relating to an account there. One of the grounds for refusal was that the account concerned was outside the jurisdiction, and conflict of jurisdictions should be avoided.

The more recent case of *Mackinnon v Donaldson, Lufkin and Jenrette Securities Corp* [1986] Ch 482 concerned an ex parte order under s 7 obtained by the plaintiff against an American bank (which was not a party to the litigation); the plaintiff was alleging fraud against a certain company and individual defendants. The order required the bank to produce books and other papers, held at its head office in New York, which related to an account of one of the defendants, a Bahamian company, which had been struck off the Bahamian register of companies since the issue of the writ and had ceased to exist. In addition the plaintiff issued a subpoena duces tecum against an officer of the London branch of the bank. The bank moved to have the ex parte order and subpoena discharged on the grounds that they exceeded the court's jurisdiction, and infringed the sovereignty of the United States. Hoffman J, discharging the order and the subpoena, said that on principle, the court should not, save in exceptional circumstances, impose on the foreigner and in particular a foreign bank which would owe a duty of confidence to its customer regulated by the law of the country where the customer's account was kept, a requirement to produce documents outside the jurisdiction concerning business transacted outside the jurisdiction. He said that the need to exercise the court's jurisdiction with due regard to the sovereignty of others is particularly important in the case of banks, who are in a special position because their documents are concerned not only with their own business, but with that of their customers. They owed a duty of confidence to their customers regulated by the law of the country where the account was kept.

'If every country where a bank happened to carry on business asserted a right to require the bank to produce documents relating to accounts kept in any other such country, banks would be in the unhappy position of being forced to submit to whichever sovereign was able to apply the greatest pressure.'

As will be seen, the English courts' approach to jurisdictional conflicts of this nature is somewhat different from that of the US courts. Their policy appears to be that apart from exceptional circumstances, they will voluntarily restrict their own jurisdiction within their own territorial limits and, in the interests (inter alia) of comity, leave matters outside those territorial limits to the courts of the relevant jurisdiction. The appropriate procedure would be to utilise the provisions of the Evidence (Proceedings in Other Jurisdictions) Act 1975 (referred to below) which was enacted in the United Kingdom to give effect to the provisions in the Hague Convention on the Taking of Evidence Abroad in Civil or Commercial Matters 1970. It is also interesting to note that in a decision of the New York Federal District Court in *Laker Airways v Pan American World Airways* [1985] ECC 15, 38, 336, Mr Justice Brieant quashed a subpoena served on two English banks at their New York offices requiring them to produce documents held in England which related to transactions which took place in England. Mr Justice Brieant was apparently of the view that the subpoena was 'inappropriate' and constituted 'an end run around the Hague Convention'.

Compulsion by Statute

The Jack Report listed no less than 19 statutory provisions in England which either require or permit disclosure of confidential information by bankers without the consent of the customer. The list, which is not claimed to be exhaustive, is contained in Appendix Q to the Report. The list includes the Bankers' Books Evidence Act 1879, the Financial Services Act 1986, the Insolvency Act 1986, the Drug Trafficking Offences Act 1986, the Taxes Management Act 1970 and the Income and Corporation Taxes Act 1988, the Police and Criminal Evidence Act 1984, the Criminal Justice Act 1988, and the Charities Act 1960, to which can now be added the Prevention of Terrorism (Temporary Provisions) Act 1989, which came into effect since the Report's publication. Only some of these will be considered here.

Most of these provisions entitle the relevant statutory body to compel a bank to produce information relevant to any matter which it is authorised to investigate. The most obvious example is the Inland Revenue which has wide powers in this connection. The penalties for failure to comply with requests for disclosure from statutory bodies under statutory powers vary with each piece of legislation and will normally be provided for in the relevant legislation.

Income and Corporation Taxes Act 1988, s 745

Section 745 gives the Inland Revenue wide investigatory powers if they suspect that the provisions of the Taxes Act preventing or counteracting the transfer of assets abroad for the purpose of evading English tax have not been complied with. In such cases, the banks are under an obligation to furnish particulars of any banking transactions between the bank and the customer. In the case of *Clinch v Inland Revenue Commissioners* [1973] 2 WLR 862, the court considered the effect of a notice served by the Commissioners under s 481 of the ICTA 1970 (the predecessor of ICTA 1988, s 745). The facts of the case were briefly this. Clinch was the managing director of a wholly-owned subsidiary in England of NT Butterfield & Son (Bermuda) Ltd. As such, he specialised in the management and trusteeship of international funds etc and many of his customers were persons who wanted to transfer money to Bermuda to avoid English income tax or to transfer part of their capital abroad. The Inland Revenue Commissioners served Clinch with a notice under s 481 requiring him, in any case where he had acted for an English customer, to furnish them (inter alia) with details of transactions resulting in the formation or management of a foreign company, partnership, trust or settlement and the names and addresses of such customers or their agents. Clinch maintained that the notice was void because it was merely a 'fishing expedition' and did not identify with sufficient particularity the customers or transactions in which the Inland Revenue was interested. Alternatively, the notice was invalid because compliance with it was unduly oppressive or burdensome. The court held that in the circumstances the notice was within the Inland Revenue's powers, although the court could intervene if it went substantially beyond that which was required for the purpose of enabling the Commissioners to decide whether or not in their opinion tax had been unlawfully evaded. The burden of proving oppression is therefore a heavy one. It should be remembered, however, that such a notice can only be served on someone in England and only be complied with by such a person in relation to documents and files in his possession in England.

Insolvency Act 1986, s 236

This section applies in the case where an administration order is made in relation to a company, an administrative receiver is appointed, the company goes into liquidation or a winding-up order has been made by the court. The court has the power to summon before it (inter alios) any person whom the court thinks capable of giving information concerning the promotion, formation, business, dealings, affairs or property of the company.

The court is further empowered under s 236(3) to require any such person to submit an affidavit to the court containing an account of his dealings with the company and produce any books, papers or other records in his possession or under his control relating to the company. Failure to comply with the order could result in a warrant being issued for that person's arrest and the seizure of any books, papers, records or goods in his possession. This section has been used against banks and is wide ranging and potentially penal in effect.

Banking Act 1987, s 84

Section 84 provides for the disclosure of information by a bank to various persons, including the Secretary of State or one of his inspectors, the Director General of Fair Trading or one of the Self Regulatory Organisations within the meaning of the Financial Services Act 1986 'if the Bank [meaning the Bank of England] considers that the disclosure would enable or assist that person to discharge the functions specified'. These include functions under Part XIII of the Companies Act 1985, under the Financial Services Act 1986, and under the Consumer Credit Act 1974.

Police and other Criminal Investigators: Recent years have seen a spate of new and varied legislation in this area. Notably, the Criminal Justice Act 1988 permits banks to disclose confidential information simply on suspicion of a customer's involvement in any one of a long list of specified offences. This directly overrides the view of Bankes LJ in his judgment in *Tournier*'s case that the giving of information to the police in regard to a customer suspected of a crime would be unwarranted.

At the end of 1988 the Basle Committee (which is composed of representatives of the central banks and supervisory authorities of the Group of Ten countries) issued a statement of principles designed to assist in suppressing money laundering through national and international banking systems. This statement of principles was circulated by the Bank of England in early 1989 and again in November 1989 with a letter drawing the attention of UK banks to a number of statutes which allow disclosure of customers' transactions and confer exemption from actions by customers for breach of confidentiality. Some of the more recent statutes relating to criminal investigations deserve closer consideration.

Police and Criminal Evidence Act 1984

Section 9 of the Act provides that a constable may obtain access to special procedure material for the purposes of a criminal investigation by making an application under Sch 1 to the Act. 'Special procedure material' is defined as 'material other than items subject to legal privilege and excluded material, in the possession of a person who acquired or created it in the course of any trade, business, profession or other occupation and holds it subject to an express or implied undertaking to hold it in confidence'. This would clearly include a bank. The police are entitled to apply for such an order at any stage if they believe that the material will assist their investigation of a serious arrestable offence.

The case of *R v Crown Court of Leicester, ex parte DPP* [1987] 3 All ER 654, in which the police applied for an order under s 9(1) granting them access to bank and building society accounts of a suspected person, confirmed that the police are not required to give notice of such application to any person suspected of or charged with the offence or to serve a copy of the application on him. (The case arose out of Judge Jowitt's refusal to grant police access because the suspected person had not been given prior notice of the application).

Further, the recent Court of Appeal cases of *Barclays Bank plc v Taylor; Trustee Savings Bank of Wales and Border Counties v Taylor* [1989] (*Financial Times* 23 June) made clear that where the police have obtained an order under s 9(1) a bank is obliged to comply with it, is not in breach of the duty of confidentiality by so doing and is under no obligation to oppose the application, probe the evidence given in respect of it or give notice to its customer that the application was being made.

Financial Services Act 1986—Insider Dealing

Sections 177 and 178 of this Act supplement the provisions in the Company Securities (Insider Dealing) Act 1985. Under the original legislation, there were no provisions for the investigation of suspicious events relating to stocks and shares. Under s 177, the Secretary of State may appoint inspectors to carry out investigations to establish whether there has been any contravention of the Insider Dealing Act, who then report back to the Secretary of State.

The Act gives the inspector the following powers:

(I)   to require the production of documents from any person who may be able to give information relating to the relevant company;
(II)   to require attendance before him of any such person;
(III) to require such a person to give all reasonable assistance in connection with the investigation; and
(IV)   to examine such a person on oath.

Any statement made by such a person may be used as evidence against him.

Section 177(8) specifically restricts these rights in relation to banks by stating that:

'Nothing in this section shall require a person carrying on the business of banking to disclose any information or produce any documents relating to the affairs of the customer unless—

(a) the customer is a person who the inspectors have reason to believe may be able to give information concerning the suspected contravention; and
(b) the Secretary of State is satisfied that the disclosure or production is necessary for the purposes of the investigation.'

There are two new penalties for failure to comply with the request by inspectors. The court may either treat it as a contempt of the court under the Contempt of Court Act 1981 or direct that the Secretary of State may exercise his powers under this section in respect of the person. Under these powers, the Secretary of State may issue a notice directing that the person is no longer authorised to carry on investment business within the meaning of the Financial Services Act. He may be restricted from carrying on business for a certain period of time or certain specified activities may be restricted or prohibited. These restrictions could clearly have far-reaching and very damaging effects on any bank made subject to them.

Drug Trafficking Offences Act 1986

There are three sections under this Act which are of considerable importance to the banks and their employees.

First, s 27(1) provides that for the purpose of an investigation into drug trafficking, the police and Customs may apply to a Circuit Judge for an order in relation to 'particular material or material of a particular description'. The order which the judge may make under s 27(2) is that the person who appears to the judge to be in possession of the material to which the application relates shall produce it to a constable for him to take away or give the constable access to it within such a period as the order may specify. Once the order is served on the person specified in the order, that person is obliged to comply. Section 27(9)(b) provides that the above order shall have effect notwithstanding any obligation as to secrecy or other restriction upon the disclosure of information imposed by statute or otherwise. From the point of view of a banker/customer relationship, a bank would be obliged to comply notwithstanding its duty of confidentiality to its customer. If such an order is not complied with, the constable may apply to the Circuit Judge for a warrant authorising him to enter and search the premises.

Secondly, under s 31 of the Act, a new offence has been created of 'prejudicing an investigation' into drug trafficking. This is clearly intended to deter anyone who might 'tip off' a suspect, for example a financial adviser or bank alerting a customer that his affairs are being scrutinised. The offence carries a maximum term of five years' imprisonment. If an order under s 27 has been made or applied for, and that person, knowing or suspecting that the investigation is taking place, makes any disclosure likely to prejudice the investigation, he is guilty of the offence.

Perhaps the most important of the new offences is created by s 24, which is aimed at intermediaries who assist traffickers and benefit from their crimes by 'laundering' the proceeds. It makes it an offence for a person (e g a banker), knowing or suspecting that a customer carries on or has carried on trafficking in drugs or has benefited from this, to enter into or otherwise be concerned with arrangements for:

(I)   retaining or controlling the proceeds of drug trafficking,
(II)   placing funds so obtained at the customer's disposal, or
(III)   using funds to acquire property by way of investment.

It is not necessary actually to know that the investor is a drug trafficker. Suspicion is sufficient. However, no offence is committed if the belief or suspicion is disclosed to the police as soon as possible, and under s 24(3) such disclosure 'shall not be treated as a breach of any restriction upon the disclosure of information imposed by contract'. The real difficulty for the bank is obviously when and in what circumstances to suspect someone of drug trafficking. A bank which fails to disclose its suspicion is guilty of an offence, the sanction for conviction being imprisonment for up to 14 years or a fine or both.

This is the first piece of legislation which requires a bank to disclose information to the police on its own initiative, thus imposing a very onerous duty on the bank. Additionally, it is only concerned with the proceeds of drug trafficking, which gives rise to the added difficulty of proving that a suspicion is linked to drug trafficking, although already legislation with similar provisions concerning the proceeds of terrorist activities has been introduced. It may be only a matter of time before other offences will be created in this way.

Prevention of Terrorism (Temporary Provisions) Act 1989

This Act, which only came into effect on 22 March 1989, requires (inter alia) banks to disclose, on suspicion, confidential information concerning the location of funds which might be used for or derived from possible terrorist offences.

There are two offences of particular concern to banks. Section 9 makes it an offence to solicit, receive or accept contributions of money or other property, intending that it shall be used for, or in furtherance of or in connection with, acts of terrorism or having reasonable cause to suspect that it may be so applied or used. It is also an offence to give or otherwise make available money or property, or to be concerned in or have reasonable cause to suspect it may be so used.

Section 11 makes it an offence to enter into or otherwise be concerned in an arrangement to control or retain terrorists' funds.

A let-out is provided in s 12 which provides that an offence is not committed under ss 9 and 11 if the person who entered into such a transaction or arrangement acted with the consent of the police or disclosed promptly and on his own initiative to the police a suspicion about the money or property concerned. (A defence is available in relation to the offences in this part of the Act where a person has a reasonable excuse for his failure to make such disclosure). Further, a person may disclose to the police a suspicion that any money or property is derived from terrorist funds notwithstanding any contractual restriction on the disclosure of information. This specifically overrides the bankers' duty of confidentiality to his customers.

Criminal Justice Act 1987

This is not considered in the Jack Report, but s 2(10) should be noted as another, potentially wide ranging instance where the obligation of confidence in a banking relationship may be overridden.

The Act empowers the Director of the Serious Fraud Office to investigate any suspected offence which appears to him on reasonable grounds to involve serious or complex fraud (s 1(3)). Under s 2 any person can be required to answer questions or otherwise furnish information or produce documents in respect of any matter relevant to an investigation.

Section 2(10) provides as follows:

'A person shall not under this section be required to disclose information or produce a document in respect of which he owes an obligation of confidence by virtue of carrying on any banking business unless—

(a) the person to whom the obligation of confidence is owed consents to the disclosure or production; or
(b) the Director has authorised the making of the requirement or, if it is impracticable for him to act personally, a member of the Serious Fraud Office designated by him for the purposes of this sub section has done so.'

By s 2(1) the Director can make such a requirement for the purpose of an investigation under s 1, in any case in which it appears to him that there is good reason to do so for the purpose of investigating the affairs, or any aspect of the affairs, of any person.

There are no specific provisions in the Act which allow the authority of the Director to be questioned. Section 2(13) provides that any person who without reasonable excuse fails to comply with a requirement placed on him shall, on summary conviction, be guilty of an offence and liable to imprisonment or to a fine. Judicial Review of the Director's power of investigation was unsuccessfully sought by the person under investigation in *R v Director of Serious Fraud Office, ex p Saunders* [1988] Crim LR 837. In that case, the court rejected the argument that the Director's powers under s 2 lapsed once a suspect had been charged; the Serious Fraud Office was entitled to continue the investigation thereafter. It was said, strictly obiter, that the Serious Fraud Office was entitled to obtain (inter alia) self-incriminating material in the possession of a third party including material arising out of civil proceedings (although the court expressed reservation as to the extent to which the latter could be required in view of the subject's constitutional rights against self-incrimination).

There is little helpful authority on what would constitute a 'reasonable excuse' under s 2(13) for failure to comply with a requirement for information from the Serious Fraud Office. In *ex p Saunders* the court said that an undertaking given by the third party to the Vice-Chancellor not to disclose the documents concerned to any person without leave of the court was a reasonable excuse for non-compliance. It is, however, most unlikely that a bank receiving such a requirement would be able to question the decision of the Director to authorise it.

Statutory interventions such as those described above cumulatively place a considerable burden on banks and make substantial inroads into the whole principle of customer confidentiality as conceived by *Tournier* and which were of great concern to the Jack Committee.

Treaties and Subpoenas—Extra-territorial aspects of the compulsion by law exception

It is now appropriate to turn to the extra-territorial aspects of bank secrecy and the disclosure by compulsion of foreign law. Examples often given include those of an American branch of a British bank asked by a United States Court to supply information maintained with their head office in London, or of the New York office of an American bank requested by a New York Court to provide information regarding a customer's dealings with branches in the United Kingdom. Such information may clearly be confidential. The dilemma for the bank is that in complying with the order of the United States court, it may breach its duty of confidentiality to its customer giving rise to a legal action which could be commenced by the customer; failure to comply may leave the officers of the bank open to criminal charges.

Two methods are commonly used to obtain such information—letters rogatory and subpoenas.

Letters Rogatory

'Letters rogatory' or 'letters of request' involve a request for evidence made by the foreign court which is seeking the information to the court in the place where records are maintained, in order to obtain the information without directly or indirectly infringing the sovereignty of the other country. The use of such letters rogatory is regulated by the Hague Convention on the Taking of Evidence Abroad in Civil or Commercial Matters 1970. This led to the enactment in the United Kingdom of the Evidence (Proceedings in Other Jurisdictions) Act 1975. Section 1 of the Act enables an English court to make an order for the obtaining of evidence in civil proceedings in other courts or tribunals upon a request from that court or tribunal, if the evidence requested relates to proceedings 'which either have been instituted before the requesting court or whose institution before that court is contemplated' (s 1(b)).

Such an order only requires the person to whom it is addressed to produce documents which are specified therein and which are in his possession, custody or power. The Act also provides that a person shall not be compelled to give any evidence which he could not be compelled to give in civil proceedings instituted under the jurisdiction of the court which makes the order. The intention is that the extent of disclosure to a foreign court does not exceed that which would be available in English proceedings.

The Act was considered by the House of Lords in the leading case of *In re Westinghouse Uranium Contract* [1978] 2 WLR 81. In that case Westinghouse Electric Corporation was the defendant in proceedings for a breach of contract in the United States, having failed to complete a contract to build power stations and supply them with uranium. Westinghouse's defence to these proceedings was, broadly, that the contracts were frustrated due to the steep increases in the price of uranium. Westinghouse also alleged that there was an international cartel among uranium producers which would, of course, have been contrary to the United States anti-trust laws. Westinghouse wished to adduce evidence of the existence of the cartel in its defence and also instituted proceedings against the alleged members of the cartel including Rio Tinto Zinc Corporation, an English company ('RTZ'). The United States Court for the District of Virginia issued letters rogatory to the High Court in England seeking orders for representatives of RTZ to attend for oral examination in London. RTZ claimed privilege on the grounds that their evidence might expose them to penalties under arts 85 and 86 of the Treaty of Rome.

By art 14 of Regulation 17 made pursuant to art 85, the European Commission is empowered to make all necessary investigations into undertakings and associations of undertakings to ensure compliance with art 85, which prohibits anti-competitive agreements. Officials authorised by the Commission, upon production of authorisation in writing specifying the subject matter and purpose of the investigations and the penalties provided in the Treaty where production of the required books or other business records is incomplete, may (inter alia) examine books and other business records of an undertaking. It is possible that this provision could be used to compel banks to disclose information not only about themselves but also about their customers.

RTZ's claim of privilege was upheld by the English Court of Appeal. The United States Federal Judge upheld a claim by witnesses to privilege under the Fifth Amendment. The US Department of Justice then applied for an order in the US Court compelling testimony in return for the provision of immunity on the grounds that it was required for a Grand Jury investigation into violations of the US anti-trust laws and with the view to issuing criminal proceedings.

The House of Lords upheld RTZ's claim of privilege and also held that the provisions of the Evidence (Proceedings in Other Jurisdictions) Act 1975 did not enable an English court to make an order to provide evidence to be used for investigatory purposes such as Grand Jury proceedings. The 1975 Act does extend to the obtaining of evidence for the purposes of criminal proceedings, but specifically limits this to proceedings which have been instituted. Grand Jury proceedings were held not to be criminal proceedings which had been instituted, rather they were merely investigatory proceedings, and consequently the English courts will not recognise or assist proceedings of this nature.

The issues at stake in the Westinghouse case were considered so important that the Attorney General intervened to bring to the notice of the House of Lords the policy of HM Government, which was opposed to extra-territorial recognition of the US investigatory jurisdiction (at least in relation to English companies or persons). It is clear that the House of Lords was concerned by the fact that an order giving effect to the District Court's request would expose British citizens to proceedings conducted in the US in respect of acts performed outside that country.

However, in the case of *Société Nationale Industrielle Aerospatiale v US District Court for the Southern District of Iowa* [1987] 107 S CT 2542, 55 USIW 4842, the United States Supreme Court has decided that the Hague Convention is optional rather than mandatory. In other words, although applicable, it is not the exclusive method of obtaining documents or testimony from outside the US. Briefly, the facts of the case were that following a plane crash in Iowa, the pilot and the passengers sued several defendants in the Iowa Federal District Court. The main Defendant was Aerospatiale, a French corporation which was the manufacturer. There were no jurisdictional objections to the litigation being conducted in the US. After some preliminary discovery (which did not require foreign discovery), there was further discovery and Aerospatiale objected to the Plaintiff's request for documents, interrogatories and admissions on the grounds that the Treaty was the exclusive basis of seeking evidence located in France and, under the Treaty, the trial court should have forwarded the Plaintiff's request to the appropriate French minister who would have probably denied or limited the scope of the discovery because it violated part of the French Penal Code. The Code provides that subject to treaty exceptions, technical commercial documents cannot be disclosed for use in foreign litigation. Aerospatiale argued that it could not comply with the order for discovery without violating French law.

The defendant appealed to the Eighth Circuit Court of Appeal, which confirmed the trial court order and stated its reason for allowing discovery without need to have recourse to the provisions of the Hague Convention thus: 'the better rule, which has been adopted by the vast majority of [US] courts, is that when the District Court has jurisdiction over a foreign litigant, the Hague Convention does not apply to the production of evidence'. However, subsequently the Supreme Court reversed the Appellate Court's findings and remanded the matter to the trial court. The majority opinion of the Supreme Court was that the Treaty was optional rather than mandatory. This effectively means that US courts do not have to resort first to or even apply the Convention. The United States is apparently the only party to the Treaty to consider the Treaty requirements optional.

This decision obviously has serious repercussions for international comity, as the Supreme Court's dissenting opinion recognised:

'Some might well regard the Court's decision in this case as an affront to the nations that have joined the US in ratifying the Hague Convention ... [which thus] ignores the importance of the Convention by relegating it to an "optional" status, without acknowledging the significant achievement in accommodating divergent [national] interests ...'

Subpoenas from other Jurisdictions

Foreign courts can ignore issues of comity by serving a subpoena on local offices of international banks in order to obtain information relating to the overseas branches. Often, the bank is thereby placed in the position of refusing to comply and being held in contempt of court, or obeying it and then infringing the secrecy laws of the country in which the information is maintained.

For example, in *First National City Bank v Inland Revenue Service* [1960] 361 US 948, a United States decision, an officer of First National City Bank was jailed for contempt by a US court for failure to comply with a subpoena ordering production of documents relating to a customer of the Bank's branch in Germany, the documents also being in Germany. The Bank's officer pleaded that compliance with the subpoena would be a breach of the German duty of confidence. The court, after receiving evidence about the effect of the penalties under German law, had no sympathy with him, but the court did indicate that its attitude might have been different if the penalties under German law had been criminal rather than merely civil. On the evidence before it, the court concluded that they were merely civil, though there seems to have been some disagreement on those points.

The qualification of compulsion by law in relation to foreign subpoenas was considered more recently in England in the case of *XAG v A Bank* [1983] 2 All ER 464. The plaintiffs (X), a multinational Corporation incorporated under Swiss law and based in Switzerland, and Y, an American subsidiary of X incorporated in Switzerland but with a major branch in New York, were concerned with oil marketing. Both had accounts with the London branch of the American bank, the defendant. A Grand Jury subpoena was served on the bank to produce all documents relating to any accounts maintained by the plaintiffs at the London branch. The bank declared its intention to comply with the subpoena, whereupon the plaintiffs sought and were granted an injunction in the High Court to restrain the bank from producing the documents, on the grounds that to do so would be a breach of the bank's duty of confidence to the plaintiff. An order was then obtained from the New York District Court, ex parte and in camera, requiring the bank to comply with the subpoena. The plaintiff successfully brought proceedings in the High Court to continue the injunction until trial.

Leggatt J held, first, that since the accounts of the company were opened and maintained in London, the banker/customer relationship was centred in London and English law was the proper law of the banking contract between the plaintiffs and the bank. Second, in determining whether the injunction should be continued, the court had to determine the balance of convenience with regard to:

(I)   the fact that the order of the New York Court would take effect in London in breach of both a private interest (the contract between bank and customer) and the public interest in maintaining the obligation of confidentiality imposed on banks conducting business in the City of London;

(II)   the effect of the subpoena of the New York Court and the fact that under the United States' doctrine of foreign government compulsion, the New York Court would not hold the Bank liable in contempt for complying with the injunction issued by the English court which had jurisdiction over the branch where the documents were located, and would treat the English injunction as adequate excuse for non-production;

(III) the fact that although the court would not be 'enforcing' a foreign revenue or penal law, if the New York subpoena were permitted to be enforced in London, nevertheless the mere fact of not impeding it would involve a measure of assistance and approbation which would involve the court tolerating a breach of the obligation of confidentiality which it would normally, in the public interest, maintain.

He summarised the balance of convenience thus:

'On the one hand, there is involved in a continuation of the injunction impeding the exercise by the US court in London of powers which, by English Statutes, would be regarded as excessive, without in so doing causing detriment to the Bank: on the other hand, the refusal of the injunctions, or the non-continuation of them, would cause potentially very considerable harm to the [group], which cannot be disputed, by suffering the Bank to act for its own purposes in breach of the duty of confidentiality admittedly owed to its customers.'

A similar view was taken by the Hong Kong Court of Appeal in *FDC Co Limited v Vanguard International Manufacturing Ltd Inc and Garpeg and The Chase Manhattan Bank NA* [1984] (Civil Appeal No 65). The United States Internal Revenue Service ('IRS') was making investigations into the affairs of a company within US jurisdiction and an Italian citizen. In the course of the investigations, the IRS issued summonses to the New York head office of Chase Manhattan Bank which (inter alia) covered matters related directly to accounts maintained by the plaintiffs with Chase which were in the possession of its Hong Kong branch.

The Court of Appeal upheld injunctions restraining the Hong Kong branch of Chase from divulging documents, records and information arising from or relating to the accounts of the plaintiffs, or from producing them to its head office or any other branch out of the jurisdiction (including the IRS) or removing any such record from the jurisdiction. This was notwithstanding the fact that the US court held Chase to be in contempt of the various summonses and had imposed fines of US$15,000 per day. The Hong Kong court refused to treat the fact that the bank had been exposed to considerable financial penalties and possible loss of banking licence as a ground for abrogating the normal rule of preserving the confidence between a bank and its customers. It is interesting to note that the majority of the Court of Appeal were of the opinion that for the purpose of this case, the Hong Kong branch of Chase should be considered as an entirely different entity, separate from the New York branch. This view has since been confirmed in the English decision of *Bank of Tokyo Ltd v Karoon* [1987] AC 45.

The decision in the *FDC* case should be compared to the *XAG* case; in the latter case the possible detriment to the bank in being exposed to contempt proceedings for failing to comply with a subpoena was regarded as a material factor. At least one commentator has come down on the side of the *FDC* decision as being the correct view on this point.

Finally, it should be noted that the balancing test has also been applied in relation to letters rogatory. In *In re State of Norway's Application* [1986] 3 WLR 453 Kerr LJ regarded as significant factors to weigh in the balance the nature, scope, quality and effect of a foreign court order or request.

Where there is a Duty to the Public to Disclose

This final exception in *Tournier* should be mentioned for the sake of completeness. Bankes LJ said that many instances might be given where a bank is justified in disclosing its customers' affairs on the grounds that there is a duty to the public to do so. He did not however indicate what these instances were. Scrutton LJ said that a bank 'may disclose the customer's account and affairs . . . to prevent frauds or crimes' and Atkin LJ considered that the right to disclose exists 'to the extent to which it is reasonably necessary . . . to protect the Bank, or persons interested, or the public, against fraud or crime'.

Since *Tournier*, the passing of such statutes as the Police and Criminal Evidence Act 1984, the Criminal Justice Act 1988, and the Financial Services Act 1986, have imposed duties of disclosure in circumstances where offences are suspected, or in order to assist the police generally in the investigation of crime. This has happened to such an extent that the 'disclosure under compulsion by law' exception in *Tournier* may now, effectively, be nothing more than a reference to those cases where a duty to the public to disclose has been recognised and imposed by statute. One has to assume that these statutory intrusions into the bank's obligation of confidence have taken place because the banks have construed their duty to the public far more narrowly.

The Jack Report recommends that this exception should now be deleted as 'statutory specification of this type of disclosure has now been carried so far that it is hard to see in what circumstances the generalised provision, with its uncertainty of application, could any longer be needed, given that emergency legislation could always be enacted in time of war'.

However, the case of *Libyan Arab Foreign Bank v Bankers Trust Co* [1988] 1 LLR p 259 illustrates that this exception may not yet be completely moribund. The case concerned the United States Presidential order of 8 January 1986 freezing Libyan assets under the control (inter alia) of overseas branches of United States banks. One of the claims made by the plaintiffs involved the scope of this exception to the duty of confidentiality. The issue arose because Bankers Trust in New York had had discussions with the Federal Reserve Board on 8 January about Libyan Arab Foreign Bank's accounts. The defendants relied on three of the four Tournier exceptions—that their own interest required them to do so, that the plaintiffs should be taken to have implicitly consented, or that there was a duty to the public to disclose. Staughton J rejected the first and second grounds, but accepted (tentatively) the third. He said:

'But presuming (as I must) the New York law on this point is the same as English law, it seems to me that the Federal Reserve Board, as the central banking system in the United States, may have a public duty to perform in obtaining information from banks. I accept the argument that higher public duty is one of the exceptions to a banker's duty of confidence, and I am prepared to reach a tentative conclusion that the exception applied in this case.'

Summary

Having discussed in some detail the four exceptions contained in *Tournier*, this is a convenient place to consider the recommendations made in the Jack Report regarding these exceptions. The Committee found that although the Tournier rules essentially remain valid, considerable doubt as to how they should be interpreted in the conditions prevailing today necessitates a statutory codification of the rules which at the same time will bring them up to date. This statute should make clear that the duty of confidentiality applies to any provider of banking services, and that it covers all information which the bank has acquired about the customer in the course of providing bank services to him.

The Report made the following recommendations with regard to each exception:

(I)   Duty to the public to disclose: for the reasons discussed above, the Report recommended that this exception be abolished.

(II) Disclosure under compulsion of law: this exception should be statutorily codified to incorporate all existing statutory exemptions.

(III) The interests of the bank require disclosure: the Report recommended that this exception be specifically limited to the cases of:
  (A) disclosure to a Court in the event of legal action to which the bank is a party;
  (B) disclosure as between banking companies within the same group (disclosure being limited to what is reasonably necessary for the

specific purpose of protecting the bank and its subsidiaries against loss); and

(C) disclosure for the purposes of or in connection with, and insofar as may be necessary for, the proposed sale of the ownership of the bank itself, or a substantial part of its undertaking.

(IV) Disclosure made with the consent of the customer: This exception should be altered to provide for express consent alone, which should be in writing and state the purpose for which the disclosure should be given. A standard of best practice should then provide for two further requirements for the mechanics by which a bank is to obtain its customers' express consent. First, express consent should not be sought in a way that puts the customer under pressure to give it, and second, in the limited case of banks' opinions where consent in tacit form may be obtained, a letter should be sent personally by the bank to all its customers seeking their consent for this specific purpose.

The Jack Report recommended that a new exception be included 'where there has been a breakdown of the banker/customer relationship arising through customer default' (default being defined as the case where no security has been given and no satisfactory response has been received from the customer within 28 days of a formal demand for repayment). Disclosure should be expressly limited, even in these circumstances, to the release of information about debts to approved credit reference agencies.

With regard to a customer's remedies for breach of the duty of confidentiality, the legislation should spell out that damage for breach of confidentiality under any of these rules should include compensation for distress, embarrassment or inconvenience, regardless of whether financial loss could be proved.

Finally, a standard of best practice should enjoin banks to explain clearly to all their customers the confidentiality rules as set out above. They should also require banks to remind customers of their right of access under the Data Protection Act 1984 to computer data about them held by the banks.

Whether the recommendations made in the Jack Report will ever find their way onto the English Statute book is a matter, at present, for speculation. What is clear, however, is that the rule and exceptions laid down by Bankes LJ in *Tournier*'s case are no longer adequate to deal with the changing face of society and modern banking practice, and that some kind of statutory intervention would be welcomed by those concerned in this area of law.

INSIDER TRADING AND CHINESE WALLS

The final topic is one which, although not falling squarely within the boundaries of the bank's duty of confidence, is nevertheless of great concern to banks and to the financial market generally, particularly in the context of securities dealing and mergers and acquisitions. Insider trading is often seen as a victimless crime which undermines the whole credibility and reputation of the securities market. For many years, the City conducted a system of self-regulation which relied on an unwritten code of fair play between bankers. Over the years, under governmental pressure, the systems of voluntary regulation have improved steadily, with the establishment of the City Panel on Takeovers and Mergers as the major supervisory body.

With the implementation of the Conservative government's policy of privatisation and wider share ownership, self-regulation was not felt to be sufficiently effective to safeguard and, most importantly, be seen to safeguard, the new type of investor, the 'man in the street', against abuses which were said to be rife. The government therefore embarked on a programme of strengthening the powers of and widening the role of self-regulatory authorities together with imposing a degree of statutory regulation contained in the Company Securities (Insider Dealing) Act 1985, the Financial Services Act 1986 and the Companies Act 1985.

The self-regulatory aspects had previously been dealt with in the main by the City Code on Takeovers and Mergers, but this has now been radically expanded by the setting up of Self-Regulatory Organisations ('SROs') under the umbrella of the Securities Investments Board (SIB), which in turn answers to the Secretary of State for Trade and Industry. The various SROs regulate the affairs of their members who include Investment banks and Securities Houses (TSA), firms dealing in broking, futures and options and providing investment management advice in these fields (AFBD), independent intermediaries advising on collective investments such as unit trusts or life assurance (FIMBRA), investment managers, unit trust managers and pension fund managers (IMRO) and life assurance companies and unit trust managers (LAUTRO). Investment and securities houses are regulated by The Securities Association ('TSA') whose rules, in particular regarding Chinese Walls, will be considered in more detail below.

Insider dealing first reached the statute book in the Companies Act 1980. The provisions have now been replaced by the Company Securities (Insider Dealing) Act 1985 and Part VIII of the Financial Services Act 1986. Insider dealing in corporate securities involves the utilisation of unpublished price sensitive information obtained through a privileged relationship to make a profit or avoid a loss by dealing in securities the price of which could be materially affected by public disclosure of that information.

Section 1(1) of the Act makes it a criminal offence for an individual who is or has at any time within the preceding six months been knowingly connected with a company, to deal on a recognised stock exchange in securities of that company if he has information which:

(I)   he holds by virtue of being connected with the company,
(II)   it would be reasonable to expect him not to disclose (except in the proper performance of the functions attaching to his position), and
(III)   he knows is unpublished price-sensitive information in relation to those securities.

This is known as primary insider dealing, where the information must be acquired by virtue of the insider's connection with his own company.

Of more importance to banks is the prohibition on secondary insider dealing or 'tippee' trading. Sections 1(3) and 1(4) deal with the situation where an individual obtains insider information from an individual who is or was during the preceding six months connected with the particular company, and the 'tippee' must know or reasonably believe that the individual has such information by reason of his connection with the company and that, because of the informant's position with the company, it will be reasonable to expect him not to disclose that information. If the 'tippee' then uses that information and deals on the Stock Exchange or investment exchange, he may be guilty of an offence (subject to certain defences).

It should be noted that, in order to be a 'tippee', the information must be obtained directly from the person connected with the company or indirectly through any number of people forming a chain between 'tippee' and insiders. One can therefore very clearly envisage the situation, in the context of a bank, where the mergers and acquisitions section obtains some unpublished price-sensitive information from a client company, which is then passed to its dealing arm, who proceed to trade in the shares on the bank's own account on the strength of that information.

There has been a paucity of case law dealing with secondary insiders under the Company Securities (Insider Dealing) Act 1985, leading to suggestions by some commentators that the Act has not succeeded in its aim of catching 'tippees'. The first case in which a prosecution was brought against a 'tippee' was *Attorney-General's Reference (No 1 of 1988)* [1989] 1 All ER 321.

In 1980, the T family decided to sell their interest in 1 million shares in a public company and instructed its merchant bankers to act on their behalf. After a number of false starts, F appeared as a prospective purchaser and after a number of discussions with DT (a member of the family) spoke at DT's request to a Miss H-M of the merchant bank. However, DT did not regard F as a serious purchaser and, in December 1985, agreed to sell the shareholding to Diamond Ltd, at a price of 54p per share. He telephoned Miss H-M to inform her and agreed that she should inform F as she was still dealing with him.

At about 4.30 pm on 5 December, she telephoned F to tell him of the deal made by DT and that it was likely the deal would go through and that an announcement would be made soon, although she did not impart the price. She also told him that this information was highly sensitive and confidential and as a result of the conversation he would be regarded as an 'insider'. F then proceeded to instruct his stockbroking firm at about 4.30 pm on the same day to purchase shares in the company, which were later sold on 10 January 1986 at 98p per share.

When charged with offences under s 1(3) of the Act, F's defence was that the section provides that the accused must have 'knowingly obtained directly or indirectly' the unpublished price-sensitive information; and he had not 'obtained' it because 'obtaining' meant taking positive steps to get the information. In the present case he had merely received it in a passive role and although he had acted upon the information, he had not taken any positive steps to obtain the information. The trial judge accepted this defence and acquitted F.

The Attorney General referred the issue to the Court of Appeal who, overruling the trial judge, were unanimous in their view that Parliament had intended that a recipient of price-sensitive information, who dealt in the relevant securities, had 'obtained' the information, whether he had procured it or came to it without any positive action on his part. This would clearly catch the bank employee overhearing a conversation in the lift at work and, realising that what he was hearing was price sensitive, dealt in securities on the strength of it. The Court of Appeal's decision has now been upheld by the House of Lords. The decision of the House of Lords is expected to give rise, subject to evidential difficulties, to a large number of further prosecutions under s 1(3) of the Act.

The use of so-called Chinese Walls (ie the internal segregation of information between departments) has been advocated by regulatory authorities operating under the SIB umbrella as the only practical solution to the kind of problem illustrated in the above case. Taking the TSA rules (the TSA being an organisation whose members include banks) as an example, they recommend two procedures for the segregation of information: Chinese Walls and an Independence Policy. Neither of these are compulsory, although TSA members are not permitted to claim to operate an Independence Policy if they do not in fact do so.

Rule 1220.01 of Ch IV, Part XV, in essence, provides that a Chinese Wall exists between one employee and another employee of the same firm (or of a connected company) if the firm has written rules and procedures which are likely to ensure that the first employee will not be provided with or allowed access to information acquired by the second employee until such time as that information is generally known in the city in which the employee is based. The rules and procedures must be drawn up and carried out in such a way which achieves this result and the member firm must require their employees to comply with this rule. The TSA has power to notify a member firm that it shall not be regarded as having Chinese Walls and such notification may set out conditions that the member firm must satisfy before the notification will be lifted.

The Independence Policy (explained in Rule 1100.02 of Ch IV, Part XII) broadly requires the employees of the firm, in acting for a customer, to disregard any other relationship, arrangement or interest which may influence their advice to that customer. The TSA has explained in its synopsis of the Rules that an Independence Policy is a means of ensuring that employees disregard interests or relationships of which they are aware, as opposed to a Chinese Wall which is a mechanism for restricting the flow of information.

In the context of take-overs in particular, Rule 1100.01 (Ch IV, Part XII) of the TSA rules prevents an employee of a TSA member firm from providing corporate finance facilities (which would include acting as an adviser in a take-over) to a client where he knows of a material interest in any transaction or investment involving another person unless that relationship, arrangement or interest has been fairly disclosed to the client. However, this rule appears to be of limited practical application in a takeover situation. First, it is difficult to see how it could apply in practice in a takeover except where both parties in the takeover are concurrently clients of the bank; and secondly, it does not in any event apply to any firm which has a written independence policy in force with which its employees are required to comply (provided that compliance in the particular case can be proved).

It is clear, from the decisions of the English courts in the so-called concurrent agency cases, that if an agent, while acting for a principal, starts to act for a second principal whose interests conflict with those of the first principal, he cannot continue to act for both simultaneously. However, he will be permitted to act for both principals if he informs both of the circumstances of his involvement and obtains their consent to his acting for both simultaneously.

The City Panel on Take-overs and Mergers was faced in 1987 with a problem as to whether the internal segregation of information is sufficient where a merchant bank acts at two different times in relation to the same company in a take-over. The issue was considered in the Tozer Kemsley and Millbourn (Holdings) plc/Molins plc ruling: in November 1985, an offer was made by a management buy-out consortium to acquire the whole of the share capital of Molins; the merchant bank engaged by the consortium as financial adviser received material confidential information relating to Molins in the normal course, including long-term financial projections. The bid did not proceed and the merchant bank ceased to have any material involvement with Molins. In May 1987, Tozer engaged that same merchant bank to act for them in relation to their bid for Molins. The merchant bank did not initiate the offer and its personnel acting for Tozer were different from those who acted for the consortium in 1985. Further, steps were taken to isolate confidential documentary information previously obtained from Molins, so that it could not be available to those advising Tozer.

The Panel had to determine whether, in all the circumstances of the case, the possession of relevant confidential information (if it were found to be that) required that the merchant bank should cease to act for Tozer in connection with the offer. Although the Panel did not make a formal ruling, as the issue was not covered either by the General Principles or by the rules of the Code, it considered it appropriate to express its views. The general issue of principle was whether it was proper to resolve potential problems of conflict of interest by taking steps internally to isolate information within a corporate finance organisation. The Panel recognised that a potential conflict of interest could only be avoided by the strict segregation as between corporate finance, market-making and investment advisory functions as required by the regulatory authorities. It considered

'. . . that it is inappropriate for a corporate finance organisation or other advisor to seek to resolve problems of conflict of interest simply by isolating information internally. The organisation should respect that confidence [of the client] by declining to act if necessary rather than by adopting internal measures to keep information separate.'

The Panel noted that there will often be internal formal discussions which lead to the dissemination of such information within the organisation, which emphasises that it is not sufficient simply to isolate documents or assign different personnel to act.

The Panel further considered that the long-term information received by the merchant bank in 1985 had not in this case become out of date, although this fact could be relevant in similar cases. The Panel concluded that, in this particular situation, the merchant bank should have declined to accept instructions from Tozer, although it emphasised that this view was formed in the context of a novel and difficult situation, and that the merchant bank had minimised the risk of any actual abuse of the information in their possession. The offer was held to be still current and continuing, as the Panel considered that a greater disadvantage could be suffered by the shareholders of both Molins and Tozer if the offer were interrupted by the merchant bank resigning than by their continuing to act.

The conclusion to be drawn from this ruling is that the Panel has clearly attempted to differentiate between mere internal isolation of information and the adoption of strict segregation procedures as required by the various self-regulatory organisations created under the Financial Services Act. The implication of the ruling is that each particular instance of potential conflict of interest will turn on the facts of the particular case. It would appear that the more exhaustive the measures of segregation that are taken, the less likelihood there is of the Panel ruling that conflicts of interest have arisen.

Summary

There will no doubt be disputes relating to the possible misuse of confidential information between present or past customers on the one hand and banks and other organisations on the other hand, when those banks/organisations have, where they are required to do so, set up a system of Chinese Walls or adopted an independence policy.

Clearly, there will be those customers who will not be persuaded that Chinese Walls/independence policies are completely effective in ensuring the confidentiality of the customer's information. There has already been a recent shift by some substantial customers away from their bankers where another member of the banking group was perceived to be acting against the customer; it would appear that the main feeling was that the bank had shown a lack of loyalty to the customer. The consequences of a substantial customer removing its considerable business from a bank may be a factor in a bank's decision whether it or a member of its group acts for that customer's competitor. However, that sanction would not be available to a past customer nor perhaps to a less substantial customer, who would be left with having to seek redress in the courts to restrain an alleged misuse of confidential information.

A customer seeking injunctive relief would have to give a cross-undertaking in damages in the event that the injunction was granted and the party against whom the injunction was granted subsequently had the injunction discharged either before or at trial.

As a grant of an injunction is a form of equitable relief which it is in the discretion of the court to grant or refuse, the court when considering an application for an interlocutory injunction founded upon an arguable claim (i e before the trial of the action) applies a test as to where the balance of convenience lies; namely, which party would suffer more if an injunction were to be granted or refused. In addition, the court has to be satisfied that monetary damages would not be an appropriate remedy.

A fundamental point which the court would have to decide is whether the Chinese Walls erected and the independence policy adopted by the bank/organisation would justify the refusal of an interlocutory injunction and subsequently at trial whether the existence of the Chinese Walls or the policy would provide a good defence.

In an unreported case in 1976 (known as the *Charles Ball* case), Charles Ball, when employed by merchant bank 'A', was involved in advising company 'D' in relation to a third party's attempted takeover bid of company 'D'. This was in 1975. He then moved to merchant bank 'B' and in the intervening period company 'D' had published its report and accounts. Several months afterwards, in 1976, company 'E' advised by merchant bank 'B' made a takeover bid for company 'D'. As a result, company 'D' sought an interim injunction against Charles Ball and merchant bank 'B' to restrain them from being involved in the takeover bid. It was clear that Mr Ball had been involved on behalf of company 'D' when employed by merchant bank 'A', although he claimed in his affidavit that he had no confidential information and, if he had, it was not made available to merchant bank 'B'.

The judge deciding in favour of company 'D' remarked that it was necessary 'for the good of the law and the City that doubt should be removed by preventing Mr Ball acting'. The Chinese Wall argument was apparently not well received.

It will be interesting to see the outcome of such disputes in the future when viewed in light of the self-regulatory steps required by the SROs under the umbrella of SIB. It should be noted that an alternative procedure which a customer may be able to adopt in appropriate circumstances is to complain to the SRO of which a customer's bank/organisation is a member in respect of any threat of or actual misuse of confidential information.

7 France

Philippe Giroux

'To live happy, let's live in the dark.' What a famous French author said about love may also be true of business. That was at least what businessmen seem to have thought for centuries. An extreme example of such attitude was given in the nineteenth century by Savary, who reported that several tradesmen had preferred to lose a trial rather than open their accounting books in court.

Bankers are obviously in a privileged position to get important information about their customers who certainly expect them not to disclose such information unless compelled to do so.

However, the problem of abuse of confidential information has now become much wider than that of the information entrusted to bankers as holders of bank accounts. Banks and financial institutions now provide various services which involve different kinds of information and conflicts of interests are bound to arise.

NATURE AND EXTENT OF BANKER'S DUTY OF CONFIDENCE

Source

In as early as 1810 the Penal Code imposed sanctions upon persons such as physicians or 'all other persons who are in possession, by virtue of their . . . profession . . . of secrets confided to them' who reveal these secrets (Penal Code, art 378).

In 1922 it was held that this provision applied to stockbrokers, but it remained doubtful for more than a century whether it could apply to bankers. In the first part of the twentieth century a tendency grew in favour of the application to bankers of the confidentiality duty imposed by art 378.

The 1973 law on the Banque de France specified that the agents and employees of the Banque de France were bound by a duty of confidence and that the sanctions of art 378 of the Penal Code would apply in case of breach of such duty.

Finally, when the whole organisation of banks was revised in 1984, it was made clear that art 378 applied to 'any member of a board of directors, and, if any, of a supervisory board and any person who in whatever capacity takes a part in the management or in the operation of a bank or is employed by it' (art 57 of the Law of 24 January 1984).

This confidentiality duty does not apply to all pieces of information which banks may get. In France as in many other countries, it is customary for instance to ask banks for 'references' on the financial situation of a company with which one is intending to do business.

According to French law, the confidentiality duty of banks only covers precise information on the amount shown by an account or operations effected by the customer, as opposed to general information relating to the customer's solvency.

Civil or criminal?

The breach by a bank's manager, officer or employee of his confidentiality duty is a criminal offence and may be punished by imprisonment of from one to six months and by a fine of from FF500 to FF15,000.

Remedies

Should the breach of the duty of confidence cause a damage to the customer, the latter may claim damages. The general rules of tortious liability laid down by art 1382 of the civil code will apply, which means that it will have to be established that there has been a fault, a damage and a causal link between the fault and the damage.

EXCEPTIONS TO BANKER'S DUTY OF CONFIDENCE

Customer's Consent?

While the criminal courts refuse to admit that a professional can be released from his duty of confidence by his customer, civil courts have adopted diverging views on this issue which remains unsettled.

When Suing the Customer?

There does not seem to be any case law on the question as to whether a banker could disclose certain confidential information when suing its customer. However, in a case involving a tax adviser, the Paris Court of Appeal held that the duty could be waived for the needs of proceedings concerning the adviser's fees, to such extent only as was necessary for the defence of his interests (Paris, 11 January 1985).

This solution could probably be extended to proceedings brought by a bank against its customer, bearing in mind that the information disclosed should be restricted to that strictly necessary.

Compulsion of Law

Civil Proceedings

Whereas a banker may not invoke his duty of confidence when requested to give evidence before a criminal court, he may refuse to testify before a civil or commercial court. There are however three exceptions to this rule:

(I)   in the case of the liquidation of a matrimonial property;
(II)   in the case of insolvency or bankruptcy proceedings where the president of the commercial court or the supervising judge ('juge-commissaire') may request information from banks on the financial situation of the debtor; and
(III) in the case of the attachment of an account ('saisie-arrêt') by a customer's creditor (art 559, para 4 of the old Civil Procedure Code) where the bank is bound to confirm to the bailiff ('huissier') in charge of the attachment whether the debtor holds an account with the bank, what is the amount of money on this account and whether there have been previous attachment proceedings.

Regulatory Authorities

Domestic Authorities

The banker's duty of confidence will not prevail against inquiries from the 'commission bancaire', which is the regulatory authority for banking institutions, nor to the Banque de France (art 57 of the Law of 24 January 1984), nor to the 'Commission des Opérations de Bourse' (COB), which is the equivalent of the American Security and Exchange Commission (art 5 of the Ordinance of 28 September 1967), nor of course to tax authorities. All these authorities have access to all accounting documents, including particulars of any customer's account. The fact that the information relates to an account held outside France is not relevant provided that the information is available in France.

Foreign Authorities

The professional duty of confidence may override claims of foreign authority, except possibly if it relies on an international treaty such as a bilateral tax treaty or the 1970 Hague Convention on the obtaining of evidence abroad. The Hague Convention provides that evidence may be obtained either through diplomatic or consular agents, who do not, however, have any compulsion power, or through the French Ministry of Foreign Affairs (which conveys the request to the Ministry of Justice which itself conveys the request to the Public Prosecutor who conveys it to the competent French court). But even in this case, it is doubtful whether a French judge would receive evidence where this would constitute a breach of a professional duty of confidence under French law.

In addition to the professional duty of confidence, a bank may invoke arts 1 or 1 bis of the Law of 26 July 1968.

Article 1 provides that the conveyance of economic, commercial, industrial, financial or technical information to foreign public authorities is a criminal offence where the communication of such information could interfere with the sovereignty, security, essential economic interests of France or with public order. This offence applies to any natural person of French nationality or residing in France as well as to any manager, representative, agent or employee of a legal entity having its registered office or a branch in France. This provision would therefore apply to any manager or employee of a foreign bank having a branch in France.

Article 1 bis provides that when commercial or financial information is requested from any person with a view to adducing evidence for any judicial or administrative proceedings abroad, the request and the communication of such information are criminal offences.

The prohibition applies to 'any person'. Therefore, if a French national who resides in France, visits a foreign country and discloses information for the purpose of judicial proceedings in that country, the Law of 26 July 1968 would probably apply, if the information was obtained in France (answer to written question no 4356, official journal, Senate Debate, 4 June 1987, p 390).

Both articles apply subject to international treaties and therefore may not be invoked if the procedure laid down by the 1970 Hague Convention were relied upon.

A foreign authority seeking information to be found in France could request the French analogous authority to provide it with such information. For example, the American Federal Bank Examiners or the SEC could request the French Commission Bancaire or the Banque de France or the COB to provide it with information concerning an American bank having a branch in France. The Commission Bancaire, the Banque de France and COB could obtain the information, notwithstanding any duty of confidence owed by the bank (art 57 of the Banking Law of 24 January 1984 and art 5 of the Ordinance of 28 September 1967).

The question, however, arises as to whether the French authority could be in breach of its own duty of confidence when conveying the information to the analogous foreign authority.

As regards Commission Bancaire and Banque de France, the information may be given to the foreign authorities in charge of the surveillance of credit establishments, provided that reciprocity exists and subject to the conditions that these authorities are themselves bound by a professional duty of confidence with the same guarantees as in France (art 49 of the 1984 Banking Law). As regards the COB, it may convey information to any analogous authority of another member State of the European Community which is bound by a professional duty of confidence as well as to any analogous body of a foreign state provided that reciprocity exists and that the foreign authority is bound by a professional duty of confidence with the same guarantees as in France (art 5 of the Ordinance of 28 September 1967).

A bill which was approved by the Council of Ministers in March 1989 purports to restrict the conveyance of information to foreign authorities by providing that the COB must refuse to convey the information to the foreign analogous authority where there could be an interference with the sovereignty, the security, the essential economic interests or to the public order in France or when any penal proceeding has begun in France on the basis of the same facts and against the same persons, or when these persons have already been subject to a final judgment on the same facts.

Police and other Criminal Investigators?

Prior to the 1984 Banking Law, the police were not entitled to conduct investigations within banks. Article 57 of this law now states that the duty of confidence will not justify non-disclosure to 'the judicial authority acting in the course of criminal proceedings'. The question therefore arises as to whether the police may be regarded as a 'judicial authority'. Article 75 of the Penal Procedure Code provides that officers and agents of 'police judiciaire' (who are defined in art 20 of the Penal Procedure Code) are authorised to conduct preliminary investigations either upon the Public Prosecutor's instructions or upon their own initiative. Such investigations are, in both cases, conducted under the control of the Public Prosecutor who is a judicial authority.

The view is thus taken by some authors that the police are now authorised to request information from banks. Others think that the police may be regarded as a 'judicial authority' only when acting upon the Public Prosecutor's instructions. In practice it is advisable for the bank to request the officer or agent to sign a declaration specifying his role and whether he is acting upon the Public Prosecutor's instructions.

INSIDER DEALING

The temptation is great for employees or managers of banks or financial institutions to use the information they collect for their own benefit or for the benefit of related persons. Two methods are conceivable in order to prevent these practices, namely penal provisions and rules of professional conduct. In France the first method has been the only one for a long time but the need for rules of professional conduct is now widely admitted.

The Offence of Insider Dealing

It has been a criminal offence since 1970 for the managers of a company or persons who get information about a company in the course of their profession to use such information before it has become public in order to effect transactions. This results from an amendment to the Ordinance of 28 September 1967, which established the COB to supervise the quoted securities market and public offerings.

We will examine in turn:

(I)   the persons who may be liable,
(II)   the nature of the information concerned,
(III)   what is meant by the 'abuse' of such information,
(IV)   the intention which must be established, and
(V)   the sanctions imposed upon offenders.

Persons who may be Liable

Article 10.1 of the Ordinance of 28 September 1967 as amended, which defines insider dealings, is aimed at 'persons finding themselves in possession of privileged information in the course of their profession or of their duties'. It is therefore necessary that the information be obtained by reason of the exercise of the profession or duties and not by mere luck or through friendly or family relationships.

Bank managers and employees are obviously in a privileged position to get information about the transactions which their customers contemplate and there are examples of bank managers abusing such information. Thus in 1978 a bank manager who was in charge of the supervision of the personal bank account of a customer got to know that the customer intended to take over a company if the results of the parliamentary elections were what he expected. The bank manager bought for his own account 90 shares after a meeting with the customer and 155 shares on the day following the elections. He was sentenced to three months' imprisonment with remission of sentence and to a fine of FF 20,000 (Trib. Corr. Paris 13 January 1978).

Nature of the Information

The content of the information concerned is defined very broadly as any information 'about the perspectives or the situation of an issuer or on the likely evolution of a security or of a futures contract'. The courts have held that this covers, inter alia, the preparation of a take-over bid.

'Abuse' of the Information

The abuse must take the form of a transaction effected on the market. Therefore if a bank advises and leads a lending syndicate to a company purporting to make a take-over bid for one of the bank's customers, there will be no offence of insider dealing, although there may be a breach of the duty of confidence.

The offence of insider dealing is however defined broadly in that (a) it is not necessary to establish a causal link between the information and the transaction effected, and (b) it is an offence for a person in possession of privileged information not only to effect a transaction directly or through an intermediary but also to enable a third party to effect the operation.

a) Until recently it was necessary to establish that the person in possession of the privileged information had made an abusive use of it, which meant that he had effected transactions 'on the basis' of such information.

Article 10.2 of the 1968 Ordinance as amended by a law of 22 January 1988 now provides that the privileged person must 'effect on the market, or intentionally permit the realisation, directly or through an intermediary, of one or more transactions'.

Privileged persons are therefore now under the obligation to refrain from effecting any transaction until the information becomes public, because if they did, the abuse of such information would be presumed.

b) The prohibited transactions may be effected by the privileged person directly or, more often, through a man of straw who, as the COB noted, is often a non-resident company (often located in a tax-haven). The Commission has therefore called for the conclusion of international treaties.

Co-operation between the appropriate national authorities is obviously necessary, although confidentiality should be ensured. The COB is at present authorised to provide information to equivalent entities in the EEC and also to foreign authorities outside the EEC, provided that the assistance is reciprocal and the foreign authority subject to a duty of confidence. Similar provisions apply to the Commission Bancaire and Banque de France.

We have seen that it is an offence for a privileged person to enable a third party to effect a transaction. This 'third party' may be a customer or an employee of the same financial institution. Thus, a bank manager having privileged information concerning a company who advises a customer to effect transactions on securities of such company or uses this information when managing the securities held on behalf of customers will be liable. Similarly a bank employee dealing with the account of a customer who passes some information on to another employee dealing with the managing of securities accounts will fall within the ambit of the 1967 Ordinance.

Intention

Where the person in possession of privileged information effects a transaction himself or through an intermediary, he will be liable if he was aware of the fact that the information had not yet been disclosed to the public. Where the information is passed on by the privileged person to a third party, it must be established that the informer knew that the third party would act upon it.

Sanctions

Offenders may be punished by imprisonment of from two months to two years and/or by a fine ranging from FF 6,000 to FF 5 million. However, and this is unique in the French legal system, the fine may not be inferior to the profit made and may reach four times this profit, even though the fine would then exceed FF 5 million.

Professional Rules of Conduct

Large financial institutions raise a special problem which is partly due to the variety of services they now provide which include dealing with securities owned by their customers. Moreover, they often effect transactions on their own behalf and so do their employees. Conflicts of interests may therefore arise between several clients as well as between the financial institution itself and its customers.

This problem led the COB to issue a recommendation in March 1974 in which it stated that financial intermediaries must ensure that confidential information remains confidential vis-à-vis third parties as well as vis-à-vis other persons working within the same institution. As a consequence, departments dealing with securities should be, as far as possible, kept separate from the other departments.

In 1983 the stockbrokers' supervisory body ('Chambre Syndicale des agents de change', now replaced by 'Conseil des bourses de valeurs') issued a professional code applicable to its members.

More recently, in early 1987, the COB decided to set up a working committee ('groupe de travail sur la déontologie des activités financières') composed of 12 members including a representative of the Ministry of Economy, a representative of the Ministry of Justice, a member of the COB and experienced professionals. The committee's work has been summarised in a report which was published by the COB in March 1988 (COB 'Rapport général due groupe de déontologie des activités financières' supplément au Bulletin mensuel no 212 mars 1988).

We shall analyse first the contents of the professional rules laid down by the committee and second the means which were recommended in order to ensure compliance with these rules.

The Rules

The committee expressed the view that the financial institutions ought first to analyse the various 'professions' they exercise, i e that of broker, merely trying to find a seller or a purchaser, that of managing customers' portfolios and that of 'market-maker'. The financial institutions should also try to analyse possible conflicts of interest between different customers or between customers and the institution or its employees. Each institution should then try to set up a body of internal rules, the implementation of which would be ensured by the institution itself. These rules should be based upon two important principles which are the customer's interest and market integrity.

The Committee concentrated upon four particular issues, which were:

(I)   transactions effected by professionals for their own account;
(II)   the management of customers' portfolios;
(III)   market-making transactions;
(IV)   option and futures markets.

We shall concentrate upon the first two issues which are the most relevant to our topic.

Transactions Effected by Professionals for their own Account

Before the Committee was set up, the Law of 22 January 1988 already provided in art 19 that financial institutions had to set up internal regulations dealing with:

(I)   the conditions under which their employees may effect transactions on the market for their own account,
(II)   the conditions under which they must inform their employer thereof,
(III)   the obligations imposed upon them in order to avoid undue disclosure of confidential information.

The Committee indicated that the position of relatives of persons effecting transactions on their own behalf should also be studied.

It expressed the view that it would be advisable to request these professionals to use an account opened with their employer. Where this is not possible and an account is opened with another institution, measures should be taken to enable the employer to ensure that professional rules of conduct have been duly complied with. The institution where the account is opened should avoid executing orders which its own employees would not be authorised to make or which they would only be authorised to make under certain conditions.

Portfolio Management

The Committee recommended that the managers of financial institutions providing such services should make a declaration to the appropriate supervisory body which would be signed by their representatives and would list the obligations resulting from the management of portfolios on behalf of customers.

The agreement between the institution and the customer should specify whether or not the customer's portfolio could comprise securities in which the institution or its group may have interests.

If the operations effected by the institution on its own behalf are substantial, they should be dealt with by persons who will not be in charge of the management of the customers' portfolios.

All measures should be taken by the institution to ensure that records are kept of all transactions on the portfolios managed on behalf of customers. Where part of the remuneration of the person in charge of customers' portfolios depends on the results obtained, that remuneration should be independent from any profit made by the institution.

Where a transaction involves an offer which may be accepted by a limited number of persons only, rules should be set up as to the order in which orders may be made amongst the various customers' portfolios or between these portfolios and the institution.

The Committee, moreover, wanted the French authorities to ensure that the above rules would be complied with by foreign institutions.

Finally, the Committee recommended that where the same institution provides different kinds of services such as that of broker, market-making transactions and management of portfolios, these services should be provided by separate departments.

Control of Compliance with the Rules

The Committee made a distinction between internal and external control. It expressed the view that compliance with the rules of conduct should, to a large extent, be entrusted to the financial institutions themselves which are in a much better position to find out about infringements. The institutions should draw up internal regulations and either set up a body of supervisors similar to the English 'compliance officers' or use the services of an external supervisor. In April 1988 the COB announced that these rules had to be implemented within one year.

As regards external control, it is entrusted to four authorities, which are the 'Société des bourses françaises' which has authority over stockbrokers, the 'Conseil du marché à terme', which supervises the futures market, the 'Commission bancaire' which has authority over banks, and the COB. A lot will depend on the measures which, it is to be hoped, are going to be taken by the COB in order to ensure the effectiveness of the above rules.

In this respect, it is interesting to note that the COB's powers have recently been strengthened by the Laws of 22 January 1988 and 2 August 1988 which have reinforced the COB's autonomy by changing the way its members are appointed and increased its financial autonomy and powers of investigation and repression powers. Hopefully, the COB will soon leave 'adolescence' to enter into adulthood.

APPENDIX

Legal provisions which are referred to in the report are set out below in chronological order.

Penal Code Article 378

Doctors, surgeons and other health officers, as well as pharmacists, midwives and all other persons who, by state or by profession or by temporary or permanent functions, hold secret information that is confided to them and reveal such information, shall be punished by imprisonment of one to six months and by a fine ranging from FF 500 to FF 15,000, except when the law obliges or authorises them to disclose such information.

Ordinance No 67–833 of 28 September 1967

Setting up a stockmarket transactions commission ('Commission des Opérations de Bourse') and relating to information of the carriers of transferable securities and to the publicity of certain stockmarket transactions:

Article 5B

In order to ensure the performance of its mission, the stockmarket transactions commission may act through agents whose powers are granted by its chairman, in accordance with a decree approved by the 'Conseil d'Etat'.

The agents may obtain any document, in whatever form, and may obtain its copy. They may convene and interview any person in possession of information. They have access to all professional premises.

Article 5

All summoned persons have a right to be assisted by a counsel of his/her choice. The terms of this summons and the conditions under which such right will be ensured will be determined by decree.

Except for judicial auxiliaries, no one can invoke a professional duty of confidence against agents of the Commission.

The officers and agents of the commission are bound by a professional duty of confidence in respect of the facts, acts and information that they may have obtained because of their functions, under the conditions and penalties set forth in art 378 of the Penal Code.

Article 5 bis

The commission may, under the same conditions, procedures and sanctions as are provided by this ordinance for the performance of its mission, conduct investigations upon request by foreign authorities performing analogous powers, provided that reciprocity exists, except in the case of a request by an authority of a State which is a member of the European Communities.

The professional duty of confidence provided for in article 5 does not prevent the Stockmarket Transactions Commission from conveying the information that it has or that it obtains upon request from authorities of other member states of the European Communities performing analogous powers and bound by the same professional duties of confidence, to said authorities.

The Stockmarket Transactions Commission may also convey information that it has or that it obtains upon the request of authorities of other states performing analogous functions, to said authorities provided that reciprocity exists, and subject to the condition that such foreign authority be bound by a professional duty of confidence with the same guarantees as in France.

The assistance requested by a foreign authority performing analogous functions for the investigation procedures or the disclosure of information that the commission has or has obtained, will be refused by the commission when the performance of the request would interfere with the sovereignty, security, essential economic interests or to the public order of France or when any penal proceeding has begun in France on the basis of the same facts and against the same persons, or when the latter have already been subject to a final judgment on the same facts.

Article 10.1 (paras 1 and 2)

The persons mentioned in art 162–1 of the Law no 66–537 of 24 July 1966, as amended, on commercial corporations and persons who, by their professional activity or by their function, obtain confidential information on the likely evolution or on the situation of a securities issuer or on the forecast of transferable securities or of a futures contracts, and who carry out or knowingly allow others to carry out one or several transactions on the market, either directly or through a nominee, before the information became public, shall be punished by imprisonment from two months to two years or by a fine ranging from FF 6,000 to FF 5 million—the fine, however, being capable of exceeding such amount, up to four times the profit made and not being less than the amount of such profit—or by both penalties.

In the event that the transactions were effected by a legal entity, its managers or its de facto managers will be criminally liable for the perpetrated violations.

Law no 68–678 of 26 July 1968

On the conveyance of documents and of economic, commercial, industrial, financial or technical information to foreign natural persons or legal entities, as amended by Law no 80–538 of 16 July 1980.

Article 1

Subject to international settlements or treaties, any French natural person or person normally residing in the French territory and any manager, agent or employee of a legal entity having its registered office or a branch in France is forbidden to convey orally, in writing or in any other manner, anywhere, to foreign public authorities, documents or economic, commercial, industrial, financial or technical information where the communication of such information could interfere with the sovereignty, security, essential economic interests of France or with the public order, as may be defined, if need be, by the administrative authority.

Article 1 bis

Subject to international settlements or treaties and to laws and regulations in effect, any person is forbidden to request, to seek or to convey, in writing, orally or in any other manner, documents or economic, commercial, industrial, financial or technical information for the purpose of establishing evidence for possible foreign judicial or administrative proceedings or in relation thereto.

Article 2

The persons referred to in arts 1 and 1 bis shall inform, without delay, the relevant Minister when any such information is requested from them.

Article 3

Without prejudice to heavier penalties imposed by other legal provisions, any violation of arts 1 and 1 bis of this law will be punished by imprisonment from two months to six months or by a fine ranging from FF 10,000 to FF 12,000, or both.

Law no 73–7 of 3 January 1973

On Banque de France.

Article 39

The agents of Banque de France are bound by a professional duty of confidence under the penalties of art 378 of the Penal Code.

Law no 84–46 of 24 January 1984

On credit establishments' activity and control.

Article 49

Any person who participates or has participated in the control of credit establishments, under the conditions set out in this chapter, is bound by a professional duty of confidence under the penalties of art 378 of the Penal Code. This duty may not be invoked against the judicial authority acting within penal proceedings. Notwithstanding the legal provisions in Law no 80–538 of 16 July 1980, the banking committee ('Commission Bancaire') and Banque de France can transmit information to the authorities in charge of the credit establishments' surveillance in other countries, provided that reciprocity exists and subject to the condition that these authorities are themselves bound by a professional duty of confidence with the same guarantees as in France.

Article 57

Any officer of a Board of Directors and, as the case may be, of a supervisory board ('conseil de surveillance') and any other person, who by some office participates in the administration or management of a credit establishment or is employed by it, is bound by a professional duty of confidence under the conditions and the penalties set forth in art 378 of the Penal Code.

Notwithstanding the instances where the law provides for it, the professional duty of confidence cannot be invoked against the banking committee, nor against the Banque de France, nor against the judicial authority acting within a penal proceeding.

Law no 84–148 of 1 March 1984

On the prevention and the amicable settlement ('règlement amiable') of the enterprises' difficulties.

Article 36

To evaluate the debtor's situation, the presiding judge may, notwithstanding any contrary legislative provisions or regulations, obtain information from the statutory auditors, the members and representatives of personnel, from public services, social security and state insurance organisations, from banking or financial establishments as well as from departments in charge of centralising banking risks and defaults in payments, setting out exactly the economic and financial situation of the debtor.

Law no 85–98 of 25 January 1985

On judicial reorganisation and liquidation of enterprises.

Article 19

The supervising judge ('juge commissaire') may, notwithstanding any contrary legislative provisions or regulations, obtain any information which may enable him to set out accurately the economic and financial situation of the debtor, from the statutory auditors, the members and representatives of personnel, from public administrations and organisations, social security and state insurance organisations, credit establishments as well as from departments in charge of centralising banking risks and defaults in payments.

Article 184

For the purposes of applying the provisions of arts 180 to 182, the court may, from its own motion or upon request of any one of the persons mentioned in art 193, request the supervising judge or, failing that, a member of the jurisdiction that it will designate, to obtain, notwithstanding any contrary legislative provision, any document or information on the patrimonial situation of the managers, natural persons or legal entities, as well as natural persons permanently representing legal entities appointed as managers mentioned in art 179, from the public services and organisations, from social security and state insurance organisations and from credit establishments.

Law no 88–70 of 22 January 1988

On the Stock Exchange.

Article 5 (para 4)

The members of the Stock Exchange Board are bound by a professional duty of confidence under the conditions and penalties set forth in art 378 of the Penal Code.

Article 19

The house rules of stockbrokers, credit establishments, bank intermediaries, establishments set out in art 8 and in art 99 of Law no 84–46 of 24 January 1984 relating to the credit establishments' activity and control, of intermediate brokers and portfolio managers set out in Law no 72–1128 of 21 December 1972 relating to intermediate brokers, portfolio managers, and collective securities investment agencies, shall include provisions governing:

– the conditions under which employees may carry out market transactions for their own account;

- the conditions under which they will then have to inform their employees on such transactions;
- the duties which are imposed upon them to prevent the undue circulation of confidential information.

Article 21

The Stock Exchange Board, the Forward Market Board ('Conseil du marché à terme'), the Stockmarket Transactions Commission and the Banking Committee are authorised, notwithstanding any contrary provisions, to convey to each other any information relevant to the performance of their respective missions. Such information is subject to the rules governing the professional duty of confidence in effect in the organisation that disclosed it.

The stockbrokers must convey to Banque de France the information relevant to the preparation of monetary statistics.

8 Germany

Wolfgang Hauser

PROTECTION OF BANK SECRECY

Source of Secrecy Obligations

West German law contains no statutory definition of bank secrecy but does afford several types of legal protection to the secrecy obligation of banks, including ultimate embodiment of bank secrecy in constitutional law.[1] The protection provided by the constitution is twofold: As regards the customer, bank secrecy is protected by art 2 of the Constitution ('Basic Law, GG') which guarantees the individual's right to an uninhibited development of his personality. As regards the bank, the secrecy obligation is also secured by art 12 GG which protects the right to choose and to exercise one's profession. Bank secrecy is considered a material element of the banking business as such and is therefore protected by the Constitution.

However, both art 2 and art 12 GG have a very general character and are subject to all restrictions that may reasonably be imposed by any Act of Parliament, as well as by rules and regulations lawfully issued pursuant to Acts of Parliament.

These provisions are not always easy to apply in practice, but the fundamental constitutional character of the bank secrecy obligation is nonetheless worthy of note, since art 2 or 12 GG may be invoked in situations in which the German concept of bank secrecy is in conflict, for example, with the informational requests of foreign states or authorities.

In most practical cases, however, the lawyer will look to criminal and especially civil law for protection of bank secrecy.

In principle, bank secrecy is protected by torts law, but such protection plays no practical role. In the end, the same can be said with respect to certain criminal law provisions which are of limited scope and apply only to board members (eg s 93 of the Stock Corporation Act) or to those few banking institutions that are incorporated according to public law (s 203, Absatz 2 of the German Criminal Code).

The core of the secrecy obligation is to be derived from contract law. It has long been acknowledged that the secrecy obligation is an implied contractual duty which the bank owes to its customer.[2]

Scope of Secrecy Obligation

The scope of the protection is very broad. The Federal High Court

---

1 There are numerous books and articles on bank secrecy in Germany. This chapter will cite only a few authors whose publications contain further references. See Canaris 'Bankvertragsrecht Großkommentar HGB' (1988) p 4 (following 'Canaris') p 25 ff; Sichtermann 'Bankgeheimnis und Bankauskunft' (1984) p 3 (following 'Sichtermann') p 40 ff.
2 See Canaris p 30 ff; Sichtermann p 111 ff.

('Bundesgerichtshof', or BGH) has defined the scope of bank secrecy as follows: 'The obligation to maintain secrecy comprises all factual information which the customer wishes to be kept secret.'[3]

The secrecy obligation does not only arise on the basis of a valid contract between the customer and the bank, but binds the bank even if for some reason the contract should not be valid, as well as during the phase of negotiations preceding signing of a contract; ultimately, the secrecy obligation does not depend on a specific contract at all, but is connected with the banking relationship as such. Of course, the secrecy obligation also survives termination of the banking relationship. Under certain circumstances, even third parties other than the customer himself may be protected by the secrecy obligation, for example the spouse of a customer or members of his business partnership. The Federal High Court has also ruled that a customer who instructs his bank to remit funds through another bank enjoys a right of secrecy vis-à-vis such other bank.[4]

As indicated above, the scope of bank secrecy obligations is very broad since the subject matter which they encompass is not defined by law, but by the customer's wishes. The bank is required to keep secret all information that the customer wishes to be kept secret. If the customer's real intent cannot be determined, his deemed intent or his objective interest is decisive; in case of doubt, the bank is well advised to assume that the customer wants to keep secret everything that the bank has learned in connection with the business relationship (including the existence of such relationship), not only facts regarding the financial or personal situation of the customer, but also value judgments of any kind that the bank is in a position to make only because of information it has received in the course of the banking relationship.[5]

Remedies for Breach of Bank Secrecy

If a bank breaches its secrecy obligation, the customer can claim damages. The claim is for the full amount of actual damages, but there is no allowance for punitive damages. The burden of proving damages and the amount thereof generally lies with the customer.

Not all kinds of damage suffered give rise to a claim against the bank; for example, if the customer has to pay additional taxes because the breach of secrecy made information available to the tax authorities, such taxes do not constitute recoverable damages, since the customer was under an obligation to pay taxes anyway.[6]

If the breach of the secrecy obligation is serious, the customer can also terminate the banking relationship immediately for cause (and claim for the damages that he suffers because of termination), or he can file a claim for injunctive relief. The latter remedy is relevant mainly when the customer and the bank cannot agree on whether the bank is under an obligation to furnish information or is at least excused from the secrecy obligation. For example, if the bank were ordered by foreign authorities to make available information that falls within the protection of German bank secrecy laws, the customer could seek to prevent the bank from disclosing that information by means of a judicial injunction.

---

3 BGH, decision of 12 May 1985 (BGHZ 27, 241–246).
4 BGH, decision of 12 May 1985 (BGHZ 27, 241–246).
5 Canaris p 34.
6 Canaris pp 46, 47.

It has even been suggested, but apparently not tested in practice, that the customer file a request for a preliminary court order that the bank records in question be seized in order effectively to prevent the bank from disclosing the information.[7]

EXCEPTIONS FROM BANK SECRECY

Customer's Consent

German banks' General Business Conditions contain an exception to the secrecy obligation in respect of requests for information submitted by another bank (for example, the bank of a supplier of the customer). A growing concern for the protection of personal data is evident in the fact that the scope of this exception has been limited in recent years. Whereas ten years ago it was generally accepted that the banks were almost completely free to answer informational requests from other banks (unless the customer had explicitly denied the bank this right), the relevant clause in the General Business Conditions has been redrafted a number of times over the last five years. Clause 10 of the General Business Conditions in its present version distinguishes between legal persons and businessmen registered in the Commercial Register, on the one hand, and all other customers, on the other. The bank may give banking information on legal persons and on registered businessmen unless they have given instructions to the contrary, but banking information on other persons and associations is given by the bank only if such persons or associations have, generally or in a particular case, expressly agreed thereto.

The banking information that may be revealed comprises general statements and comments concerning the financial situation of the customer as well as his creditworthiness and solvency, but not information as to the amounts of balances in checking accounts or savings deposits, nor as to the value of assets kept in safe custody or otherwise entrusted to the bank. Banking information is furnished only to the bank's own customers and to other banks for their own purposes and those of their customers, and the information is provided only if the party requesting it substantiates a legitimate interest therein.

Overriding Public Duty, Overriding Interest of the Bank

There may be cases in which the bank is justified in disclosing information if it learns that a customer is engaged in or wants to engage in unlawful or criminal behaviour. For example, if the bank becomes aware that a customer intends to defraud a third party, then the bank may be allowed to warn that party if this is the only way that such fraud can be prevented.

It is also acknowledged that there may be cases where the bank has a duty to inform or warn other customers and is therefore justified in disclosing confidential information. For example, the bank may be considered justified in warning other customers of a particular customer's imminent bankruptcy.

However, in all such cases the bank is required carefully to weigh the conflicting interests in good faith, and the bank may disclose information only if this balancing test legitimately indicates that the secrecy obligation is of secondary importance.[8]

---

7 Bosch 'Das Bankgeheimnis in Konflikt zwischen US-Verfahrensrecht und deutschem Recht' (1984) IPRax (following 'Bosch') pp 127, 132.
8 Canaris p 38 ff.

There may also be cases in which in connection with civil proceedings the bank is under an obligation to give information to third parties, for example to creditors of its customer. It is common in Germany to enforce a judgment claim by attaching the debtor's bank account. Upon attachment, the bank is obliged to give information to the attachment creditor in respect of the attached claim. If the bank should fail to supply this information, the creditor is entitled to recover for damages caused by such omission.

In the absence of an attachment order, however, the bank is not obliged and generally not allowed to give information to a creditor, not even regarding an account alleged to contain embezzled funds.

It is also generally accepted that in principle a bank is entitled to assign claims against a customer to another bank, for example for re-financing purposes. In case of such an assignment, the bank is also allowed to pass on pertinent information to the assignee. Nevertheless, the bank's liberty to make assignments is not unrestricted. It is questionable whether the bank may assign claims arising from a current account relationship (it is argued that there is an implied prohibition on assignment) and the bank is also prohibited from giving information to non-banks.[9]

Finally, the bank may be justified in disclosing information because of its own overriding interest. For example, if a customer makes false or defamatory statements about the bank, the bank is allowed to disclose information pursuant to its defence. Legal commentators have also argued that a bank may be allowed to disclose information if a foreign court has ordered such disclosure and the bank itself, its foreign branches or subsidiaries will be subject to punishment or serious disadvantage if it does not comply with the order. Again, a court order and the threat or fact of sanctions alone should under no circumstances be viewed as automatically permitting the bank to disclose information. Rather, the bank has to balance carefully the conflicting interests. Only if the balancing test shows the bank's interest to be clearly overriding, will the bank's breach of the secrecy obligation be excused.[10]

A final point worthy of mention in this connection is the fact that the secrecy obligation may cease to apply if foreign courts or authorities request the assistance of the German authorities in order to obtain information and if such an informational request is in accordance with the respective statutory or treaty requirements (two cases will be discussed below).

Regulatory Authorities, Reporting Requirements

According to s 44 of the German Banking Act, the Federal Banking Supervisory Authority is entitled to request from banks information on all business matters and the presentation of books and documents, as well as to carry out audits without special cause. Since the duty to provide information covers all business matters relating to the bank, the Federal Banking Supervisory Authority may request not only information on internal matters, on the development of expense and income accounts, or on items upon which the bank is required to report regularly (such as large loans, intra-entity loans etc), but also may seek information about the bank's business relations with individual customers. The bank is not permitted to cite bank secrecy, but the information given to the Federal Banking Supervisory Authority must be kept confidential under a law

9 Sichtermann p 183.
10 Canaris pp 42, 43.

imposing criminal penalties on Authority employees who violate a duty of secrecy.

Section 44a of the Banking Act, which came into effect on 1 January 1985, goes even further. Section 44a, para 1 provides that legal provisions regarding the transmission of data are not to be applied to communications between a bank and an enterprise domiciled in another country which holds directly or indirectly at least 25% of the share capital of the bank, if transmission of the data is necessary in order to comply with consolidated banking supervisory requirements applicable to the foreign-domiciled enterprise.

Section 44a, para 2 contains a special provision regarding banks in other member states of the European Community. At the request of a banking supervisory authority in another member state of the European Community, the Federal Banking Supervisory Authority is required to check the correctness of data that have been transmitted by a bank in fulfilling consolidated banking supervisory requirements; alternatively, it must allow the requesting authority, a chartered accountant or an expert to check these data. It is furthermore foreseen that audit rights may be granted to banking supervisory authorities by means of a treaty.

Bank secrecy can also lose its protection in antitrust proceedings. Under the German Antitrust Act, the Federal Cartel Office may demand information from commercial enterprises including banks, and in case of urgency may even search premises and confiscate records. However, the right to obtain information and to search and confiscate records extends to parties not directly involved in the cartel law proceedings only if there is reason to believe that a punishable violation of the antitrust laws has occurred and that evidence of this violation may be available from such third parties; furthermore, searches can only be ordered by a court in the event of imminent danger of disappearance of evidence (Antitrust Act, s 46). Finally, the kind of information that the Cartel Office may request is limited to information that the Office needs for the exercise of its functions in a particular case; only under exceptional circumstances, therefore, can the Cartel Office legitimately request detailed information as to individual customers.

Banks also have to give information to the German Federal Reserve Bank ('Deutsche Bundesbank') and other competent authorities under the Foreign Trade Act ('Außenwirtschaftsgesetz') and in particular under its provisions regarding information on payments to and from foreign countries. Such information is required primarily for statistical and general economic policy purposes.

Civil Proceedings

In civil proceedings, the bank is obliged to comply with the secrecy obligation, and the bank's right to refuse testimony is protected by s 383, no 6 of the German Civil Procedure Act. Similar provisions apply to other non-criminal proceedings, such as labour law proceedings, administrative law proceedings etc. The secrecy obligation also prevails if foreign courts or authorities request legal assistance, whether under the Hague Convention or any other similar treaty.

Criminal Proceedings

The bank's position is different in criminal proceedings.[11] Bank secrecy is not protected by the Criminal Procedure Act ('StPO'). Unlike lawyers, doctors,

---

11 See for details Canaris p 43 ff; Sichtermann p 324 ff.

clergymen, auditors and the like, banks do not have a right to refuse to give evidence in respect of matters which were entrusted to them in their professional capacity. Banks are obligated to give evidence to courts and to the prosecutor's office.

The bank's records and documents can be seized by virtue of a judicial order, and in case of emergency, by virtue of an order from the prosecutor's office (StPO, ss 94, 103).

Furthermore, aside from the provisions in the Criminal Procedure Act, the criminal authorities often simply send a letter to the bank requesting certain information and informing the bank that seizure orders in accordance with the Criminal Procedure Act will be issued unless the bank voluntarily discloses the information in question or provides certain documents. It has been argued that banks may comply with such informational requests if the effects for the customer are not more onerous than those that would have resulted had compulsory action been taken.[12] However, this view is not entirely unproblematic, since it could lead to compliance with informational requests that might not have been fully supported by judicial orders if application had been made for such orders.

Tax Proceedings

The tax authorities have broad powers to obtain information from banks, and, as in criminal law proceedings, bank secrecy is not one of the professional secrecy obligations protected by the Tax Procedure Act ('AO') (AO, s 102). The tax authorities may request information from third parties including banks (AO, s 93) and may ask for documents and records (AO, ss 97, 104). The informational rights are not limited to investigations in respect of tax evasion, but also extend to the normal procedure for tax assessment.

However, the tax authorities may request such information only with respect to a particular person under investigation, and have no right to demand a random inspection of documents relating to other taxpayers.

Moreover, the tax authorities traditionally have been required to observe some important restrictions formerly contained in rules and regulations of the Federal Finance Ministry ('Bankenerlaß' of 31 August 1979). Recently, these internal restrictions have been strengthened and incorporated in the Tax Procedure Act. Section 30a of the AO, in effect since 3 August 1988, provides for the following:

(I)   The tax authorities in gathering information have to take special account of the confidential relationship between the bank and its customers.

(II)   The tax authorities are not allowed to request from credit institutions one-time or periodic information as to accounts of a particular kind or a particular amount for purposes of general supervision.

(III)   In connection with a tax audit of a bank, the tax authorities are prohibited from taking note of the identity of holders of accounts maintained with the bank, and the tax inspectors must not pass on information as to the identity of account holders to the tax authorities having jurisdiction over them.

(IV)   In tax assessment forms, there shall be no request as to information regarding accounts or deposits maintained by the taxpayer with credit institutions, unless such information is required either in connection with deductible costs or privileges asserted by the taxpayer or in connection with payment transactions between such taxpayer and the fiscal authorities.

12 Mallmann & Schroeter *Aktuelle Rechtsfragen zum Datenschutz im Bankverkehr* (1988) p 44 ff.

(V)   An informational request shall be sent to a credit institution only if the taxpayer has not provided the required information or if an informational request addressed to the taxpayer himself is not likely to be successful or will not elicit the required information.

For tax purposes, bank secrecy practically ceases to apply upon the death of the customer. In that event, the bank is obliged to inform the tax authorities of all accounts, the balances thereon and any other assets of the deceased customer which are in the bank's custody. While this provision originally served to determine the inheritance tax, it is now also used by the tax authorities to assess income and net worth taxes owing for past periods.[13]

Legal Assistance in Tax and Criminal Matters

There are two court cases that may illustrate that there are fairly effective forms of legal assistance that may be used to pierce the secrecy veil. The facts they presented are set out below.

Case Decided by the Federal Fiscal Court in 1979[14]

The Swedish tax authorities learned that Swedish nationals had securities deposited with a German bank, and requested the assistance of the German authorities in obtaining the names of these customers.

The German tax authority subsequently asked the bank to provide the names of these customers, but the bank refused to do so. While the court of first instance ruled in favour of the bank, the Federal Fiscal Court held that the German tax authorities had the right to request such information, and that the secrecy obligation invoked by the bank did not exist in this case. The Court based its decision on the German–Swedish Treaty Regarding Assistance in Tax Matters of 14 May 1936, which contains a very general provision to the effect that the tax authorities are obliged to assist each other.

The court therefore concluded that under this treaty, the tax authorities had the right to request the same information as if s 93 of the German Tax Procedure Act were to apply directly.

The Federal Fiscal Court also decided that information required by foreign tax authorities should not be considered a 'business secret' within the meaning of the German–Swedish Treaty. The Court pointed out that the Swedish tax authorities are themselves subject to a secrecy obligation in respect of tax matters. It is interesting to note that the Federal Fiscal Court did not consider it relevant that the Swedish authorities publish tax lists showing the income tax obligation of citizens. The court held that there are no indications that such tax lists give any clue as to how the tax authorities obtained the information on which they based the tax assessments.

The Federal Fiscal Court did not decide whether the German–Swedish Double Taxation Treaty also would have furnished grounds for requesting the same information. It has been argued that the protection awarded to 'business secrets' or 'professional secrets' in double-taxation treaties[15] means that bank secrecy is absolutely protected, and that no legal assistance needs to be granted by German

---

13 Canaris p 45.
14 Federal Fiscal Court, decision of 20 February 1979 (Bundessteuerblatt 1979, Teil II, 268–274).
15 See for instance art XVI of the German/US double taxation treaty, art 26 of the OECD 1977 model agreement.

tax authorities with regard to matters that are covered by bank secrecy in Germany.[16] Other commentators, however, point out that 'trade secrets' or 'business secrets' should be interpreted narrowly in order to allow for an effective exchange of information between tax authorities to prevent tax fraud, and that therefore only such information which is of economic importance and which can be used for practical economic purposes should be protected.[17] Some double-taxation treaties, such as the German–Swiss treaty and the treaty between Germany and Luxembourg, expressly mention bank secrecy or state that the authorities are not allowed to pass on information that they have received from banks.

Section 117 of the Tax Procedure Act establishes certain rules that allow for exchange of information and international assistance by the German tax authorities even in the absence of a double-taxation treaty. In respect of the member states of the European Community, an additional special law[18] which reflects an EC directive provides for the exchange of tax-related information. Bank secrecy is protected to the extent that it is protected by German law. Therefore, information from banks can only be collected and exchanged so far as permitted by the Tax Procedure Act, especially s 30a (see above).

Two decisions by the District Court of Kiel of 1982 dealt with a German–American relationship[19]

The plaintiff was a German company under criminal investigation in the United States. A Grand Jury in Michigan issued three subpoenas directed at the defendant, a German bank with its main office in Frankfurt and, inter alia, branches in New York and Kiel. These subpoenas ordered that the defendant deliver a number of documents to the Grand Jury.

The plaintiff, a customer of the bank, requested and received from the Kiel District Court an injunction forbidding the defendant to comply with the subpoena.

The court ruled that bank secrecy is ultimately embodied in certain constitutional rights of a customer as well as of the bank. The court further held that the customer's rights could only be limited or wiped out by actions of German courts or authorities permitted under German law. In the court's view, orders by American authorities should not be considered equivalent to German court orders when the defendant was a German company with its main office in Germany.

The defendant argued that it would be subject to severe sanctions in the United States if it did not comply with the subpoena. The court in Kiel took the view that it was hardly conceivable that an American court would hold a defendant in contempt for behaviour that a German court had ruled to be lawful.

The Kiel court was wrong: the American judge did not respect the preliminary injunction issued by the Kiel court.

However, shortly thereafter an agreement was reached between the bank and the US District Attorney's office that the subpoena proceedings would be stayed and that the US authorities would file a request for judicial assistance with the competent German authorities. The request for judicial assistance turned out to

---

16 Sichtermann p 497.
17 Tipke/Kruse, AO 13, Auflage, s 117, pp 52, 57; Klein/Orlopp, AO 30, Auflage, s 117, p 250.
18 EG-Amtshilfe-Gesetz of 19 December 1985 (BGBl I 2436, 2441).
19 Decisions of 30 June 1982 and of 23 August 1982 (RIW 1983, 206, IPRax 1984, 146, 147).

be an effective means, since the documents requested were furnished to the US authorities only one month after the request was made.[20]

The German Act on International Assistance in Criminal Matters ('IRG') of 23 December 1982 contains a number of important provisions according to which a bank can be compelled to disclose information that would otherwise be protected by the bank's secrecy obligation. According to s 67 of the IRG, the German authorities can seize objects and documents and order a search of premises provided the following requirements are met:

(I)   The documents or objects are admissible as evidence in foreign criminal proceedings (or have been obtained by the suspect through his criminal behaviour).
(II)   The illegal behaviour in question would also be punishable under German law.
(III) The foreign state submits an attachment order or confirms that an attachment order would be issued if the objects were located in that foreign state.

An attachment order can be issued by the German authorities even before the foreign state's formal assistance request is received. The attachment or search order is issued by the local court ('Amtsgericht') and, in case of imminent danger of disappearance of evidence ('Gefahr im Verzug'), also by the prosecutor's office.

The IRG Act does not apply to matters that are covered in treaties between the Federal Republic of Germany and a foreign country; therefore, the IRG Act has little or no practical bearing on tax matters that are covered by a double-taxation treaty.

Since it is a requirement that the matter under investigation by the foreign authorities would also constitute an unlawful punishable act under German law, judicial assistance would not be available in Germany in connection with insider trading which is not (yet) unlawful in Germany (see below).

The forms of assistance available under the IRG Act are not limited to attachment or search orders, but may extend to any kind of support, including, for example, provision of information, service of documents and also interrogations. Such general assistance is, unlike attachment and search orders, not subject to the requirement that the matter would also be punishable in Germany.

The lawfulness of assistance is subject to judicial review by the Circuit Court ('Oberlandesgericht').

INSIDER TRADING, CONFLICTS OF INTEREST

Insider Trading

In Germany, there are no statutory rules regarding insider trading. Insider trading is therefore subject neither to criminal nor to civil sanctions by operation of the law.

Rather, a number of industry and trade associations, including the Federal Banking Association, all stock exchanges, the Federal Industry Association, the Federal Association of Insurance Companies etc, have worked out Insider Rules

20 Bosch p 134.

which contain especially rules on insider trading and recommended that these Rules be accepted by their members. It is therefore only by virtue of a voluntary contractual agreement that the Insider Rules become binding. The names of those companies and banks who have not accepted the Insider Rules are reported in the official gazettes of various stock exchanges in Germany. It is reported that some 90% of the companies whose shares are registered in or traded on German stock exchanges have accepted the Insider Rules (measured in terms of registered share capital).

Section 1 of the Insider Trading Rules as amended in June 1988 provides that insiders may not deal in insider shares on the basis of information they have obtained in their capacity as insiders. They are also prohibited from divulging insider information to third parties unless compelled by law or by an overriding legitimate interest.

The term 'insider' refers in every case to insiders of a particular company. Section 2 of the Insider Trading Rules defines as 'insiders', inter alia, the legal representatives and supervisory board members of a company and of its domestic affiliates, major shareholders (owning more than 25% of the share capital), and employees and other agents of the company, such as lawyers and auditors. Credit institutions as well as their board members, employees and agents can also be insiders of a particular company if they are involved in capital increases or capital decreases, profit and loss absorption agreements, mergers and acquisitions, takeovers, or loans granted to the company, and if they usually obtain knowledge of insider information in connection with such involvement. Companies that have accepted the Insider Trading Rules are also obliged to require compliance by those considered their insiders.

'Insider shares' are shares, warrants, option rights etc which are admitted to trading with official quotation or to the regulated market on a domestic stock exchange and which are issued by a domestic company ('Company 1') or a domestic affiliate thereof or by another domestic company ('Company 2') which is to become an affiliate of Company 1 through, eg, a merger or a takeover bid.

'Insider information' constitutes awareness of any circumstances which are not yet public knowledge and which may have an effect on the valuation of the insider shares. Information as to proposed capital increases, mergers, takeovers, acquisitions and the like is always considered to be insider information.

Alleged violations of the Insider Rules are investigated by a committee of inquiry established in co-operation with the competent stock exchange.

Insiders who have accepted the Rules and who have committed a breach thereof are required to hand over the financial benefits they have derived from the forbidden insider trading to the company of which they are an insider or, respectively, in the case of a bank, to the company whose insider shares were the subject of the trading. This payment obligation applies not only to insiders, but also to the companies for whose benefit they have acted (provided, of course, that those companies have accepted the Insider Rules). The financial benefits that have to be paid over to the company concerned may be the profits obtained, but also the losses avoided.

It is apparent that the German Insider Rules constitute a relatively weak barrier against the undesirable use of insider information. There are indications that this situation will soon change, since the Commission of the European Community is reportedly working on a directive regarding uniform statutory rules against insider trading that it plans to submit to the Council in a few months.

Conflicts of Interest

One can conceive of numerous situations where a bank and/or its board members might encounter conflicts of interest, for example, because of contractual relationships between the bank and each of the parties to a transaction or a dispute, or because an executive board member of the bank also serves as a member of the supervisory board of another company. Such conflicts of interest have to some extent been discussed in the legal literature,[1] but hardly had to be decided upon by a court. There are, therefore, no firm and established rules as to what a bank and its board members have to do in order to avoid or to resolve such conflicts of interest.

It is, for example, clear that a bank is not allowed to disclose confidential information that it has obtained in the course of its relationship with a particular customer in order to assist another party which wishes to acquire shares in the customer. Because of this prohibition on disclosing confidential information, it would be very difficult for the bank to act as adviser to an unfriendly bidder. It is not clear whether or not a bank could finance a take-over bid which the customer's management considers unfriendly. One view is that a change of ownership does not violate a company's interests, but may only affect the management's interests which interests are, however, not protected, and that a bank is therefore free to finance a bidder for a bank customer's shares. Other authors have argued that a bank must refrain from such financing because of an implied duty of loyalty that it owes to its customer.

It is debated whether a concept of 'Chinese Walls' would help to avoid and solve such conflicts of interest. While there is a decision by an Appeal Court which says that there is no general rule that a bank is obliged to establish internal informational barriers and to segregate, for example, the loan department from the investment department,[2] some legal authors have argued that there are situations where the erection of 'Chinese Walls' may not only be useful but required.

In the absence of clear rules, each such situation which involves a conflict of interest and which raises the question what information the bank may or may not use or pass on to a third party has to be examined on a case-by-case basis and in the light of the nature of the information and the interests at stake. The bank has to balance very carefully the different interests and the explicit or implied duties that it owes to the parties involved. Even then, there may not always be a right decision.

---

1 A series of articles on these topics were published in 1981. See Heinsius 'Anlageberatung durch Kreditinstitute' (1981) 145 ZHR p 177; Kübler 'Anlageberatung durch Kreditinstitute' (1981) 145 ZHR p 204; Lutter 'Bankenvertreter im Aufsichtsrat' (1981) 145 ZHR p 224; Werner 'Aufsichtsratstätigkeit von Bankenvertretern' (1981) 145 ZHR p 252.
2 OLG Köln, decision of 11 November 1984, ZIP 1985, p 209.

9 Greece

Yanos Gramatidis

There are express provisions of Greek law establishing bank secrecy and the exceptions to bankers' duty of confidence. Such provisions are based on fundamental principles laid down by the Greek Constitution of 1975 and aim at the combined protection of the interests of the individual and of those of the national economy. There are also other provisions of criminal character establishing a professional duty of confidentiality and such provisions apply practically to any professional abusing confidential information entrusted to him by clients.

THE GREEK CONSTITUTION

Article 19 of the Greek Constitution of 1975 establishes the fundamental principle of the protection of free communication and correspondence. Such provision establishes also the obligation of the state and its servants to respect the secrecy of ideas and correspondence moved in any conventional way (ie by telephone, telex, fax, telegram etc). Such protection is also extended to foreign nationals since art 4 of the Civil Code provides that Greek and foreign nationals enjoy the same civil rights.

Such constitutional protection extends to communication and correspondence of any kind and, indeed, to bank secrecy and the duty of confidentiality. Such interpretation has been constantly supported by Greek jurisprudence.

THE GREEK CRIMINAL CODE

In the past, and in the absence of specific legislation related to the protection of bank secrecy, the duty of confidentiality of banks in connection with the transactions of their clients was created by custom, while such secrecy had already been legislated in other countries. In addition to certain provisions establishing and protecting specific forms of secrecy, there was the general provision of art 371 of the Penal Code.

Article 371 of the Penal Code is based on art 19 of the Constitution mentioned above. By its first paragraph, it imposes the sanctions either of a fine or of up to one year's imprisonment to physicians, lawyers, other persons and their assistants confided with private secrets because of their profession or special capacity, who reveal such secrets to third parties in any way. Because of the general character of the provision of this article, no distinction could be made between Greek and foreign nationals.

By general acceptance, a secret is something which should not be revealed, in other words what is to become known in a limited circle of persons. Professional as well as bank secrecy is in this category.

The provision of para 1 of art 371 of the Penal Code is the completion of the constitutionally established protection of the secrets of private life. In this case, the protection of the general interest, of the professional faith and of the profession or capacity acquired by certain categories of persons, requires the obligation of confidentiality on their part. No doubt, it is a special crime (delictum proprium) committed only by persons exercising a certain profession or having a certain capacity because of which they are confided with private secrets. The professions mentioned in art 371 of the Penal Code are simply indicative, thus making it possible for any person exercising a certain profession or having a certain capacity to be covered by the relevant provision.

The wording of art 371 of the Penal Code provides the following prerequisites of criminal responsibility:

(I)   The existence of a private secret, in other words of an actual fact concerning only the private, family, individual life and property of a natural person or a legal entity of private law.

(II) Such private secret to have been confided to the person responsible by those persons concerned or in any other way. The case in which the person responsible became aware of a private secret because of his profession or a certain capacity should also be included. Therefore, not any private secret is protected by such provision, but only the so-called professional secret which one confides to certain professionals or to other persons because of their special capacities. Confiding is any announcement, either verbal or in writing, in which secrecy is either expressly demanded or is expected ipso jure.

(III) The existence of guilt of the person responsible, consisting in the knowledge that such secret is a private one and in the will to reveal the same to third parties.

It has been accepted that the death of an individual enjoying a private secret lifts the obligation to professional confidentiality. However, such a conclusion should not be correct, since the protection of the private and professional secrecy has been established in the frame of the protection of the general interest, of the professional faith and of the stability of transactions. Therefore, such protection should not be lifted by the person enjoying a private or professional secret, since such secret, in addition to its connection with a specific person, is connected in a wider way with the duty of confidentiality of a general nature of specialised professionals and persons having special capacities vis-à-vis society as a whole. The faith of society in the principle of secrecy should remain firm. It is a pity that the Penal Code further provides in para 2 of art 371 that criminal charges are raised only in the case of filing of individual complaints, thus connecting even more the private and professional secret with the person damaged and not with the damage to the general principle of secrecy.

Finally, in para 3 of the same article it is provided that the act is not unjust and will remain unpunished if the person responsible aims at the completion of a duty or at the protection of a lawful or other justified interest of crucial importance, either public or of his own or finally of a third party which could not be otherwise protected. It is obvious that such provision is in accordance with the principle established in art 19 of the Constitution, providing that special statutes should establish the guarantees under which the Greek Courts are not bound by secrecy for reasons of national security or in order to identify extremely serious crimes.

The prerequisites for the application of such provision are:

(I)   the completion of a duty, and

(II) the protection of a lawful or other justified interest of crucial importance.

Completion of a duty exists in any case dictated by a provision of law. On the other hand, lawful interest is the security and trust in the frame of any transaction, while protection of a justified interest is an objectively necessary protection to be determined freely by the judge.

THE SPECIAL STATUTE ON BANKS' DUTY OF CONFIDENTIALITY

Legislative Decree 1059/71, as amended by art 10 of Law 1858/89, establishes the secrecy of bank deposits. Article 1 of this law provides that deposits of any kind with financial institutions are secret. Further, in art 2, para 1, such law imposes a sanction of at least six months' imprisonment upon the bank employees, managers etc violating such secrecy.

Greek jurisprudence[1] has accepted that bank deposits covered by secrecy are meant to be deposits of money. Deposits in joint accounts are also covered by the same protection, whereas art 1 of Legislative Decree 1059/71 provides that secrecy covers deposits of any kind. Article 12 of Legislative Decree 1321/72 provides that, in connection with shipping banks, the principle of secrecy established by art 1 of Legislative Decree 1059/71 is extended also to banking activities and relations of any kind vis-à-vis any authority or third parties in general, with the exception of the control and supervision exercised by currency, judicial and tax authorities who, however, are themselves under an obligation of secrecy. That means that not only money deposits with shipping banks are secret and beyond attachment, but also all claims in general deriving from bonds, bills, bank transfers etc of their own depositors. As a result, providing information either in an extra-judicial way or before courts on the part of a bank in connection with deposits made with it is strictly prohibited.

Exceptions to the Principle of Secrecy

Jurisprudence, however, has accepted that secrecy does not apply to the following cases:

(I)   Secrecy does not apply in the case of a bankruptcy receiver (according to Greek Law) of a foreign company lawfully established in Greece seeking relevant information from a bank; and, therefore, such receiver can lawfully apply for an order for the bank to provide him with all information available in relation to the accounts of the bankrupt;[2] and

(II) secrecy does not apply in the case of the heirs of joint account holders and of the creditors of an inheritance.[3]

Further art 1 of Legislative Decree 1059/71 provides that secrecy does not apply vis-à-vis the Central Bank in the exercise of its powers related to the control of the banking system in Greece and to compliance with the existing currency, credit or exchange regulations. All powers and authorities of the Central Bank are included in Law 5076/31 which, in art 18b, provides that all banks are subject to the control and supervision of the Ministry of National Economy and the Central Bank.

Article 3 of Legislative Decree 1059/71 establishes an express exception from the principle of secrecy, providing that the provision of information related to

---

1 Athens Court of Appeal Judgment 2–257/85.
2 Piraeus Single Member Court of First Instance Judgment 3629/84.
3 Athens Court of Appeal Judgment 2–257/85.

bank deposits is permitted only on the basis of a judgment of a national court, duly justified, to the extent that such information is considered to be absolutely necessary for the identification and punishment of actions characterised as crimes committed in Greece or violations of the legislation related to the protection of national currency. It is evident that the above decree is also an expression of the possibility of deviating from the principle of secrecy provided by art 19 of the Greek Constitution.

It is interesting that, on the basis of the above provision, the principle of secrecy declines only before a judgment of a Greek Court duly justified and in the frame of identification and punishment of actions characterised as crimes committed in Greece. Therefore, the principle of secrecy cannot be ignored in the case of crimes committed abroad. Crime under Greek Law is any act punishable with death or life or temporary imprisonment. The duration of a temporary imprisonment does not exceed 20 years and is no less than 5 years.

The Consent of the Customer

Further, art 2, para 1 of Legislative Decree 1059/71 provides that the consent or approval on the part of the depositor enjoying secrecy in no way can revoke the criminal character of the action, while para 3 of the same article provides that bank employees, managers etc, when called as witnesses in a civil or criminal trial, are never examined about secret deposits even if the depositor enjoying such secrecy consents. From the combination of such provisions, one concludes that the secrecy and the duty of confidentiality exists in favour of the depositor,[4] however, it also exists in favour of the public interest since the criminal character of the violation of secrecy is not lifted with the consent of the party concerned. It is evident that this view has been adopted to encourage deposits with banks and to reinforce faith in banking transactions. Such view cannot imply that the secrecy exists in favour of the bank.[5]

Extent of Confidentiality to Foreign Banks

In the past, there was doubt as to whether deposits with foreign banks operating lawfully in Greece were characterised as secret. Before the application of art 10 of Law 1858/89, which amended Legislative Decree 1059/71, art 1 of the latter provided that all deposits with Greek banks are characterised as secret. Such wording had created many problems, since prima facie it suggested that it was the will of the legislature to limit the obligation of secrecy only to Greek banks and not to extend it to foreign banks operating in Greece.

Part of Greek jurisprudence,[6] and also of legal science,[7] supported the view that such secrecy should be limited only to Greek banks based on the grammatical interpretation of the relevant provision and on the argument that such limitation had been inserted to favour the national banks and capital. However, according to the prevailing view,[8] bank secrecy and confidentiality should also be extended

---

4 Athens Court of Appeal Judgment 7060/76; Athens Single Member Court of First Instance Judgment 8169/87.
5 Athens Court of Appeal Judgment 7060/76.
6 Athens Single Member Court of First Instance Judgment 9164/76; Piraeus Single Member Court of First Instance Judgment 1296/77; Supreme Court Judgments 1224/75, 1225/75.
7 L Roilos *Nomiko Vima* (1978).
8 Athens Court of Appeal Judgment 7960/76; Piraeus Court of Appeal Judgment 534/87; Supreme Court Judgment 1275/75; Athens Single Member Court of First Instance Judgment 8169/87; Piraeus Single Member Court of First Instance Judgment 3629/84.

to foreign banks operating in Greece through central offices or branches and being governed by Greek Law. The basic argument in favour of such a view was that the existence of secrecy only in favour of depositors of Greek banks and not a favour of depositors of foreign banks operating in Greece (such depositors also being Greeks to a large extent) would be contrary to the principle of equality between Greeks established by art 4, para 1 of the Greek Constitution and of art 4 of the Civil Code providing that Greek and foreign nationals enjoy the same civil rights. Further, the same principle of equality provided by art 4 of the Civil Code should impose the same equal treatment between Greek banks and foreign banks operating in Greece. Limitation of the secrecy of deposits only to Greek Banks would violate the principle of equality and would also create unequal conditions of competition between Greek banks and foreign banks operating in Greece in violation of fundamental provisions of the Treaty of Rome. However, the new wording of art 1 of Legislative Decree 1059/71 solved the problem and there is no doubt any more that the replacement of the term 'Greek Banks' by the term 'financial institutions' is the expression of the will of the legislature to extend bank secrecy and confidentiality also to foreign banks lawfully operating in Greece.

Attachment of Bank Deposits

In connection with the principle of bank secrecy and confidentiality established by art 1 of Legislative Decree 1059/71, the interesting question as to whether bank deposits can be attached has been raised.

Article 982 of the Code of Civil Procedures provides that movables belonging to a debtor and being in the possession of a third party can be attached. On the basis of this general possibility, art 985, para 1 of the Code of Civil Procedures provides that, within eight days from the service of the note of attachment upon the third party, the latter is under the obligation to declare (a) whether the asset attached actually exists, (b) whether the asset attached is in his possession and (c) whether any other attachment has been made on the same asset, in which case he should mention the particulars of the party which caused the attachment as well as the amount for which such attachment took place. Finally, in para 3 of the same article it is provided that the omission of such a declaration has the same effect as a negative declaration. In this case, the third party (the bank) will be liable to compensate the party which executed the attachment.

The basic argument in favour of the attachability of bank deposits is the unfair results to which a rule against such attachability would lead. Such results would be against society as a whole, since it would be possible for debtors of bad faith to defraud their creditors by liquidating their assets and depositing part of such assets with banks, and for criminals to enjoy the product of their crimes. Such results would also be against the interests of the banks, since art 464 of the Civil Code provides that non-attachable claims are also unassignable and art 451 of the Civil Code provides that unassignable claims cannot be subject to set-off. Therefore, banks could not lawfully set off their claims (in the case of loans and in any other case) against the claims of their clients deriving from deposits, nor demand the assignment of a client's account in full payment of a loan or of a guarantee or of any other facility granted by such banks without the consent of the client/debtor.

The basic legal argument in favour of the attachability of bank deposits is that the bank secrecy, established by art 1 of Legislative Decree 1059/71, is already limited by the application of art 371, para 4 of the Penal Code, which permits the violation of secrecy by a person aiming at the completion of a duty or the protection of a lawful or other justified public or private interest which could not otherwise be protected.[9] This is further supported by the argument that the interpretation of Legislative Decree 1059/71, as providing for non-attachability makes such law anti-constitutional, since art 20 of the Greek Constitution provides that anyone is entitled to legal protection from the Greek courts. Therefore, if bank secrecy and confidentiality were extended to the attachment of assets in the possession of banks, an adequate and effective means of satisfaction of the right included in the deed of enforcement would be lost. As a result, creditors would be deprived of the constitutionally provided legal protection in the form of compulsory enforcement.[10]

However, up to now Greek jurisprudence, with few exceptions,[11] while constantly supporting the principle of attachability, has also maintained that, as a result of the secrecy of bank deposits, the omission of the statement provided by art 985 of the Code of Civil Procedures does not amount to a negative statement and the creditor pursuing an attachment has no right to raise objections against such an omission. The same jurisprudence has therefore concluded that an attachment of a deposit with a Greek bank is unacceptable and, therefore, null and void.[12] Such a view is definitely the prevailing one, but it is based on an interpretation rather than an express legislative provision.

In the same context, the interesting question whether an insurance placement is attachable or not has also been raised. This is the act of lawfully blocking property assets of an insurance company for the protection of the interests of those insured with it.[13] An insurance placement consists of several property assets, including money deposits with a bank of the choice of the insurance company and in the name of the latter. Such money deposits are ipso jure blocked, once they are part of an insurance placement, and such blockage consists of the termination of the management of such deposits by the insurance company and the prohibition of their free disposal. Such provisions have been established on the basis that the above-mentioned property assets aim at the protection of the interests of those insured and, therefore, such assets are not covered by the legislation related to private deposits and to the transactions of insurance companies with financial institutions.

Circular K4-5390/20.11.84 of the Ministry of Commerce provides that an insurance placement consisting of cash is absolutely irrelevant to the secrecy of bank deposits since, in the case of an insurance placement, what is actually brought into the bank, pursuant to the law, is the insurance placement consisting of cash as such and this is not the same as the deposit of moneys on the part of the depositing insurance company. Therefore, so that beneficiaries should benefit from the insurance placement, this should be achieved by following the provisions of art 985 of the Code of Civil Procedures and the attachment should take place against the bank in possession of the funds involved. Omission or refusal to submit a relevant declaration on the part of the bank pursuant to art 985 of the Code of Civil Procedures could not be based on the provision of Legislative Decree 1059/71 establishing the secrecy of bank deposits. In addition, such a refusal on

9 Thessaloniki Multi Member Court of First Instance Judgment 2575/72.
10 Mitsopoulos *Civil Procedures* and L Roilos *Nomiko Vima* (1978).
11 Athens Court of Appeal Judgment 1467/75; Thessaloniki Multi Member Court of First Instance Judgment 2575/72.
12 Athens Court of Appeal Judgments 3455/85, 257/85; Supreme Court Judgments 1224/75, 1225/75.
13 Article 7 para 1 of LD 400/70.

the part of the bank would establish immediately its liability to compensate the party enforcing the attachment.

It should be noted that Greek jurisprudence took the view that non-attachability refers only to claims over money deposits and does not include deposits of shares, bonds or other titles. In addition, it should be concluded that moneys in the possession of a bank but not deposited in a specific bank account at the time of the attachment (ie bank transfers) do not enjoy the protection of secrecy and, therefore, of non-attachability.

Finally, it has been accepted that the non-attachability of bank deposits is also extended to foreign banks lawfully operating in Greece, for the same reasons that bank secrecy is also extended to them as mentioned above.

REMEDIES

Violation of bank secrecy and of the duty of confidentiality established by Legislative Decree 1059/71 would impose all criminal sanctions provided by art 2, para 1 of such law, as well as civil sanctions on the basis of the application of art 914 of the Civil Code.

More specifically, art 914 of the Civil Code provides that whoever unlawfully and culpably causes damage to another is liable to pay compensation. Whether an act is unjust (tort) is not stipulated by art 914 of the Civil Code; such act is judged on the basis of other provisions. In the case of bank secrecy, an act is considered to be unjust or unlawful, according to the provision of art 914 of the Civil Code, when the same violates the provision of art 1 of Legislative Decree 1059/71.

The person damaged must establish the elements of liability, being:

(I)   the damage,
(II)   the unlawfulness of the act,
(III)   the culpability on the part of those who caused the damage, and
(IV)   an adequate connection between the fault and the damage.

The burden of proof rests on the party damaged.

Under the term 'damage', the legislator means direct damage (in other words, the decrease of the existing property of the person damaged), but also indirect damage, even in the case where the person who caused the damage could not have foreseen such a consequence. Finally, by the same term the legislator means the loss of income or profits, in other words the income or profits which would be expected to have been gained in the normal course or because of special circumstances and, in particular, on the basis of preparatory measures taken. The person who so damaged another would also be liable to interest on the total amount of damages and such interest would be calculated from the moment of service of the relevant lawsuit.

Culpability includes malice (being the most onerous case) and negligence. Malice exists when he who caused the damage desired the (unlawful) result. Negligence exists where the person who caused the damage did not pay the attention which he should and could have paid to avoid the (unlawful) result, in other words when his will became 'inactive'.

Finally, under the term 'adequate connection' between the act and the damage, the legislature means that the act must not simply have caused the damage on the basis of a logical cause (in the sense of the conditio sine qua non), but that such act had generally the tendency and the ability to lead to the damage in the usual course of events and conditions (causa adequata).

Unfortunately, there are no interesting cases concerning the establishment of the obligation to pay compensation as a result of violation of the Greek legislation related to bank secrecy and the duty of confidentiality.

10 Italy

Marcello Gioscia

The basic approach regarding confidentiality of banking transactions in Italy should be that the right to the maintenance of secrecy belongs to bank clients and not to banks themselves. Thus, subject to certain limitations and exceptions, banks owe a duty to their customers to refrain from revealing information concerning banking transactions.

THE BANK'S DUTY OF CONFIDENCE

Sources of Law

While there is no doubt that banking transactions have historically been accorded confidential treatment and it is generally agreed that such confidentiality is mandated by Italian law, there is no consensus on the sources of law from which the banker's duty to maintain confidentiality arises. There is no body of law in Italy which is explicitly applicable to the rights and obligations that arise in connection with secrecy in banking transactions and, therefore, such rights and obligations are founded upon various sources of law each of which is subject to objection.

Article 47 of the Italian Constitution

Article 47 of the Italian Constitution states: 'the Republic encourages and protects saving in any form'. Based on this constitutional principle it is argued that an obligation to maintain confidentiality in banking transactions arises because effective encouragement and protection of saving requires a strict prohibition on the free transmission to third parties of information concerning bank clients and their transactions. In this context, bank secrecy is thus based more on the public policy requiring protection of the banking system and the national economy, than on the private right of the individual to such protection.

Law 375 of 12 March 1936 (the 'Banking Law')

Article 10 of the Banking Law provides: 'all information concerning credit institutions that is submitted to the Bank of Italy for review is protected by "official secrecy" with respect to public administrations'. The last paragraph of art 10 further provides: 'officers and all employees of the Bank of Italy are bound by official secrecy'. While it has been argued that art 10 of the Banking Law codifies the right of the individual to have maintained, and the obligation of credit institutions to maintain, confidentiality with respect to any banking services rendered to clients, it is also argued that the secrecy obligation of art 10 applies to the Bank of Italy and not to the credit institutions in that the relevant information is not that of individual clients, but rather of the banks who are subject to the control of the Bank of Italy. Thus, the beneficiaries of the secrecy obligation are the credit institutions and not their individual clients. Notwithstanding the latter argument, art 10 of the Banking Law does not seem to permit a distinction between information relating to specific individual clients and information generally concerning credit institutions, because the phrase 'all information concerning credit institutions' would appear to encompass both and thus to provide official secrecy protection to both types of information. This reasoning has been accepted by many Italian legal writers.[1]

Article 77 of the Banking Law regulates the situation where a court evaluates the claims presented by creditors of credit institutions which are in the process of mandatory administrative liquidation. While the court is entitled, where convenient, to review the lists of unsecured and preferred creditors in the interest of protecting secrecy, such lists may not be revealed to the parties to the case. According to some legal writers, the legislators intended to codify already existing banking practice and thus create a confidentiality obligation.

Customary Practice

Secrecy protection has historically accompanied banking transactions. It has been argued, therefore, that this constant repetition of uniform behaviour gives rise to a legal rule which is tacitly generated by collective will. Article 1374 of the Italian Civil Code (the 'Civil Code') requires the parties to a contract to act not only according to the terms of the contract but also in accordance with the consequences that derive from law or, in the absence of law, common practice and equity. Customary practice in the absence of specific law thus subjects banks to the obligation to maintain secrecy. This argument has been accepted by Italian case law.[2]

General Norms of Fairness (arts 1175, 1337 and 1375 of the Civil Code)

According to some legal writers, the rights and duties of confidentiality do not arise from the special circumstances of banking transactions, but rather from legal norms generally applicable to all contractual relationships. Article 1175 of the Civil Code provides that the debtor and creditor in any given transaction must act in accordance with the norms of fairness. Article 1337 of the Civil Code provides that during negotiations occurring in the precontractual phase of a transaction, the parties must act in good faith. Finally, art 1375 of the Civil Code provides that the fulfilment of a contract must be conducted in good faith. These provisions, in conjunction with the protection accorded by law to the privacy of persons in their dealings with third parties, arguably establish an obligation on banks to maintain confidential, and a right of clients to have maintained confidential, information with respect to their banking transactions.

Criminal Law

According to some old judicial decisions, protection of bank secrecy may also be

---

1 See, among others, Ruta *Il segreto bancario nella realtà giuridica italiana Banca borsa e titoli di credito* (1982) 1037.
2 *Gentili v Banca Morgan Vonwiller* Supreme Court 18 July 1974, no 2147. The Supreme Court stated:

'On the basis of a custom constantly followed, a binding usage having the force of law has been established with regard to the observance of so-called bank secrecy. Such a usage is to be considered as an integral part of the agreements concluded by the bank with its clients, whose interests are entrusted to the bank with the confidence that such interests will be guarded from indiscretion. Consequently, with regard to the relationship between the client and the banker, the latter has the contractual obligation not to disclose to other parties all such information which is to remain secret, according to the customer's intentions, express or implied.'

founded on art 622 of the Italian Criminal Code (the 'Criminal Code') which punishes the disclosure as well as the use of the so-called 'professional services'.[3]

This crime does not protect third parties and covers only information which has been transmitted to the bank in direct connection with the services requested of the bank by the client. Actual damages are not necessary, but a risk of damage must exist. Further, disclosure of information with 'cause' (e g by court order) or use of such information without 'profit' (not necessarily financial gain) would not constitute a crime.

Some legal writers are of the opinion, however, that violation of confidentiality with respect to bank clients does not constitute a crime under art 622 of the Criminal Code, given that such information is not a 'secret' as contemplated by the provision. Such writers argue that the provision protects information revealed during the course of obtaining personal professional services and that, given the sophistication and impersonal nature of banking services, such services are not included. Also, bank officers and employees may not be considered professionals in the sense required by art 622 of the Criminal Code. This represents the most recent view on the issue and the Italian Supreme Court, in *Gentili v Banca Morgan Vonwiller*[4] in fact, has reasoned that bank secrecy is not founded on criminal law stating:

'The attempt to include it within the scheme of professional secrecy contradicts the decisive argument that the criminal provision requires an individual and professional activity, while banking activities are carried out by business entities and are of a commercial nature.'

While Supreme Court dicta are not decisive and the issue as to whether violation of bank secrecy is a criminal offence remains open, in Italy, the Supreme Court's reasoning represents a clear indication of a new trend limiting the scope of bank secrecy to the civil arena.

Article 326 of the Criminal Code prohibits public officials or persons entrusted with public service from revealing, in violation of the duties inherent in their position or service, information which should remain secret.[5] The crime is punishable by six months' to three years' imprisonment. It is generally agreed, however, that this provision does not apply to bank officials or employees. It is true that a recent decision of the Supreme Court[6] recognised that such officials and employees are entrusted with a public service and concluded that when such officials or employees misappropriate the funds with which they are entrusted, they commit the crime of embezzlement. However, the fact that bank officers and employees are entrusted with a public service is not sufficient for application of art 326, insofar as information concerning bank clients may not in any way be

---

3 Article 622 states:

   'Whoever, having knowledge, by reason of his status or office, or of his profession or art, of a secret, discloses such secret, without just cause, or make use of it for his own profit or for the profit of others, is punished, if a damage may arise from such action, with imprisonment of up to one year or with a fine ranging from Lire 60,000 to Lire 1,000,000. The crime is punishable upon request of the offended person.'

4 See note 2 above.

5 Article 326 states:

   'A public officer or person charged with a public service, who, by violating the duties pertaining to his office or service, or by any way abusing his position, discloses official information which ought to remain secret, or in any manner facilitates the disclosure thereof, shall be punished by imprisonment.'

6 *In re Carfi* [1981] Supreme Court (Plenary Session), 10 October.

considered a secret of the nature protected by the criminal provision. The purpose of the provision is to avoid general dissemination of official secrets whose secrecy is necessary for the protection of administrative functions interpreted strictly. Because the interests protected by bank secrecy are private in nature and only indirectly concern the public interest, revealing bank client information may not in any way be considered to violate the criminal provision in question.

CUSTOMER'S REMEDIES FOR BREACH OF CONFIDENCE

Criminal Penalties

Violation by bank officers and employees of the confidentiality of information concerning bank clients is not expressly subject to criminal penalties. As indicated above neither art 622 nor art 326 of the Criminal Code seems to apply to violations of bank secrecy and therefore the penalties provided for therein are inapplicable.

There is, however, another, more complex, hypothesis for criminalising violations of bank secrecy. Article 2622 of the Civil Code provides that directors, officers, liquidators and statutory auditors of a company who, without just cause and for their own profit or the profit of others, make use of information obtained by them by reason of their position within the company in a way that creates a risk of damage to the company, are punishable by imprisonment of up to one year. The company must initiate the cause of action.

Article 92 of the Banking Law extends application of art 2622 to managers of credit institutions including department heads, head managers of branch offices and persons entrusted by the bank with duties of a general management nature.

This provision, however, 'criminalises' the unauthorised revealing of privileged corporate information regarding the activity of the credit institution as a company and not the revealing of information concerning the relationship between the credit institution and its clients. According to the prevailing doctrine, 'risk of damage to the company' includes only direct damage that may occur to the credit institution itself and not indirect damages that may occur in the event a client of the institution succeeds in holding it liable for damages resulting to the client from violation of his right to secrecy.

Civil Penalties

Article 1218 of the Civil Code provides that any obligor under a contract who does not perform the exact obligation required by the contract, is liable for damages to the other party to the contract, unless he proves that performance of the obligation was rendered impossible through no fault attributable to the obligor.

As stated above, art 1374 of the Civil Code obligates the parties to a contract not only to the express provisions of the contract but also to all consequences of the contract that derive from law or, in the absence of law, from customary practice and principles of equity.

Because confidentiality is a customary practice connected with banking transactions, it is argued that for exact performance of the contractual obligation required by art 1218 of the Civil Code, respect by the bank of the client's expectation of confidentiality is necessary. Thus, the bank will also be liable for all damages resulting to the client from the bank's unauthorised revealing to third parties of information concerning the client and its banking transactions. In

Gentili v Banca Morgan Vonwiller,[7] the Supreme Court stated that, where a bank and its client have concluded a contract, the duty of confidentiality becomes part of the contract on the basis of the principle contained in art 1374 of the Civil Code. Furthermore, the existence of the customary practice of confidentiality implies that even in the absence of a completed contract, the gratuitous revealing of confidential information obtained during the course of its activity by a bank is a breach of a non-contractual duty or sufficient grounds for a tort under art 2043 of the Civil Code. This article provides that any culpable or harmful act that causes an unjust damage to others subjects the actor to liability for the damages caused. Finally, as provided by art 1228 of the Civil Code, the bank would also be liable for the actions of its officers and employees.

According to art 1223 of the Civil Code, damages for non-performance of an obligation are limited to those which are the immediate and direct consequence of such non-performance. However, the damages for which the bank would be liable include not only direct damage to personal assets (losses) resulting from the immediate exploitation by the third party to whom the confidential information is revealed of such information, but also damages arising from harm to personal or business reputation. Thus, damages in respect of the client's inability to conclude a transaction which had been commenced or to conclude such a transaction on substantially the same terms as were in the process of negotiation would be payable by the bank (lost profits).

Where there is difficulty in calculating the amount of damages that are nevertheless proven to have been suffered, the plaintiff may petition for liquidation of such damages by the judge on an equitable basis as provided in art 1226 of the Civil Code.

Article 1225 of the Civil Code gives the bank the right, if it or its officers or employees have not acted fraudulently, to limit its liability to those damages which were foreseeable at the time of the creation of the obligation.

As stated above, the liability of the bank requires its fraudulent or other culpable violation of the duty of confidentiality. No liability arises if the revealing of the confidential information occurs through no reason attributable to the bank itself, such as a fortuitous circumstance or the fraudulent behaviour of the third party who obtains the information without fault or assistance of officers or employees of the bank.

Obviously, no liability will arise in circumstances where confidentiality is breached as a result of specific provisions of law.

Prevailing Views on Banks' and their Officers' Responsibility

In light of the above reasoning, it appears that the prevailing views and current approach to protection of confidentiality in banking transactions can be summarised as follows:

(I)   Officers and employees of credit institutions are criminally liable only if their breach of their duty of confidentiality prejudices the relevant credit institution (see Civil Code, art 2622).

(II) Credit institutions are contractually liable for damaging breaches of the duty of confidentiality by their officers and employees (Civil Code, art 1228). They may also be liable, in the absence of contract, for violations of confidentiality committed by their officers or employees (Civil Code,

---

7 See note 2 above.

art 2049) or by official act of the organs of the bank itself (Civil Code, art 2043).

(III) Bank clients seem to include not only those who conclude a contractual relationship with a bank, but also those who commence negotiations with such bank and those who had a relationship with such bank. Those who are not bank clients have no claim against the bank for failure to respect their interests in the confidentiality of information obtained through lawful channels. Given the trend towards increasing the protection of confidential information even in the absence of a contract, when a credit institution reveals information that it has unjustly received from a professional or a party bound by an obligation of confidentiality, civil liability of the bank towards the client of the party who revealed the information to the bank may exist and be based upon a comparative evaluation of the interests of the bank in question and the damaged party. It has been argued by scholars also that this liability does not arise with respect to the breach of confidentiality by the bank, where the first breach of confidentiality was justified or where the act of such bank was not fraudulent.[8]

THE EXCEPTIONS TO THE GENERAL DUTY OF NON-DISCLOSURE

Customer's Consent

Even if criminal sanctions were to apply to breaches of the bankers' duty of confidentiality, and we are not of this opinion, art 622 of the Criminal Code would not apply to cases in which the bank client expressly or implicitly consents to the use of confidential information by the bank. Article 50 of the Criminal Code provides that infringement or endangerment of a right is not punishable, if the person who is entitled to waive such right has done so and it is a well-established principle that a person may dispose of his own secrets. Additionally, with regard to civil liability, courts have consistently held that confidentiality in banking transactions is the right of the bank's customer and may be explicitly or implicitly waived by the customer. Therefore, revealing information concerning a customer's solvency or account balance to third parties does not violate the duty of confidentiality, if done at the customer's request. A typical circumstance in which this may occur is where information is communicated to authorities in the customer's specific interest (eg in support of a request for obtaining financing facilities from the Public Administration).

Regulatory Authorities

Banks are obligated to release information to bodies which exercise policing authority over various credit related sectors. These include the Bank of Italy, the Italian Exchange Office[9] and CONSOB,[10] which regulates the stock market and certain securities transactions.

The Bank of Italy

The Bank of Italy has the power to obtain access to information concerning the management of credit institutions. Representatives of the Bank of Italy may, in

8 See R Vigo *Libertà e divieti nella circolazione delle notizie bancarie*, (1983) 186.
9 'Ufficio Italiano Cambi' established by Law 331 of 17 May 1945.
10 Commissione Nazionale per le Società e la Borsa established by Law 95 of 8 August 1974.

possession of an express warrant, obtain access to any document which is in the possession of a credit institution.[11] For this reason, they are subject to the strictest obligation to maintain official secrecy, even with respect to public admin-istrations (arts 10, 31 and 42 of the Banking Law). In this way the Bank of Italy, obtains information concerning bank clients. In addition, a recently established rule provides that information so obtained by the Bank of Italy may be communicated to the 'credit authorities' of other European Community member states. Thus, Community collaboration in the policing and control of credit institutions is effected. However, it is requested that the communication of information be made for the exclusive purpose of facilitating surveillance over banking institutions. Moreover, such information qualifies as an official secret and cannot be disclosed to third parties.[12]

The Italian Exchange Office

Banks and bankers are obligated to supply all necessary information to, and allow examination of their books and records, other documents and correspondence by, representatives of the Italian Exchange Office, an independent body which is vested with inspection and control powers for exchange control purposes.[13] The Italian Exchange Office's powers are exercisable with respect to any credit institution, but they are more easily effected with respect to banks which conduct exchange operations. Thus, the Italian Exchange Office also acquires information concerning monetary transactions effected by banks and their clients, whether such transactions are international or national are effected by Italian residents or non-residents as, practically, the distinction between foreign exchange transactions and other credit transactions is often blurred.

CONSOB

CONSOB has the power, inter alia, to conduct investigations, request information and obtain access to the documents of various entities, among which are banks whose shares are quoted on the Stock Exchange and banks which deal in the transfer of shares.[14] Requests for information are justifiable, insofar as they are directed towards ascertaining the compliance with law and the method of financing of transactions, in which the bank serves as an intermediary for the transfer of shares listed on the Stock Exchange.

Judicial Authorities

The most recent case law[15] and academic opinion has confirmed that the bank secrecy defence is generally not applicable against judicial authorities and therefore disclosure of information concerning bank clients to such authorities is not a breach of duty.

---

11 Article 31 of the Banking Law in particular provides that banks be compelled to transmit any information the representatives of the Bank of Italy might request.
12 Article 2 of the Law 114 of 17 April 1986.
13 Article 3 of the Royal Decree 794 of 12 May 1938.
14 By virtue of Decree of the President of the Republic ('DPR') 138 of 31 March 1975.
15 The Supreme Court in *Gentili v Banca Morgan Vonwiller* (see note 2 above) has confirmed the trend of lower courts. More recently see *Mostacci v Banca Nazionale d'Agricoltura* [1981] Tribunal of Rome, 20 February.

Criminal Judicial Authorities and Police Authorities

The position of banks with respect to criminal judicial and police authorities is particularly controversial. Article 348 of the Code of Criminal Procedure provides that every person has an obligation to collaborate in testifying before a criminal court. No one is exempt from this duty except, as provided in art 351 of the Code of Criminal Procedure, employees of public entities which are protected by principles of official secrecy. However, employees of credit institutions are not excepted and they do not, therefore, have the right to refuse to testify before a criminal court.[16]

Searches and seizures conducted on bank premises are governed by art 340 of the Code of Criminal Procedure. According to this article, a judge may order the seizure of specifically identified items which relate to a crime and are located on bank premises. If, on the other hand, the relevant items have not been identified, the judge may solicit the co-operation of the bank and order it to permit access to documents in its possession or to communicate information which the bank is able to deduce. In the event that these requests do not result in adequate information, the judge may order a search of the bank premises and effect any seizures which may become necessary.

Generally, police authorities may not search for and attach deposited funds on their own initiative, even where there is strong evidence indicating connection with an illegality. Furthermore, art 340 of the Code of Criminal Procedure prevents judges from instructing the police to inspect bank records. The inspection may be performed only by a judge. This rule, however, has been subject to various exceptions. For example, the delegation of the conduct of such investigations to the police has been accepted in connection with monetary-related crimes. In addition, legislation which was enacted a few years ago[17] involving the institution of preventive measures against mafia-related crimes, allows certain judicial and police authorities to use the services of the tax police to request credit institutions to provide information and copies of documents that they have in their possession and to seize such items from bank premises.

Civil Judicial Authorities

Adversaries of banks or of bank clients may have an interest in obtaining the testimony of bank employees or in submitting to the court, in support of their case, documents in the bank's possession. Given the silence of the Code of Civil Procedure, it is held that the bank, whether plaintiff, defendant or third party, may be subject to an order to produce or permit inspection of documents on the same basis on which such methods of proof are generally obtained. Analogously, employees of credit institutions may be called to testify in civil judicial proceedings on the same basis as other witnesses may be called to testify.

Article 249 of the Code of Civil Procedure provides that the same persons who may refuse to testify in criminal proceedings may also refuse to testify in civil proceedings. Whereas bank employees may refuse a judicial order to testify on the basis of 'justifiable reasons' (Code of Civil Procedure, art 256), professional

---

16 Articles 348, 351 and 310 of the Code of Criminal Procedure have been replaced respectively by arts 198, 201 and 255 of the New Code of Criminal Procedure which will enter into force as of October 1989. In particular art 198 provides for the duty of the witness to appear in court in compliance with the court's order to testify.
17 Article 14 of Law 646 of 13 September 1982.

secrecy is not a 'justifiable reason' (Criminal Code, art 622), given that, in a civil proceeding, the privilege not to testify is limited to those professionals listed in art 351 of the Code of Civil Procedure and bank employees are not listed therein. Bank employees may argue only that their testimony would be irrelevant to the case.

Similarly, an order to produce documents directed to a bank not directly involved in a case may be objected to on the grounds that such production would 'gravely prejudice' the bank.[18] This may be the case, for example, where the production of a document entails the disclosure of privileged information which is irrelevant to the case at hand. Article 212 of the Code of Civil Procedure permits the bank to provide an extract of the document instead of the original. If even this production gravely prejudices the bank, the judge's production order is not binding.

Finally, as to litigation between a bank and its customer, it is generally held that a bank may introduce that part of the customer's record which pertains specifically to the dispute.

Tax Authorities

The government[19] was authorised to introduce rules which override the bankers' duty of confidentiality, but only in cases of particularly grave damage.[20] The tax legislature also established that the tax authorities may not, because of the tax exceptions to the protection of bank secrecy, obtain information with respect to anyone other than the subject of an investigation. If the bank independently supplies documents and information, however, the tax authorities may use them for tax purposes.[1]

Principles of bank secrecy for tax purposes presuppose that a banking relationship between the taxpayer and the credit institution existed or exists. Suppliers, landlords and contractors, are not considered 'clients', while depositors and borrowers, on the other hand, are considered 'clients'. However, it is hardly persuasive to argue, as some commentators have attempted to do, that bank secrecy for tax purposes should be linked to the public interest protecting savings.

Those who use auxiliary or connected banking services are not protected by any obligation of confidentiality with respect to direct investigations. Such protection would conflict with the rationale of bank secrecy, which is connected only to the credit activities of banks. Deviations from this principle have been introduced in cases relating to direct taxes[2] and to value added taxes.[3] Under these rules credit institutions are obligated to transmit 'copies of the accounts of the taxpayer with details of all transactions connected with such accounts including guarantees issued by third parties'. Credit institutions may also be required to respond to questionnaires, thus releasing 'additional specific

18 Articles 118 and 210 of the Code of Civil Procedure. Some legal writers maintain that the evaluation of the prejudice should be made in comparison with the absolute necessity of the document to prove the facts in question, so that the order to exhibit a document cannot be objected if no other evidence is available.
19 By virtue of Law 825 of 9 October 1971 (under which the government was authorised by Parliament to enact new tax legislation).
20 Law 825, art 10 of 9 October 1971.
 1 DPR 463, art 3 of 15 July 1982.
 2 DPR 600, art 32 of 29 September 1973, as amended.
 3 DPR 633, art 51 of 26 October 1972, as amended.

information relating to the client's accounts'. If banks do not respond to requests for information within the time established or there are 'founded suspicions' that the bank's response is not complete or correct, the tax authorities may gain access to the bank premises to 'obtain directly the information requested'.

Exchange of Information Among Banks

Bank secrecy is also limited by the exchange among banks of credit information. Generally, the banking community's interest is considered superior to the interests of individual clients. Therefore, courts have held that the bankers' duty of confidentiality is not violated when a bank informs another bank on the coverage of a draft or cheque, even if the information communicated reveals that a particular cheque was drawn on insufficient funds. Banks are also permitted to exchange general information regarding their clients. Furthermore, it is known that banks that are associated or connected by ownership, management or contract customarily exchange all or practically all information concerning clients.

Treaties and Subpoenas from Jurisdictions

Criminal Procedure

Italy adheres to the European Convention on Judicial Assistance in Criminal Matters signed at Strasbourg on 20 April 1959,[4] which provides for the gathering of evidence by judicial authorities of one signatory State at the request of judicial authorities of any other signatory state. In addition, arts 658–660 of the Code of Criminal Procedure[5] regulate the examination of witnesses and the carrying out of letters rogatory by foreign judges. Obviously, in these cases the Italian judge applies Italian rules of procedure. When, therefore, as a consequence of a decision or a request of a foreign judge, an Italian judge orders a bank to testify or to produce certain documentation, in light of the above discussion, the bank must comply with the order.

Civil Procedure

Italy adheres to the Hague Convention on Civil Procedure of 1 March 1954.[6] In addition, Italy is a signatory of many bilateral conventions concerning civil procedure which contain provisions similar to those set forth in the Hague Convention.[7] Furthermore, art 802 of the Code of Civil Procedure provides that evidence may be collected in Italy in accordance with foreign judicial decisions or requests upon prior authorisation of the competent Italian Court of Appeals. Thus, a bank requested by an Italian judge to testify or to produce documents on the basis of a decision or a request of a foreign judge may raise the defence of bank secrecy only within the limitations set forth above.

---

4 The said Convention has been implemented by Law 215 of 23 February 1961.
5 These articles have been replaced by art 723–729 of the New Code of Criminal Procedure.
6 The said Convention has been implemented by Law 4 of 3 January 1957.
7 See, among others, the Convention with Yugoslavia signed in Rome on 3 December 1960 and the Convention with the United Kingdom signed in London on 17 December 1930.

INSIDER DEALING

The proposed new laws[8] on insider dealing form part of a series of draft legislation aimed at the better regulation of the securities markets. The pending insider dealing law prohibits the purchase and sale of shares listed on the stock exchange or admitted to trading in other markets using information obtained by virtue of being a shareholder of the company or in the exercise of one's professional, official or public duties. The communication to third parties, without justified motive of such information and the advice to third parties to effect sales or purchases of shares on the basis of such information is also prohibited. People who have obtained information, directly or indirectly, with knowledge of its privileged status, from people who possess such information by reason of their office or profession are also prohibited from trading-related securities.

The currently pending version of the insider trading bill provides for imprisonment of up to one year and fines from 10 million to 100 million lire or up to triple the amount of profits realised in respect of violations of the law. These sanctions would also apply to cases where the violation occurs outside Italy as long as the violation relates to shares listed on an Italian stock exchange or admitted to trading in an Italian market.

Privileged information is defined as specific, precise, non-public information, which if made public would affect the price of shares quoted on the stock exchange or admitted to trading in other markets. The draft legislation also provides that CONSOB shall oversee enforcement of the law and may request the collaboration of the governmental organisations. Under the said law, CONSOB is required to collaborate and exchange information with the competent authorities of other EEC member states and may also collaborate with non-EEC member states.

---

8 Since 28 September 1989, a unified bill has been under the scrutiny of the VI standing committee (finance committee) of the Chamber of Deputies.

11   Luxembourg

Alex Schmitt and Luc Frieden

INTRODUCTION

Banking secrecy in Luxembourg is based on the client's right to have all dealings with a financial institution kept confidential. In other words, no one working in a bank may divulge any information whatsoever about any matters dealt with in the course of his job. The confidentiality extends to all details relating to transactions made by the bank with or for the clients, including knowledge on whether somebody is a bank client, temporarily or permanently, or whether the bank transacts business for him only in Luxembourg or abroad as well. This duty for banks not to disclose information regarding its customers applies both vis-à-vis the state and other third parties.

The extent to which private information is protected in a particular jurisdiction reflects a certain type of society. The difficult balancing between the sometimes conflicting interests of the collective and of the individual has tended to favour the protection of the right to privacy. Banking secrecy has thus, almost naturally, become a cornerstone of the Luxembourg international financial and banking centre.

Brief Historical Overview

Up to the years following the 1939–45 war many legal authors defended the view that the provision on professional secrecy of the Criminal Code did not apply to banks. In the late 1960s, however, the legal writing, encouraged by the banking community, came more and more to the conclusion that bankers exercise an officially regulated profession that is subject by law to a duty of secrecy in the interest of the collective and public order.

It was not until 1981 that the Luxembourg courts had an opportunity to decide on the issue. The commercial division of the Luxembourg District Court decided on 26 June 1981 that banking secrecy had always existed in Luxembourg, which had indeed been confirmed in the meantime by the Law of 1981 on the control of the financial sector (see below). The issue to be decided was whether a bank could disclose confidential information, should this be necessary to protect its own interests. The court decided that the bank had such right. However, even in this situation, the possibility of disclosure must be interpreted restrictively.

The highest judicial authority of Luxembourg, the Superior Court, confirmed the existence of the principle of banking secrecy on the basis of the 1981 Law in a landmark case of June 1983. It further appears from this case that banking secrecy serves private interests, but also that it affects public order and the interests of the society.

Banking secrecy is not peculiar to Luxembourg law. However, the fundamental difference with the situation in other jurisdictions is that, in Luxembourg, banking secrecy is protected by criminal law. This was most importantly confirmed by the Law of 23 April 1981 on the control of the financial sector. While introducing exceptions to the duty of bank secrecy, the law expressly confirmed ex post that the professional secrecy duty of the Criminal Code also applies to bankers, thereby setting an end to sometimes conflicting views in legal writing in the past. In 1989, the principle of banking secrecy as against tax authorities was also expressly asserted by law.

LEGAL BASIS OF BANKING SECRECY IN LUXEMBOURG

Article 458 of the Luxembourg Criminal Code, which dates back to Napoleonic times, prohibits doctors, surgeons, health officers, pharmacists and other persons to reveal any secrets entrusted to them by virtue of their status or their profession.

To decide who was meant by persons entrusted with such secrets by virtue of their status or profession, the courts invented the concept of 'necessary confidant' and it was generally admitted that bankers belonged to that category. Article 16 of the Law of 26 June 1981, which implemented into Luxembourg law the first EC banking directive, finally gave legal backing to this position. The provision confirming ex post that the Criminal Code provision extends to bankers has now become art 31 of the Law of 24 November 1984 on the control of the financial sector, as amended.

Another legal basis for banking secrecy is found in the Decree of 24 March 1989 regarding banking secrecy in tax matters. The decree prohibits tax authorities from requesting information on individual customers from professionals of the financial sector (see below).

A third legal basis for the banker's duty of confidence lies in his duty not to communicate personal data recorded on computers of the bank. This duty arises under the Law of 31 March 1979 on the storage of nominative data on an EDP basis.

Finally, the banker is under a general duty of discretion under tort and contract law. In case of breach of that duty, the victim of the abuse of confidential information may claim damages if the conditions set out by art 1382 of the Civil Code on liability in tort, or, as the case may be, if the rules on liability in case of breach of contract, are fulfilled.

The Scope of Protected Confidential Information

Any information that is not publicly known and to which the bank has access as a result of doing business with the client, is considered to be confidential. All individual and nominative data, as opposed to statistical data or other generally available information, is protected.

Confidentiality also extends to information exchanged between banks if it relates to individual confidential data. It is, however, generally admitted that a bank may deliver to a correspondent bank information regarding the general reputation of a given person.

Finally, it should be mentioned that, in accordance with the above-mentioned 1984 Law, every employee of the bank, from the office clerk to the bank manager and the members of the board, is subject to this duty of secrecy. The same is true for the bank's external auditors.

The Legal Use of Confidential Information

In its 1983 landmark case on banking secrecy, the Luxembourg Superior Court, while solemnly reaffirming the duty of strict confidentiality, recognised that there may be exceptions to the secrecy rules either in the public interest, for instance in criminal proceedings to facilitate the investigation, or in the private interest, for instance to allow the bank to defend its own rights in court.

Indeed, the Criminal Code itself provides for two exceptions with regard to the general professional secrecy duty. As explained above, this criminal provision has been interpreted by the law on the control of the financial sector, as amended, to apply to bankers. Moreover, the latter law itself, as well as some other laws, in accordance with the criminal code, provide for other cases where confidential information may be legally used by the banks.

The following paragraphs outline the use of confidential information in relation to the state, as tax, administrative, or judicial authority, other individuals, including the mother company or the bank's employees with regard to privileged inside information, and third countries with respect to inquiries on criminal or tax matters. It should, however, be said from the outset that all exceptions to banking secrecy have to be interpreted restrictively and that the list of legal exceptions to the secrecy obligations is restrictive.

CONFIDENTIAL INFORMATION AND THE STATE

Article 458 of the Criminal Code provides for two exceptions to banking secrecy: first, the banker may disclose confidential information if he is summoned as a witness in court proceedings; second, if he is expressly required to disclose confidential information by law.

With respect to civil and commercial proceedings, the Superior Court of Luxembourg decided in 1976 that any person who is subject to a duty of professional secrecy under art 458 of the Criminal Code may disclose confidential information if summoned as a witness, but the court may never force him to do so. Although the case did not involve a banker, it is fair to believe that this position equally applies to bankers as they are covered by the same provision. It is therefore for the banker to decide whether and what information he wants to disclose. It should, however, be said that the disclosure of information that is not strictly relevant to the question put to him as witness may render him liable for breach of duty of confidentiality.

A similar position was taken by the Luxembourg Superior Court in the above mentioned case of 1983, which opposed the Herstatt Bank Luxembourg to two of its customers. In this case, the bank was summoned as a party and not as a witness. The two customers claimed the repayment of the balance of three current accounts with Herstatt Bank, the amounts in question resulting from transactions in precious metals and foreign currencies. The bank, which was in the process of being wound up, refused to reimburse, claiming that the amounts resulted from fraudulent transactions contrary to honest practices of banking. To prove its allegations, the bank submitted documents. The customers thereupon asked the court to disregard the documents, as the bank could not disclose them under its duty of secrecy. The court first reaffirmed the principle of banking secrecy on the basis of the law on the control of the financial sector. It went on to say that the Criminal Code, to which the latter law expressly refers, provides for two exceptions to the secrecy rules in the public or private interest. Therefore it concluded on appeal that the lower court had rightly decided that a banker may, in a litigation in which it is a party versus its customer, disclose confidential information to protect its own interests. The court, however, stressed that this exception to the secrecy rule must be interpreted restrictively, that the disclosure may only occur in litigation before a court and that this must be limited to the necessities of the complaint.

Even in criminal court proceedings, bankers may refuse to disclose specific information. The same applies to the criminal investigations by the competent judge ('juge d'instruction') before whom the bankers may be called to testify. In practice, however, banks often co-operate with the judicial authorities in criminal proceedings. Banking secrecy in criminal matters is of course often subject to international treaty obligations regarding judicial assistance in criminal matters (see below).

The banks may further sometimes be required to disclose confidential information by the state in its administrative capacity, either as banking supervisory authority or with regard to foreign exchange transactions.

Banking supervision is entrusted in Luxembourg to the Monetary Institute (IML). The IML has a right of access to all files of credit institutions registered in Luxembourg. However, the Law of 20 May 1983 on the IML expressly provides that all employees of the Monetary Institute are subject to the Criminal Code provision on professional secrecy.

Foreign exchange transactions are free in Luxembourg. However, certain forms have to be filled in by the banks regarding such transactions under the rules of the Belgian-Luxembourg Exchange Institute (Luxembourg has been in an economic union with Belgium since 1921). The forms to be completed for such purposes will remain within the bank, and the Exchange Institute will only be given coded information on the transaction. The Institute will therefore usually not know the name of the customer. It is empowered to check the books of the bank to find out such information, but it may, however, not transfer such information outside Luxembourg.

The most controversial issue regarding the protection of confidential information in relation to the state is the status of banking secrecy with regard to the tax authorities.

Indeed, the whole process of Luxembourg tax law is based on the principle that the taxpayer is compelled to declare his revenue to the authorities. The taxpayer bears the consequences of incomplete or even wrong information provided to the tax authorities.

This philosophy stems directly from Luxembourg constitutional law, which is very protective of personal freedom in its regulation of the relationship between the individual and the state. Individual rights may only be restricted where the highest collective interest of society, or even of the international order, so requires. This is mainly the case where criminal offences have been committed. Hence, it has always been a practice that the secrecy rules cannot be interpreted so as to cover criminal activities and their financial implications.

The scope of the secrecy varies depending on the taxes concerned, because there are two tax authorities in Luxembourg: one in charge of indirect taxes, ('Administration de l'Enregistrement et des Domaines'), the other one in charge of direct taxes ('Administration des Contributions').

With regard to indirect taxes, art 30 of the law of 28 January 1948 provides for two important restrictions to bank secrecy:

(I)   the banks must produce any information and documents that are required by the authorities in charge of indirect taxes to calculate and collect registration and inheritance taxes; and

(II) the law provides for a right of investigation by the competent tax authorities.

Moreover, the banks are required to inform the authorities of the existence of registered shares owned by any person who died in Luxembourg. However, such obligation only exists if the deceased is a person living outside the Grand Duchy of Luxembourg, whatever his nationality. It should further be noted that the banks do not have to provide any information if the heirs produce a certificate that proves to the authorities that the inheritance is free of any inheritance tax. This latter provision applies to the transfers of property to ascendants or descendants of the deceased whose last place of residence was Luxembourg, except in case of testamentary devolution.

On the other hand, the administrative practice regarding banking secrecy vis-à-vis the Department for Direct Taxes has recently been put into black letter law. The move was prompted by the new EC draft directive, submitted to the EC Council of Ministers in February 1989. It aims at amending EEC Directive 77/799 regarding the mutual assistance of the competent authorities of the member states in the areas of direct taxes and value added tax. The new proposal allows member states to refuse to transmit certain information to the tax authorities of another member state if, according to its own national law, it may not collect that information.

The new draft directive thus only tolerates refusals to communicate based on national law, whereas under the current and already implemented EC directive, it is sufficient that national administrative practice does not allow a member state to collect the requested information. It should further be noted that the EC Commission, in its communication to the Council, is of the opinion that a Community-wide harmonisation of national legislation on bank secrecy is not possible at this stage.

To introduce legal certainty and clarity regarding this issue, Luxembourg adopted on 24 March 1989 a Grand-Ducal regulation 'clarifying bank secrecy in tax matters and delimiting the investigation powers of the tax authorities'.

Articles 1–3 of the new text set out the general principles regarding the investigation powers of the tax authorities. Articles 4–7 implement these principles by amending the relevant tax laws.

In essence, the new regulation prohibits the tax authorities from requesting credit institutions, mainly banks, as well as holding companies, investment funds and other professionals of the financial sector, to provide them with information on individual customers. The only exception is the one set out above in favour of the Department of Indirect Taxes regarding registration and inheritance taxes, to the extent the inheritance is subject to Luxembourg law.

Furthermore, the tax authorities are prohibited from requesting information on a certain category of accounts or on all accounts of a certain importance. The regulation also specifies that the control of the accounting books of the credit institution may not be used to collect information on the tax status of individual customers. Any information gathered in a way that conflicts with the foregoing provisions may not be relied on or be transmitted.

The new text does not modify the Luxembourg attitude regarding banking secrecy in tax matters, which has remained unchanged for more than half a century. It also does not create a shield for criminal financial transactions. What it does is to clarify and to give legal backing to an administrative practice which has always been applied by the Luxembourg tax authorities.

Confidential Information and Non-governmental Third Parties

Confidential information may also be used or abused in the relation of the bank with third parties other than the state. Protected data may sometimes be transferred to mother companies of the banks established in Luxembourg. Individuals may receive data stored in computer data bases, or employees may make transactions on information acquired in the process of their work.

The following paragraphs will examine under what conditions it is lawful to disclose confidential information to those persons or entities.

The Law of 27 November 1984 on the control of the financial sector, as amended, sets out what confidential information may be disclosed to the majority shareholder by the Luxembourg-based banks. Indeed, art 31 provides that the management of a Luxembourg credit institution, as defined by the above-mentioned law, may transmit to any person who holds at least 50% of its share-capital, information regarding:

(I)   the amount, the form and the maturity of credits extended to a given customer, provided the total amount of such credit facilities is equal to, or exceeds, an amount of 50 million Flux (francs) or of 5% of the company's equity, if the same is below one billion francs (these amounts are fixed by grand-ducal decree and may vary). In determining whether the foregoing limit is reached, all credit facilities are to be taken into account, whether they have actually been used or whether they merely exist as a stand-by credit or as a guarantee.

(II) the amount, the form and the maturity of liabilities vis-à-vis another bank or credit institution (local or foreign) if the liabilities equal or exceed an amount of 100 million francs (this amount is fixed by Grand-Ducal decree and may vary).

In the two foregoing instances, information may be disclosed regarding the identity of the debtor/creditor concerned, the terms and conditions of the credit/deposit involved and the events that may lead to the maturity or the anticipated maturity of the same. Disclosure in such a case will not lead to a liability of the bank.

Except for the above, no other information may be disclosed to the parent company or to qualified shareholders. This docs not include, however, information that does not contain any disclosure of individual customer data, and which are transferred, for instance, for statistical purposes. Hence, a Law of 28 January 1986 specially authorises the management of a credit or financial institution to disclose general data as opposed to individual customer data, to credit institutions that hold a participation in the share capital of the Luxembourg entity.

Confidential data stored on computers were protected by law already prior to the enactment of the statute that gave legal backing to banking secrecy rules. Indeed, a Law of 31 March 1979 on the use of nominative data in computer systems provides that all persons who by virtue of their profession gather, treat or transmit personal data are subject to professional secrecy.

This law applies indeed to banks as they generally store on EDP systems data relating to the bookkeeping of the bank and thereby automatically also personal data, such as the names of the borrowers and the depositors.

Finally, with regard to the use or abuse of confidential information by employees for their own benefit, it should be noted that to date there is no legislation regarding insider trading in Luxembourg. However, a draft bill is currently under discussion. The goal of the Luxembourg authorities is to be as close as possible to the contents of the EC Directive on insider trading, on which the Council adopted its common position in late July 1989.

However, since November 1987, insider trading has been prohibited by an amendment to the internal regulations of the Luxembourg Stock Exchange. According to those rules, information is considered to be privileged, if it is not in the public domain, is precise in nature, concerns one or more issuers of securities or one or more public issues and which would be likely to influence the price of those securities significantly. Those rules provide for a general prohibition for any member of the Luxembourg Stock Exchange, or its agents or employees, to use privileged information in directly or indirectly acquiring or selling, in Luxembourg, any securities listed on the Stock Exchange.

It should be noted that the above rules on insider trading do not apply if no approved trader is involved in the transaction. The new stock exchange regulations, as approved by ministerial decree, also provide that approved traders and their representatives are under a duty to disclose to the competent stock exchange authorities all information on such transactions, if they are invited to do so in the course of an investigation.

Finally, with regard to the use of confidential information and non-state third parties, a word should be said on the rules governing the disclosure of such information in case of death or bankruptcy of a banking customer or in case of seizure or attachment.

In case of death of the customer, the heirs will be entitled to obtain information on and to give instructions with respect to the account, if they conclusively establish their quality as sole heirs of the deceased.

In case of bankruptcy, the court-appointed receiver may obtain any information from the bank and give instructions with respect to the accounts.

In seizure or attachment cases, the bank's obligation is to block the assets of the customer upon notification of the court order. The bank must not disclose, however, to any party whether the customer has any assets with it, except when asked to appear in court to do so.

The Use of Confidential Information in Relation to Third Countries' Requests

As far as the co-operation between Luxembourg and third countries is concerned, two aspects have to be highlighted: judicial assistance in criminal matters and in tax matters.

Judicial assistance in criminal matters is governed by the European Convention on Judicial Assistance in Criminal Matters of 1959 (ratified by the Luxembourg Law of 21 July 1976) on the one hand, and by the Benelux Treaty on Extradition and Judicial Assistance in Criminal Matters of 1962, as amended (ratified by the Laws of 26 February 1966 and 2 June 1977 respectively) on the other hand.

There are indeed many similarities in both international documents. It should be noted, for instance, that the texts allow a signatory state not to comply with the request for judicial assistance if such compliance would affect the sovereignty, security, public order or other vital interests of the state.

The Benelux Treaty specifies that letters rogatory, through which the investigation is initiated and carried out, have to be executed as if the letters rogatory would emanate from the national judicial authorities.

As an express reservation to the European Convention, the Luxembourg government has stated that letters rogatory for the purpose of search or seizure will only be executed by Luxembourg if they relate to acts for which extradition is possible under the European Convention on Extradition and if the Luxembourg judge has agreed to the carrying out of the letters rogatory. The same attitude is taken by Luxembourg under the Benelux Treaty which, indeed, provides for such attitude in art 24.

Under both international documents, the Luxembourg government retains therefore the right to decide on a case-by-case approach whether or not, in the light of the facts and the general political situation, it should comply with such foreign requests, it being understood that consecutive Luxembourg governments, in the interest of the reputation of the Luxembourg banking centre, have never allowed banking secrecy to become a shield to protect criminal acts in financial transactions.

In the area of international assistance in tax matters, the European Convention expressly provides that a state may refuse to assist a foreign judicial authority if the request relates to tax law offences. The same is true under the Benelux Treaty because the latter requires, for assistance in tax offences, the entering into of a specific agreement regarding this issue. To date, no such agreement has been signed between the Benelux partners.

With regard to requests by foreign tax authorities to Luxembourg banks, one has to distinguish between requests by non-EC countries and EC member states. The requests by authorities of the latter are governed by EEC Directive 77/799 on mutual assistance in the area of direct taxes and value added tax (see above). It should be recalled that this text does allow member states to refuse certain information to the authorities of another member state, if according to its administrative practice, it may not collect that information. A new draft directive which aims at amending the 1977 Directive exclusively provides for refusals based on national law and will no longer allow those based on mere administrative practice. Under the current and proposed Directive, foreign EC tax authorities will, therefore, not receive more information than that available to Luxembourg tax authorities.

The same rule is also part of most tax treaties entered into by Luxembourg with non-EC countries. Thus confidential information is well protected as against tax authorities under international law applicable in Luxembourg.

Remedies in Case of Abuse of Confidential Information

The abuse of confidential information by the banker is a criminal offence and the victim, i e the person whose protected information has been disclosed, may claim damages in criminal courts.

The victim may, however, also choose to claim only damages in a civil court, especially if a criminal action is no longer possible under the statute of limitation.

Under the terms of art 458 of the Criminal Code, the abuse of confidential information by persons subject to professional secrecy is punished by a prison sentence of eight days to six years and a fine varying between 10,000 and 50,000 francs.

The users of confidential information for so-called insider trading at the Luxembourg stock exchange may be suspended or excluded from the stock exchange.

A final question is whether a bank's customer may agree to the disclosure of confidential information, and thereby make the use of such protected data lawful. Although there is no unanimous view on this issue in legal writing, an analysis of all aspects of bank secrecy under Luxembourg law shows that the rules on what information may be disclosed are limited as set out by law and may, therefore, not be changed by agreement between the client and the bank.

Conclusion

Confidential information on individual customers kept by Luxembourg-based banks is especially well protected as its abuse by bankers is a criminal offence. It is a powerful means of protecting individual freedom. It should, however, be understood that, as banking secrecy in Luxembourg is above all a duty of the bank as against its clients, it should not be abused as a shield for illegal transactions.

12 Netherlands

V P G de Serière

INTRODUCTION

There is no rule of Dutch statutory law by virtue of which the duty of confidentiality owed by banks to their customers is recognised. Article 10 of the Dutch Constitution reads as follows:

'1. Except as the same may be restricted by law, each person's personal living conditions shall be respected.
2. Rules shall be enacted to protect the personal living conditions with respect to the registration and disclosure of personal data.
3. Rules shall be enacted with respect to the right of persons to be informed about data which have been registered concerning them, with respect to the use which will be made of such data, and with respect to the correction of such data.'

This constitutional provision was designed to be the basis for (inter alia) a law on bank's duty of confidentiality. Such law, however, was never enacted; at present, no plans exist to introduce such law.

In the Netherlands the duty of confidentiality is based on contract. The duty is imposed on banks by virtue of the General Conditions ('Algemene Bank Voorwaarden'), which almost invariably govern the contractual relationship between Dutch banks and their clients.

On 1 July 1989, the Act Concerning the Registration of Personal Data ('Wet Persoonsregistraties') was promulgated. This Act imposes certain obligations on persons who maintain registration systems for personal data, and grants certain rights to persons whose data are so registered. In connection with, and in anticipation of, the promulgation of this Act, on 29 March 1989 the banks issued the Privacy Code of Conduct for the Banking Industry ('the privacy-gedragscode voor het bankwezen').

In 1965, a number of Dutch banks and finance companies established the Foundation for the Registration of Credit Information ('Stichting Bureau Kredietregistratie'). This Foundation provides information to banks and finance companies concerning the financial records of persons applying for new credit. The foundation operates on the basis of a regulation (established by the foundation itself) in which rules are laid down for the purpose of protecting the privacy of individuals.

The General Act Concerning State Taxes ('Algemene Wet inzake Rijksbelastingen') provides, in art 49, that everyone who is engaged in a business or profession in the territory of the state has a duty to provide to the tax inspectorate information concerning facts and circumstances which could be relevant to determine the tax obligations of third parties. The provisions of art 49 have been implemented in the so-called Code of Conduct for the Tax Inspectorate and the banks ('Gedragscode Fiscus-Banken').

The second section of this chapter will deal with the contractual duty of confidentiality. Then the Foundation for the Registration of Credit Information is further discussed. In the next two sections, the Act concerning Registration of Personal Data and the Privacy Code of Conduct for the Banking Industry are described. Then two sections discuss the relationship between the banks and the Dutch fiscal authorities. The chapter ends by summarily discussing insider dealing. Please note that this chapter does not deal with EEC law aspects.

THE CONTRACTUAL DUTY OF CONFIDENTIALITY BASED ON THE GENERAL CONDITIONS

The General Conditions were developed in 1964 by the Dutch Banking Association ('Nederlandse Bankiers Vereniging'). They are applied by all members of the association to all credit relations maintained with both private and business customers. The present revised text was established by the Association in close consultation with consumer protection agencies; it was promulgated on 1 January 1988. The banks' duty of confidentiality is generally perceived to be based on art 2 of the General Conditions, which reads as follows:

'When carrying out the orders of customers and in the performance of other agreements with customers, the bank shall take all due care and shall use best efforts to take into account the interests of the customers. Also in other respects the banks shall exercise due care with regard to transactions with its customers. The bank shall be liable if a failure to carry out the above-mentioned orders and other agreements or if a failure in the performance of any other obligation of the bank to its customers is attributable to the bank. This principle will apply notwithstanding any of the other provisions contained in these General Conditions.'

It is generally accepted that the provisions of art 2 of the General Conditions (inter alia) mean that in principle the bank is not permitted to provide information to third parties about its clients, unless its clients expressly permit the bank to disclose such information. If the bank violates these obligations, it may be liable to its customers on the basis of breach of contract or, if no contractual relationship can be construed, on the basis of tort. However, there are a number of instances in which the duty of confidentiality will not apply or will be set aside. These include the following.

Legal Proceedings

In legal proceedings (both civil and criminal) banks do not have the right to invoke the duty of confidentiality. The right of certain categories of witnesses to refuse to answer questions or to provide information in the context of legal proceedings is recognised where it concerns, for instance, notaries, attorneys and doctors, but according to consistent case law does not extend to banks. On 6 December 1955, the Supreme Court expressed its view as follows: 'that the right to refuse to provide information is only granted to professions and functions which, because of their nature, and therefore regardless of whether or not a specifically imposed duty of confidentiality exists, entail such obligations' (NJ 1956,52). Clearly, pursuant to these criteria banking is not regarded as a profession which by its nature requires a duty of confidentiality to be imposed.

Attachments

Another exception to the principle of confidentiality is that if an attachment is made against a bank, such bank will have to declare the amounts which it holds for the account of the customer against whom the attachment was made. This is provided in arts 741–742 of the Dutch Code of Civil Procedure.

Taxation

A further exception to the principle of confidentiality is the statutory right of information granted to the tax inspectorate by virtue of art 49 of the General Act Concerning State Taxes. This exception will be dealt with in detail in pp 173–174 below.

Authority of the Dutch Central Bank

The Dutch Central Bank, 'De Nederlandsche Bank NV' (herein: the 'Bank'), has a number of supervisory powers and authorities pursuant to the provisions of the Act on the Supervision of the Credit System ('Wet toezicht kredietwezen').
   Article 16 of this Act provides that

'1. The Bank is authorised to obtain information or to cause information to be obtained from any enterprise or institution which it suspects to be a credit institution within the meaning of the Act, in order to determine whether or not such is the case . . .'

Article 18 of this Act provides that

'1. The Bank is authorised to obtain information from any credit institution or to cause information to be obtained from any credit institution if the Bank considers this to be necessary in the performance of the functions given to the Bank by this Act . . .'

According to arts 16 and 18, the Bank furthermore has access to the books and records both of enterprises and institutions suspected of being credit institutions and of credit institutions themselves. The Act does, however, impose a duty of secrecy on the Bank. Information obtained from an institution or enterprise on the basis of art 16 must be kept confidential, except to the extent necessary for the Bank to exercise its rights under art 250a of the Bankruptcy Act ('Faillissementswet'). According to art 250a of the Bankruptcy Act, the Bank has certain limited authority to cause an institution or enterprise to be declared subject to a moratorium ('surseance van betaling'). Information obtained from a credit institution on the basis of art 18 must also be kept secret, except in certain clearly described restricted circumstances.
   Article 46, sub-s 1 of the Act contains a more general confidentiality provision:

'Every person who performs a certain duty pursuant to this Act or pursuant to implementing regulations of this Act, is prohibited from using or disclosing data or information provided pursuant to this Act or obtained as a result of the inspection of books or records, other than in the manner and to the extent prescribed by this Act.'

Article 46, sub-s 2 of the Act specifically authorises the Bank to disclose to credit institutions the credits granted by credit institutions to a certain borrower. This authority is obviously granted to the Bank to enable it to issue warnings to the banking industry if a particular borrower appears to be over-extended and in financial difficulties. The Bank may, however, only mention the aggregate amount of the credits concerned, and may not disclose which credit institutions are involved or which amounts are lent by any one credit institution. If the Bank makes such disclosure, the recipients of the information have a duty of confidentiality with respect to the information so disclosed.
   With respect to the confidentiality of the information obtained by the Bank in the exercise of its supervisory functions, it should be mentioned that the Bank does exchange such information with other central banks on a regular basis, pursuant to certain international arrangements between central banks and only if

the Bank can be certain that the other central bank concerned itself is under a comparable duty of confidentiality in its own country.

Finally, on this subject, it should be mentioned that a so-called framework agreement ('kaderovereenkomst') exists between the Bank and credit institutions, by virtue of which each credit institution has concluded tripartite agreements with the Bank and with the external auditors of such credit institution. According to such tripartite agreement, the external auditors are authorised to disclose to the Bank all documents and information as may be necessary for the Bank to exercise its supervisory duties pursuant to the Act on the Supervision of Credit Institutions.

All in all, it should be concluded that the Act on the Supervision of Credit institutions contains well-balanced safeguards to protect, to the extent reasonably necessary, the confidentiality of data concerning a certain customer.

Other Statutory Rules

There is a certain number of other statutes which provide to the government or certain government agencies the right to obtain information concerning customers of banks. This paper will not enumerate the relevant statutory provisions.

Finally, it should be noted that, obviously, the contractual duty of confidentiality will be set aside if the disclosure of data concerning a customer is approved by such customer. Such approval does not need to be given in any particular form, and does not even need to be given expressis verbis. For instance, it may be construed on the basis of the attitude or behaviour of the customer concerned.

What if a bank should act in contravention of its contractual duty of confidentiality? The remedies available to the customer are the same as those available in any other instance of breach of contract, but the remedy of damages is usually the only realistic possibility for the customer concerned. Often not an attractive one: to quantify the damages will in many cases be very difficult.

Obviously, the remedy of performance will normally be of no use to the customer, except where the obligation of performance is imposed for future events. To have a court pronounce such obligation is normally (obviously) a superfluous activity; but this could, nevertheless, be of some use if there is a threat of disclosure by the bank, for instance in cases where foreign government agencies are seeking information for investigative proceedings of their own. In such case, a customer may wish to obtain, in summary proceedings, an injunctive court statement as to whether or not a bank may grant such information to a foreign government agency. Another possibility is that the bank itself would seek such injunctive statement, in situations where it may jeopardise its position in the jurisdiction of the foreign government agency if it were not to comply with the request for information.

There is no published case law on this subject matter. One principal question on which it would be interesting to have a court judgment, is whether the bank could argue that its contractual duty of confidentiality has to cede to a legal duty, albeit a legal duty under a foreign jurisdiction, to disclose information. If it is accepted under Dutch law, as it undoubtedly is, that a legal duty to disclose will set aside the contractual duty of confidentiality, it is difficult to see on what grounds it can be convincingly argued that this should not apply with respect to legal duties under a foreign jurisdiction.

THE FOUNDATION FOR THE REGISTRATION OF CREDIT DATA

The purpose of the Foundation is to prevent the occurrence of payment defaults. A bank or financial institution can become a participant by payment of a yearly participation fee. Each participant is required to obtain information from the Foundation's registration system if it intends to extend credit to a customer. The system is quite popular. This is illustrated by the fact that, for instance, in 1985 on average more than 16,000 information requests were handled by the Foundation each day. There are elaborate (but internal) rules concerning the provision of information to participants and to third parties, and in addition to this, there is a complex system in place designed to protect the data banks of the Foundation.

THE ACT CONCERNING REGISTRATION OF PERSONAL DATA

This Act was promulgated on 1 July 1989. Its purpose is to protect the personal living conditions of those persons concerning whom data have been compiled in registration systems. The Act contemplates that a new government agency, the so-called Registration Chamber ('Registratie Kamer') is entrusted with supervision. The Act imposes certain obligations on those who maintain a registration system. These obligations may be summarised as follows:

(I)   The registration system may be established only for one particular purpose.
(II)   The registration system may contain only those data which have been legally obtained and which may serve the purpose for which the registration system was established.
(III)   Measures must be taken to enhance the correctness of data and to protect against loss or manipulation of data.

The personal data may only be disclosed to third parties if at least one of the following conditions is met:

(I)   Disclosure is in accordance with the purpose of the registration system.
(II)   Disclosure was authorised by the person concerned.
(III)   Disclosure is made for the benefit of research or for statistical purposes.
(IV)   Disclosure is made for urgent and important reasons.

Each person concerning whom data are registered has (inter alia) the following rights:

(I)   the right to be informed as soon as for the first time such person's data are included in a registration system;
(II)   the right to be informed about the contents of the registration;
(III)   the right to require corrections and additions to be effected;
(IV)   the right to be informed if data are disclosed to third parties; and
(V)   the right to compensation if the person maintaining the registration system violates the provisions of the Act.

The Act has been drafted in such manner that it allows for a certain measure of self regulation. Thus, in certain sectors of the economy, organisations of persons or entities maintaining registration systems, may develop and adopt codes of conduct. These codes of conduct can be submitted to the Registration Chamber, which will then determine whether or not the code of conduct complies with the requirements of the Act.

It is clear that the Act applies to the data systems relating to customers maintained by banks in the Netherlands. However, its provisions were anticipated by the banking industry. The result of this anticipation is that most of the requirements of the Act have already been put into place by banks. The Privacy Code of Conduct for the Banking Industry was developed and issued by the Dutch banking association on 29 March 1989. It has in the meantime been submitted to the above-mentioned Registration Chamber for the purpose of obtaining confirmation that it is in line with the requirements of the Act.

THE PRIVACY CODE OF CONDUCT FOR THE BANKING INDUSTRY

One of the most important provisions of the Code of Conduct is that each bank is obligated to issue specific regulations governing customer registrations. This regulation must determine which data may be included for which particular purpose, who will be authorised to have access to and work with such data, and under which conditions such data may be retrieved from the system. It must also provide for the entitlement of customers to have access to, to require correction of, and to obtain copies of registered data. If there is a dispute between the bank and a customer with respect to the Code of Conduct, the customer may lodge a complaint with the Commission for the Resolution of Disputes in the Banking Industry ('Geschillencommissie Bankbedrijf'). Alternatively, the customer may approach the ordinary courts. Decisions of the above-mentioned Commission are subject to appeal to the Registration Chamber, but at the election of the customer, and appeal may also be lodged with the ordinary courts.

THE RELATIONSHIP WITH THE TAX AUTHORITIES

Article 49, sub-s 1 of the General Act Concerning State Taxes reads as follows:

'Persons and legal entities which carry on an enterprise or independent profession in the territory of the state are required, if so requested, to make available for inspection by the tax inspector the books and other records relating to that enterprise or profession if such inspection can be relevant to determine facts which may affect the assessment of taxes of third parties.'

Without doubt the banks in the Netherlands are subject to this disclosure requirement. The term 'books and records' as used in sub-s 1 is broadly interpreted: without any doubt registration systems and computerised data banks will be considered to be part of the 'books and records' of banks.
   Article 49, sub-s 3 reads as follows:

'Persons and legal entities referred to in sub-ss 1 and 2 are obliged if requested to provide information and data to the tax inspector if such information and data can be of importance with respect to the assessment of taxes of third parties.'

Thus, in addition to being obliged to make available its books and records to the tax inspector, a bank will also be obliged to disclose other information (to the extent available to it) at the request of the tax inspector. In practice, the tax inspectors in the Netherlands will only make restrictive use of the rights accorded by art 49, on the basis of the principle that tax inspectors must take into consideration the duty of confidentiality of banks towards their customers in each case where the tax inspector will request access to information. It should be noted that information made available to the tax inspector may not be further disclosed by such tax inspector except to the extent necessary to arrive at a proper tax assessment.

In this connection, a decision of the Dutch Supreme Court dated 10 December 1974 (*in re Stad Rotterdam*) may be of interest. In an attempt to refuse to disclose information to the tax inspector, the insurance company Stad Rotterdam argued that art 49 is in violation of art 8 of the Treaty of Rome. Article 8 of the Treaty of Rome provides that each individual's private life, family life, home and correspondence should be respected. This argument was not accepted by the Supreme Court: it considered that, if indeed it were true that the provisions of art 49 would restrict the provisions of art 8, sub-s 1 of the Treaty of Rome, such restriction is permitted because art 8, sub-s 2 permits restrictions to the extent the same are 'necessary in a democratic society in the interests of the economic well-being of the country' (NJ 1975, 178).

THE CODE OF CONDUCT FOR THE TAX INSPECTORATE AND THE BANKS

The implementation of the provisions of art 49 in the relationship between banks and the tax inspectors in the Netherlands has in the past generated a number of interpretation problems. As a consequence, both the banks and the tax inspectorates felt a compelling need to clarify their mutual relationship. This resulted in the establishment of the Code of Conduct on 13 January 1984. The Code is the product of consultations between the Department of Finance of the one part and an ad hoc commission representing the banks of the other part.

Two important aspects of the Code are mentioned herein. The first is that the Code does not require the tax inspectorate to state its reasons when requesting information. Thus, the tax inspectors may request for information without giving any explanation as to why this information is requested. The consequence is that there is virtually no possibility for the banks to argue that a request for information was unduly made. The second aspect is that the tax inspectorate has agreed that it will not make a request for information, unless it has first made an attempt to obtain the required information from the taxpayer concerned himself. Because of this restriction, unnecessary infringements of the confidentiality principle are to the extent possible prevented.

By decree of 15 February 1988 the Code was amended to enable tax inspectors to require banks to provide general information (ie, not just relating to particular customers) on interest payments over deposits).

INSIDER DEALING

In the Netherlands, until the beginning of 1989, there were no statutory rules regarding insider dealing. By Act dated 2 February 1989, a new provision (art 336a) was inserted in the Netherlands Criminal Code. This article reads as follows:

'1. A person who has prior knowledge and who executes or effects a transaction in the Netherlands concerning securities quoted on an exchange which is under the supervision of the state, will be subject to either or both of imprisonment of a maximum term of two years and a fine of the fifth category, if any benefit may result from the transaction concerned.
2. The same sentence will be imposed upon the person who has prior knowledge and who, acting from the Netherlands, effects a transaction concerning securities which are quoted on a stock exchange outside of the Netherlands, if any benefit may result from the transaction concerned.

3. Prior knowledge means awareness of any special circumstance concerning the legal entity or company to which the securities concerned relate or concerning the trade in the securities:
   a. of which the person who is aware of such circumstance knows or should reasonably suspect that the same is not in the public domain and could not have been brought outside of the circle of people who have a duty of confidentiality without violation of such duty; and
   b. of which the disclosure may reasonably be expected to affect the quotation of the securities concerned.
4. An intermediary who has prior knowledge with respect to the trade in securities is not punishable as long as such intermediary acts in accordance with the rules of good faith to carry out customers' orders on the exchange.'

The text of art 336a of the Dutch Criminal Code is quite sweeping in its generality, and will therefore generate a quite considerable number of questions of interpretation. As yet, there is no case law, and there are no authoritative Dutch legal commentaries available on this subject matter. I will not in this chapter venture to address these questions of interpretation. However, a few explanatory comments may be useful to get a clearer understanding about the meaning of the text.

It should be noted that art 336a does not require that the transactions are executed as a result of the availability of the prior knowledge. Accordingly, it would seem that the mere dealing in securities while having prior knowledge with respect to such securities, will by itself constitute a criminal offence, even if the prior knowledge concerned could be proved to have had no effect whatsoever on the decision to enter into the transaction concerned.

The term 'benefit', as used in sub-s 1 of art 336a, should be broadly interpreted. Any financial gain is probably covered, including realised as well as unrealised price increases and the avoidance of potential losses. The text of art 336a makes it clear that it is not necessary that the 'benefit' actually materialises: it is sufficient that a benefit could be obtained.

Article 336a only relates to publicly quoted securities. In so far as quotation in the Netherlands is concerned, it appears that only securities quoted on official exchanges (that is to say, exchanges under the supervision of the Minister of Finance by virtue of the 1914 Stock Exchange Act ('Beurswet')). With respect to exchanges outside the Netherlands, it appears that exchanges which are not subject to any government supervision are also covered. The term 'securities', as used in art 336a, includes shares, options, warrants, depository receipts, bonds, notes, coupons etc. It should further be noted that art 336a does not require the transactions concerned to take place on the stock exchange; private security transactions are therefore also covered by its provisions.

The principle of 'good faith', as mentioned in sub-s 4, is actually derived from the Netherlands civil law. The meaning of this principle in the practical context of securities trading is unclear. The principle appears in any event to entail an obligation for the intermediary to act in accordance with the relevant securities exchange regulations.

It will be clear that the provisions of art 336a may pose a number of problems for banking institutions in the Netherlands which are active in securities trading. Chinese Wall measures have in the meantime been taken by credit institutions; these measures are perceived to be satisfactory to reduce to acceptable levels the possible applicability of this provision of criminal law.

Apart from the criminal law provisions referred to above, there is no statutory law rule regarding insider dealing. Instead, the Amsterdam Stock Exchange has issued its own set of rules in order to prevent insider dealing. This so-called Model Code to Prevent Insider Dealing only applies to managing directors, supervisory directors and certain other specifically designated persons connected with companies which are quoted on the Amsterdam Stock Exchange and which have accepted the applicability of the Model Code. Acceptance is usually effected by way of execution of the so-called quotation agreement ('noteringsovereenkomst'), or by way of separate exchange of letters between the company and the Stock Exchange Association. The Model Code is not a model of clear draftsmanship. The main objections to its provisions may be summarised as being (a) the absence of a clear definition of what constitutes insider dealing, and (b) the absence of clear procedural rules regarding the investigation into alleged insider dealing and regarding the consequences of the determination that a violation of the Model Code has occurred. An English translation of the Model Code is attached to this paper.

CONCLUSION

The duty of confidentiality to be observed by banks in the Netherlands is based on contract, not on statute. The duty is set aside wherever statutory law imposes an obligation to disclose. It is subject to doubt whether this duty is also set aside in cases where the obligation to disclose is imposed by foreign law.

MODEL CODE TO PREVENT INSIDER DEALING

Preamble

The Stock Exchange Association relies upon it that the issuer:

(I)   shall have its own codes for the confidential use of price-sensitive information;

(II)   shall enforce these codes;

(III) shall take proper care that, as soon as becomes necessary, information which had been confidential up to that moment shall be announced in such way that everyone can take note of it at the same time.

Commitment of Issuers

The issuer undertakes towards the Stock Exchange Association to impose— insofar as allowed by law—on the persons to be mentioned hereinafter the commands and prohibitions to be mentioned hereinafter, to enforce the same and to take adequate measures in the event of infringement of any such prohibition or non-compliance with any such command.

Prohibitions Imposed on Managing Directors

(1)(a) In no capacity whatsoever, whether directly or indirectly, or for his own account or for account of a third party, shall a managing director purchase or sell any of the securities issued by the undertaking of which he is a managing director (his 'own undertaking') when he is in possession of price-sensitive information in relation to such securities.

(b)   Price-sensitive information is understood to mean an unpublished matter publication of which may in reason be expected to have considerable effect on the market price of such class of security.

(c)   A managing director shall not communicate price-sensitive information to a third party, save if he does so in order to comply with a statutory obligation or in the performance of his duties as a managing director, nor shall he in the light of such information induce a third party to deal or not to deal.

(d)   The prohibitions referred to under (a) and (c) shall also apply to a class of securities issued by another undertaking whose securities are listed on the Amsterdam Stock Exchange, when by virtue of his office a managing director has knowledge of a matter as meant under (b) in relation to such securities.

(2)(a) A managing director shall be prohibited from purchasing or selling, directly or indirectly, any of the securities of his own undertaking:
  – For the period of two months immediately preceding a preliminary announcement of the undertaking's annual results:
  – For the period of 21 days immediately preceding announcement of the undertaking's half-yearly or quarterly results or the announcement of a dividend or interim dividend:
  – For the period of one month immediately preceding the preliminary publication of a prospectus for a share issue, unless the issuer shows that decision making takes less than one month, in which case such shorter period shall apply.

(b)   A managing director shall not sell any of his own undertaking's securities within six months after he purchased such securities, nor purchase any securities of his own undertaking within six months after he sold such securities.

(3)   In an exceptional case, on special grounds, the issuer may grant dispensation from a prohibition contained in article 2, if abuse of unpublished information must be considered out of the question. Both such request and the grant of dispensation must be in writing.

Restrictions Imposed on Managing Directors

(4)   When not in possession of price-sensitive information a managing director shall be free to deal in his undertaking's securities, but without prejudice to the provisions laid down in article 2 and subject to the restrictions to be mentioned hereinafter:

(a)   A managing director shall be prohibited from purchasing or selling, directly or indirectly, any of his own undertaking's securities without first notifying in writing his dealing intention; to the issuer's chairman of the managing board, the chairman of the supervisory board or another officer appointed for the specific purpose (the 'central officer') and receiving written acknowledgment hereof from the issuing undertaking. In his own case the chairman should inform the (other) managing director(s) or alternatively the central officer in writing and receive acknowledgment.

(b)   The issuer shall maintain a written record of the notification and acknowledgment.

(c)   Likewise must be promptly reported any effecting of dealings as stated in a notification referred to under (a).

(d)   Where an intended buying or selling order has not been passed by the managing director concerned to his bank or stockbroker's house and carried out the latest on the 20th day after such managing director received the acknowledgment as referred to under (a), the notification in question shall lose effect. In consequence the procedure set out under (a) has to be repeated before any such dealings by the managing director are allowed.

(e)   Contrary to the provisions in (a), prior notification shall not be required when a managing director purchases or sells rights, with the understanding that such dealings shall be promptly reported by him in the mode as stated under (c), save where such purchases or sales are effected for rounding-up purposes, in which case the managing director shall be discharged of the obligation to report.

(5)   For inspection by the members of the managing board a list must be available, to be compiled annually, showing the dealings effected by managing directors and supervisory directors in securities of their own undertaking since the effective date of this code or since the previous list.

Extension of Prohibitions and Restrictions Imposed on Managing Directors

(6)   When a managing director places investment funds under the management of a third party, he shall make this party subject to the same prohibitions and restrictions as are applicable to such managing director's own dealings in the undertaking's securities, unless by virtue of

a written agreement the third party has been given discretion and the managing director has no influence whatsoever over the management conducted by such third party.

(7)(a) A managing director shall not in the name of his own undertaking grant an option to subscribe for or acquire securities (to be) issued by the undertaking when he is in possession of price-sensitive information in relation to that class of securities, nor during the period referred to in (2)(a).

(b) Any grant by an issuer to a managing director of an option to subscribe for or acquire securities (to be) issued by the undertaking shall be regarded as a purchase by such managing director if the price at which such option may be exercised is fixed at the time of such grant.

If, however, an option is granted to a director on terms whereby the striking price is to be fixed at a later time, the purchase is to be regarded as taking place at the time at which the price is fixed.

(c) In the case of an option the six-month period referred to under (2)(b) shall begin at the time of the grant of such option.

(d) Exercising an option other than at time of price fixing shall not be subject to prohibitions or restrictions.

(e) The following exceptions shall apply to options that are granted to a managing director, the issuer being represented by another person than such managing director, or to a managing director or employee of one or more of certain categories in the issuer and/or its subsidiary within the Netherlands, if the prices at which they may be exercised are fixed at the time of the grant. Though they are to be regarded as purchases effected by such managing director such options shall be exempted from the prohibitions and restrictions contained in articles (1)(a), (2)(b) and (4)(a) and notwithstanding article (2)(b) such managing director may freely sell the securities thus acquired, irrespective of the period passed since the time of the grant of such option, on the condition that the prohibitions set out in articles (1)(a) and (2)(a) and the restrictions provided in article (4)(a) are duly observed and subject to the following: it shall not be regarded as an infringement of the prohibitions or as non-observance of the restrictions if a managing director sells the securities thus acquired within fourteen Stock Exchange trading days after he exercised the option, provided such sale is reported in the manner as laid down in article (4)(c).

(8) The prohibitions and restrictions shall be equally applicable to any purchase and sale of options on such securities on the European Options Exchange.

(9)(a) The prohibitions and restrictions shall be applicable no matter whether a managing director deals directly or indirectly, or for his own account or for account of a third party.

(b) The prohibitions and restrictions imposed on a managing director shall remain effective until six months after he has terminated his office.

Prohibitions and Restrictions Extended to Supervisory Directors

(10) The preceding provisions shall mutatis mutandis apply to a supervisory director of the issuer and to other persons who by virtue of the law or the

undertaking's Articles of Association supervise the management conducted.

Prohibitions and Restrictions Extended to Other Persons

(11)   The issuer shall designate the persons who by virtue of their office in the issuer or its subsidiary operating within the Netherlands have access to price-sensitive information ('designated persons'), in particular in the following categories:
  – executive employees in the issuer;
  – managing directors, supervisory directors or executive employees of a subsidiary of the issuer's;
  – members of a joint consultative committee established by the issuer and/or of a central joint consultative committee.
The above mentioned provisions shall mutatis mutandis also apply to the designated persons, with the understanding that, contrary to the provisions in article (4), it shall suffice for each of these persons to supply the central officer at least once every three months, at a time appointed for that purpose, with a written report of the number of the securities purchased or sold by him, directly or indirectly, in his own undertaking, as well as the times at which these transactions were effected. However, if the central officer so requests on good grounds, which he can do at any time, each of the designated persons shall promptly report his dealings.

Information to the Stock Exchange Association

(12)   Whenever in connection with suspected abuse of unpublished information an investigation is carried out by the Stock Exchange Association into dealings in certain securities, the issuer, if so requested, shall be obliged to produce the facts collected in virtue of this code for the inspection of the Compliance Officer (as referred to in article 24 of the Articles of Association), who shall be a chartered accountant, the Compliance Officer shall report his findings exclusively to the Chairman of the Stock Exchange Association.

13 Norway

Ole Christian Hoie

INTRODUCTION

Norwegian law recognises a duty of confidence owed by a bank to its customer. Under Norwegian law it is a basic principle that credit institutions are under a secrecy obligation regarding each customer's affairs towards third parties, unless the bank, in accordance with the banking laws or other laws is under an obligation to disclose information to parties to whom such disclosure obligation is owed under such laws.

The right of confidentiality belongs both to the customer and to the bank in accordance with the banking laws. With respect to finance companies which are not banks, there is a modification to this rule, namely that the obligation of confidentiality concerns only knowledge which employees and officers get with respect to other persons' affairs. In practice, the distinction probably is without much merit.

Exceptions to the basic rule, as will be shown below, are many. Both civil and criminal statutory provisions permit or compel disclosure of confidential information by banks.

THE BANK'S DUTY OF CONFIDENCE

The Law on Commercial Banks of 1961 stipulates the following secrecy rules in para 18:

'Officers, employees and auditors in a commercial bank have an obligation of secrecy about matters which they in their positions become acquainted with with respect to the bank's, or a bank customer's or another bank or its customer's relations, if they, according to this or any other law are not under obligation to disclose information. The secrecy obligation does not relate to information which the Board of Directors or someone who has a power of attorney from the Board of Directors, gives on behalf of the bank to another bank. This paragraph does not prevent banks from doing credit information business in accordance with the laws regulating such activities.'

Similar stipulations are contained in the Law on Savings Banks of 1961 and the Law on Finance Institutions of 1988.

Officers

'Officers' are members of the board of directors and members of the boards of subsidiaries of the bank, the control committee, the board of representatives and district governors (in the case of savings banks) and their deputies. The Law relates also to those members of the board of representatives who have been appointed by the government in accordance with para 11 and that member of the control committee who in accordance with para 13 in certain banks must have special qualifications and be recognised by the Central Bank of Norway. Officers are under a secrecy obligation also toward those bodies which have elected or appointed them. Thus, officers elected by the shareholders will not be permitted to give information to any further extent towards the general assembly of shareholders than to third parties. The same rule governs the obligation of officers appointed by the government towards political organs and employee representative officers towards other employees in the bank.

Employees

'Employees' are all employees, also deputy employees working for short periods of time. The secrecy obligation further exists after an individual has ended his employment or officer's position with the bank.

Auditors

'Auditors' means those persons who have been elected or employed as auditors by the board of representatives and the personnel which works under them. Persons who perform daily audits without being elected or employed by the board of representatives or by those auditors who have been appointed or employed by the board of representatives are considered to be employees.

The Savings Bank Act of 1961 and the Law on Finance Companies of 1988 must be interpreted in the same way as regards the definitions referred to above.

How Far Does the Secrecy Obligation Extend?

The secrecy obligation relates to all matters which the person concerned gets knowledge of in his position as employee or officer. It is not a requirement that the information has been received in connection with the work in the bank. The decisive point is whether the person has acquired information in his capacity as officer or auditor or not. Further, the secrecy obligation extends only to matters which are not publicly known or available at the time. Information received through radio or other means or telecommunication from somewhere else where the information is publicly known or available does not fall within the secrecy obligation. The secrecy obligation does not extend to information relating to transactions etc, which would be publicly available on investigation in publicly available protocols or registers such as the real estate register, the company register, tax protocols etc. Information involving evaluation, and which is based upon or can only be arrived at through the bank's special knowledge of its customers may not be disclosed.

The Duty to Disclose Information Internally in the Bank

The duty to disclose information internally in accordance with the Commercial Banking Act (and the Savings Bank Act) is owed by the board of directors and the auditors towards the control committee. Although nothing has been explicitly said in the Act, it must be clear that a subordinate officer is in a position to give his superiors any information required. Further, it is supposed that an employee must be in a position to give information to other employees whether or not a superior or subordinate relationship exists between these persons, on the condition that the person concerned is in need of the information related to his work for the bank. The auditors must be in a position to get information with respect to anything which is required in order to carry on a satisfactory audit.

The Obligation to Disclose Information Outside the Bank

Other laws which put banks or their officers and employees under an obligation to disclose information are:

(I)   the Criminal Procedure Act of 1981;
(II)   the Tax Law of 1911, para 66 (as applicable) and the Tax Law of 1980, para 6–4, s 2;
(III)   the Act on Civil Procedures Before the Courts of 1915, para 209;
(IV)   Laws of 13 December 1946 nos 29 and 30 (para 3 in both laws);
(V)   Law of 9 July 1948 no 3, paras 7–8;
(VI)   Law of 14 July 1950 no 10, para 7;
(VII)   Law of 26 June 1953 no 4, para 15;
(VIII) Law of 9 December 1955, para 15;
(IX)   the Law on Bank Inspection of 7 December 1956 as amended, para 3, s 2 (the Finance, Insurance and Securities Commission Act);
(X)   Law of 19 June 1964 no 14, para 28, s 3;
(XI)   Law of 25 June 1965 no 2, para 16, s 2;
(XII)   Law of 19 June 1969 no 66, para 48;
(XIII) Law of 14 June 1985 no 61, para 35; and
(XIV)   Law of 14 June 1985 no 22, paras 2–14.

As will be understood, the legal principle of bank secrecy may be affected by other laws. In order for the secrecy obligation to be waived, not only must there be a general duty to give information related to the matter, but further, there must be present an obligation to give the information in question in relation to a specific matter.

The Exception from the Secrecy Obligation—the Right of the Board of Directors to give Information to Another Bank

It is only the board of directors as such, and not any individual member of the board of directors, which may give information on behalf of the bank to another bank, or give a personal power of attorney to someone to give such information. The board, or a person who has received a power of attorney from the board, must give the information on behalf of the bank and not as private individuals.

'Another bank' means commercial banks, savings banks, state-owned banks and the Norwegian Central Bank. This terminology is used in the Commercial Banking Act and in the Savings Bank Act, both dating back to 1961. Since then, laws have been enacted with respect to other financial institutions, which are not banks as per the definitions in the Banking Act. Reference is made to the Law on Finance Institutions dated 1988, para 15, which uses the expression, 'which the board gives to other credit institutions . . .'. The Banking Act uses the expression 'other banks'. Based upon developments, practice and enactment of laws with respect to other financial institutions than banks, the expression 'bank' must be given a broader interpretation, and in principle relates to all credit institutions regulated by law.

Does the expression 'banks' also include foreign banks and financial institutions? Internationally, the expression 'bank' is subject to definition in each country concerned. According to the terminology in many other countries, Norwegian financial institutions as regulated by the Act of 1988 will be defined as banks. Foreign banks, and financial institutions falling within the definition of 'financial institutions' in the 1988 Act, must be regarded in the same way as Norwegian banks and finance institutions in this context.

Discussion of Practical Situations

The secrecy obligation is not in force in relation to a person who is empowered by law or by agreement has the same right to act towards the bank as the customer himself has. A bank may therefore give information with respect to a customer's relationship with the bank to someone who has a specific power of attorney to act on behalf of the customer, for instance his lawyer.

A married person does not have such a right without special power of attorney in relation to his/her husband/wife. Consequently, the secrecy obligation is in force if a married person requests information regarding the other party's financial affairs in connection with divorce proceedings.

A guardian has the power to ask for information regarding his ward's financial affairs, and a publicly-appointed manager of an estate (bankruptcy estate or death estate) may demand all financial information relating to the deceased or the debtor.

Persons having an interest in a death estate as inheritors, may have a personal interest in receiving financial information relating to the deceased or his estate and dating back to the time prior to the death or the opening of the estate. Such persons will, however, not receive such information automatically from banks on request. The Ministry of Justice gave a written statement in this respect in 1975 and stated as follows:

'The Ministry of Justice is of the opinion that a commercial bank probably is under no obligation to give any individual part owner of an estate information with respect to the deceased or a death estate's bank accounts relating to the period prior to the time of death.

No rule relating to an information obligation follows from the Act of Settlement of Estates and the Ministry has found no other basis for such a rule. The situation is different if the inheritant is actually acting on behalf of the estate itself.

On the other hand, one is of the opinion that the bank normally will not be bound by any secrecy obligation in accordance with the Commercial Banking Act, para 18 if an inheritant asks for information. An inheritant may have a justifiable interest in and need for information relating to the deceased's financial dispositions, and one cannot find any decisive reasons indicating a different solution, unless the request relates to information of a more personal character. Information asked for by the inheritant would in any case be subject to release if all the inheritants or their attorney should demand it in or if the estate becomes subject to public settlement. If the bank has to act as a witness in any court case relating to the estate's assets, the bank would normally not be bound by any secrecy obligation in accordance to para 18.'

Secrecy Obligation in Relation to Police

The secrecy obligation is also in force in relation to the police. The police may, however, ask for a court decision lifting the secrecy obligation. A bank will have to make an individual evaluation as to how far the bank should assist the police when the police are making inquiries regarding punishable crimes. In such matters, it has been assumed that banks should be of assistance to the police. It is difficult to draw any valid general distinction in these matters. If the bank is an interested party to the prosecution, the bank must give whatever information which is relevant to the prosecutor. The same is valid in relation to the bank's external lawyers when the bank enters into legal court proceedings against its own customers.

Credit Information

The Banking Act and the Finance Institution Act contain a general exemption from the secrecy obligation related to credit information activities carried out by the bank or financial institution in accordance with laws pertaining to such activities.

The exemption was included in the Acts when the Law on Registration of

Personal Information was enacted on 9 June 1978. This enactment was meant to confirm the situation regarded to be in force prior to the enactment of the new law. The banks decided to discontinue their credit information activities, and consequently this exemption is not relevant.

Breach of Confidence–the Bank Client's Remedies

The client has two direct remedies for breach of confidence and one more indirect: he may sue for damages after disclosure has been made, or he may apply to the court for an injunction to avoid disclosure. If disclosure has been made contrary to the criminal act, disclosure may be regarded as a punishable criminal offence.

Injunction

Disclosure will often be made as the first step in a process, whereafter an injunction may not be a valid remedy. It is, however, in theory possible to get an injunction to avoid further disclosure. An injunction in this case would mean an order by the court prohibiting the bank from making certain disclosures prior to having received a court order in normal civil proceedings permitting this disclosure to be made. An injunction may be obtained 'ex parte' or 'inter partes'. In both cases, the court must be satisfied that an unauthorised disclosure is threatened. If the injunction is granted, the applicant will have to put up security to cover damages to the other party in the event that the injunction is subsequently discharged, and the bank has suffered damage as a result of the injunction.

Damages

Although it may be difficult to measure a customer's loss in monetary terms as regards disclosure from his bank, damages may be awarded in accordance with the ordinary rules on damages under Norwegian law.

Criminal Offence

If the breach of confidence may be construed as a criminal offence, the person or the body in the bank which has disclosed information may become subject to public prosecution in accordance with the criminal act.

INSIDER DEALING/CHINESE WALLS

On 14 June 1985 a Law on Dealing in Securities was enacted. Under this Act, the trading/dealing in securities may only be done by securities' broker firms. Banks which want to act in this capacity as brokers must establish separate securities' departments for this purpose. By an Act which was passed in the summer of 1989, the earlier principle of 'Chinese Walls' to be established within a bank, separating the securities' trading from the bank's other activities has been further enhanced by rules which among others stipulate the following (in part the below references are to regulations under preparation):

(I)   the securities department must be organised as a separate company;
(II) employees or officers in the bank may not act as chairman of the board of the company;
(III) employees or officers may not constitute a majority of the board members;

(IV)   the bank and its securities company must perform their activities from separate buildings/offices; and
(V)   separate data services and switchboard services are a requirement.

Under the 1985 Act no one who has confidential information pertaining to public companies may buy or sell listed securities in those companies, if it can be assumed that his knowledge may be of importance to the pricing of the securities in question.

A company dealing in securities is under supervision by the Finance, Insurance and Securities Commission, and such a company is under obligation to give to the Commission any information which the Commission asks for in relation to the company's business, and it is specifically stated in the Act that the Commission may demand information which would otherwise be subject to any secrecy obligation.

14   Spain

Juan Fernández-Armesto and Linda Hiniker

THE BANK SECRECY PRINCIPLE

It is widely accepted under Spanish law that a bank has a duty to protect and preserve the confidentiality of its client's accounts as long as the bank possesses the information in question as a result of the commercial relationship between the two parties. While aspects of this principle are clearly based on legal regulations,[1] the general concept is based upon the custom and practice of the banking industry.

Legal Basis of the Bank Secrecy Principle

There is some controversy in academic circles as to the legal basis of the bank secrecy principle. Many legal scholars have concluded that this principle is founded upon art 18.1 of the Spanish Constitution, which guarantees the 'fundamental right to privacy', not only in one's personal life, but also in terms of information related to one's economic situation.[2] Others look to contractual principles and consider an 'implied contractual term' which governs the banking relationship between the parties as the basis of the obligation to maintain the secrecy of a client's financial data.[3] Finally, still others look to tradition and 'moral obligation' as the basis for this principle.[4]

In short, the debate seems to be composed of those who wish to see further inroads made into the protection accorded by the principle (those who find little basis for it aside from tradition) and those who believe that bank secrecy should be more strictly respected.[5] Whatever is considered the de jure basis for this broadly-respected principle, it is clear that de facto, the non-legal basis of the principle is the element of confidence necessary to ensure an effective working relationship between a bank and its customer.[6]

Legislation Applicable to Investigations by Spanish Authorities

As previously mentioned, the existence of and limits on the bank secrecy principle have been codified to a certain extent. Such specific regulations have generally

---

1 As can be seen below, the limits and the extent of the bank secrecy principle have been developed in the context of investigations by tax and judicial authorities and in terms of the special powers of the Bank of Spain.
2 See art 18.1 of the Spanish Constitution and Jaime de San Román and Rafael Sebastián Quetglas 'El Secreto Bancario' in *Cuadernos de Derecho y Comercio* 17/85, p 193.
3 Garrigues *Contratos Bancarios* (1975) pp 49–50.
4 José Manuel Otero Novas 'El Secreto Bancario, Vigencia y Alcance' *Revista de Derecho Bancario y Bursátil* 21/86, p 729.
5 See generally, Alejandro Vergara Blanco 'Sobre el Secreto Bancario' *Revista de Derecho Financiero y Tributario* (March–April 1988), p 369.
6 See generally, 'Byelaws of the Bank of Spain', which makes the first written reference to the bank secrecy principle. Most experts believe that the custom within the industry to protect the confidentiality of client accounts was grounded to a large extent on said statute.

been promulgated to define the proper scope of investigations carried out by tax and judicial authorities and to define the special function of the Bank of Spain.

Right of Tax Inspectors to Investigate Client Accounts

'Ley de Medidas de Reforma Fiscal'

The first written reference to take note of the existence of the bank secrecy principle can be found in art 23 of the Byelaws of the Bank of Spain. This article specifically prohibits the Bank of Spain from providing any type of information concerning the checking accounts, deposits or transactions of a bank client to anyone other than the client itself, its legal representative or by virtue of a judicial order.[7] By recognising a judicial order to be a justifiable limit on the bank secrecy principle, this article attempts to balance the rights of the individual by protecting the privacy of bank accounts and the right of the state to investigate potential misbehaviour by stating that 'judicial measures' are a legitimate limit on the bank secrecy principle.

This article is important primarily because many believe that the custom then common in the banking industry to maintain the confidentiality of bank accounts, became institutionalised with the publication of said Byelaws. However, these Byelaws did not significantly affect the power of the Spanish authorities to investigate a client's bank account. Rather it was not until 1977, with the 'Ley de Medidas de Reforma Fiscal',[8] that the rights of the authorities to inspect client accounts, specifically, were established.

The Tax Reform Law essentially obliges banks and other financial institutions (such as credit entities) to provide the numbers of 'asset accounts' (e g checking accounts, savings accounts etc) and loan accounts they hold as well as lists of the securities on deposit in the bank. In all cases, the law requires that information that will allow the tax authorities to identify the owner of the accounts be provided. Such information must be provided to the tax authorities regarding any person who is being audited or for use in a criminal prosecution (i e in a prosecution of a 'monetary offence'). Failure of a bank to provide such information can be severely sanctioned.[9]

In terms of further limits on the powers of the tax authorities the law provides that:

(I)   the authorisation to investigate a client account must come from certain specific regulatory bodies;

(II)   the account to be investigated must be specified (though apparently no justification for the investigation is necessary);

(III)   certain formalities must be complied with (e g the presence of the affected party is sometimes required).[10]

Case Law

After this law was promulgated, taxpayers and banking groups brought numerous cases that challenged the validity of the Tax Reform Law. Of these

---

7 Note that under the decision of the Spanish Supreme Court of 28 November 1928, the prohibition contained in art 23 is applicable to private banks.
8 Hereinafter the 'Tax Reform Law'.
9 Article 44 of the above-mentioned law provides for sanctions ranging from a warning to liquidation of the entity.
10 See Enrique Piñel López 'El Tribunal Constitucional y El Secreto Bancario' *Revista de Derecho Bancario y Bursátil*, 17/85, p 123; Law 50/77 and Ministerial Order 14/1/78.

cases the most important and most controversial was decided by the Constitutional Court on 23 July 1983. This case was brought by a group of banks, which challenged the law (and implementing legislation)[11] on the grounds that it violated a citizen's right to privacy as guaranteed by art 18.1 of the Spanish Constitution. Although the court agreed that the bank secrecy principle was grounded on the constitutional right to privacy, the law was upheld.

The most important findings of the court were as follows:

(I)   The bank secrecy principle is guaranteed by art 18.1 of the Spanish Constitution which guarantees the right to privacy.

(II) This protection however only prohibits arbitrary and limitless intrusions into a protected sphere.

(III) Thus, in view of the obligation of each taxpayer to contribute to the support of the state[12] and the limited scope of the legislation, Law 50/1977 does not violate the Spanish Constitution per se.

(IV) However, abusive actions that do in fact violate the right to privacy (ie that do not fall within the limited scope of actions permitted by the legislation) are unconstitutional.

Current State of Affairs

The law in this specific area has not changed much from the doctrine elaborated by the Constitutional Court in 1983.[13] The current legal regime essentially provides that the Spanish tax authorities can only investigate specific taxpayers after having obtained a prior resolution from the appropriate administrative authority (distinct from the inspecting authorities and usually the 'Delegado de Hacienda') and such investigation must have a limited scope.

Banks in turn must report to the tax authorities:

(I)   all operations involving borrowing or lending on the money market;

(II) all operations subject to withholding (such as interest on checking accounts and promissory notes). In this case, the reporting must be done quarterly and annually and must provide information concerning the quantities withheld;

(III) movements in the 'asset' and loan account of taxpayers under the circumstances described above.[14]

Investigation by Judicial/Law Enforcement Officials

Another area in which the limits of the bank secrecy principle are clearly indicated is in the context of a judicial investigation. Article 602 of the Spanish Code of Civil Procedure,[15] clearly states that parties involved in litigation must present private documents and correspondence relevant to the trial.

With respect to third parties, the situation is less clear. Article 603 of the SCCP provides that judges must respect the confidentiality of a non-litigant's bank account. However, it is also clear that judges have the power to review data relevant to a trial, even if such data would be normally protected by the bank

11 See Ministerial Order 14/1/78.
12 Article 31.1 of the Spanish Constitution.
13 See Law 50/1977 as updated by Law 10/1985 of 26 April, Law 14/1985 of 29 May concerning the tax regime applicable to certain financial assets and the implementing regulations thereto contained in Royal Decree 2027/1985 of 23 October.
14 See also Jaime de San Román and Rafael Sebastián Quetglas, p 187.
15 Hereinafter the 'SCCP'.

secrecy principle.[16] Furthermore, art 603 requires non-litigants to turn over privileged documents when:

(I)   one of the parties to the litigation requests the document;
(II)   the presiding judge determines that the information is relevant to the trial; and
(III) after hearing the testimony of the third party who seeks to prevent turning over his documents, the judge determines that in spite of the arguments of the third party the documents should still be presented to the court.[17]

Special Status of the Bank of Spain

The basic function of the Bank of Spain is to oversee the compliance of Spanish banks with the applicable legal rules. In order to facilitate this process, art 49 of the 'Ley de Ordenamiento Bancario' obliges banks to provide information concerning specific operations, activities or business deals to the Bank of Spain. The Bank of Spain is then empowered to investigate the 'structure' of said bank accounts but cannot investigate specific client accounts.[18]

With respect to the information they do obtain, Bank of Spain officials are subject to the bank secrecy principle to at least the extent established by the Spanish regulations.[19] These regulations specifically hold that information and documents that are in the possession of Bank of Spain officials must be kept confidential.

They further specify that Bank of Spain officials cannot publish, communicate nor exhibit privileged information to third parties without the express consent of the interested party.[20]

INSIDER TRADING

Until very recently, insider trading had not been considered to be either an illegal activity or a crime in Spain. Moreover, financial transactions were often facilitated by social relationships, tips and, in some cases, rumours. This unrestricted flow of confidential information was further encouraged by the lack of legal provisions regarding insider trading.

During the past few years, however, the problem of the use and abuse of confidential information has become of increasing interest in Spain. The reason for this interest can be attributed in part to the scandals concerning insider trading that have occurred on an international scale and in part to the perception that non-institutional investors were at a disadvantage on the international markets, because of the frequent abuse of confidential information by insiders.

Legal Provision Prior to Law 24/1988[1]

Prior to the current Securities Law, the only reference to insider trading contained in Spanish law was found in art 12 of Royal Decree 279/1984 dated 25

---

16 See generally art 2 of the 'Ley Orgánica del Poder Judicial'.
17 See generally, Novas, p 770. Note that in certain cases, the presence of the third party is required and the removal of documents from the place in which they are stored is prohibited.
18 See Novas, p 770.
19 See Royal Decree 12987/1988 of 20 June.
20 Note that information can be provided to the 'Fondo de Garantia de Depósitos', but this institution, as a related entity of the Bank of Spain, is also subject to the confidentiality principle.
1 Hereinafter the 'Securities Law'.

June 1984 (RD 279/1984) which regulates tender offers. Pursuant to this article, anyone who knows that a tender offer is being prepared shall not (i) disclose such information, nor (ii) buy or sell the relevant securities except in accordance with the conditions under which the tender offer will be launched. However, this law establishes no sanctions in case of breach of its provisions.

Insider trading has never been included as a specific crime in the Spanish Criminal Code. Several attempts to classify insider trading as a legally-defined crime such as fraud, violation of secrets or arrangements to alter prices, have been made by several authors. However, none of these crimes clearly applies to insider trading.

The Current Securities Law: Provisions on Insider Trading

The current Spanish Securities Law introduces major changes into the structure and regulation of Spanish stock exchanges. One of its most relevant innovations is Title VII: 'Conduct Rules', which for the first time in the history of Spanish stock transactions regulates insider trading.

Prohibited Activities

Articles 81–82 of the current Securities Law deal specifically with the problem of Insider Trading. For example, art 81 specifically provides that:

'anyone who has access to privileged information should refrain from carrying out, either directly or indirectly, any operation on the market involving securities to which said information relates. Furthermore such information may not be provided to third parties or used to recommend the acquisition, or transfer of the aforementioned securities.'

In short, under art 81, anyone possessing confidential information shall be deemed an insider, regardless of how he obtained it or what his profession or occupation is.[2] It also prohibits:

(I)   directly or indirectly trading the securities to which confidential information relates;
(II)   providing such information to any third party; and
(III)   tipping off any third party.

Concept of Confidential Information

In addition to defining what is meant by an insider and specifying prohibited activities, art 81 also defines the concept of confidential information. Under this article, information is confidential if it:

(I)   is unknown to the public;
(II)   is precise; mere vague rumours are not deemed confidential information;
(III)   relates to one or more securities; even though Law 24/1988 does not so specifically state, such information should refer to the issuers of such securities;
(IV)   could be somehow relevant to the listing of the security; thus, any transaction involving a security the quotation of which has been suspended would not be forbidden.[3]

2 Note that the Spanish law is much broader than other laws on insider trading such as EEC Directive 88 (549) which has a more limited definition of an insider.
3 Again it is likely that future regulation will elaborate this point.

Disclosure of Information

Article 82 of the current Securities Law requires the issuers of securities to disclose to the public any fact or decision that may influence the listing of such securities as soon as possible. However, art 82 also provides that if the issuer considers that publication could be harmful to their interests, it may so inform the Comisión Nacional del Mercado de Valores.[4] The CNMV may then decide whether or not to accede to said request.

Chinese Walls

In addition to addressing the problem of insider trading, the current Securities Law considers the related problem of the use of confidential information by law firms, brokerage firms or investment banks for the benefit of the firm at the expense of the interests of their clients. Article 83 of the current Securities Law specifically addresses this problem by requiring 'Chinese Walls' to be established within any entity (i) trading on the securities markets, or (ii) rendering advisory services concerning investments in securities.

Pursuant to art 83, such entities must ensure that confidential information known by the personnel of any of their departments is not transmitted to the personnel in any other departments so that no conflict of interest amongst such departments arises. The article does not however specify exactly how these Chinese Walls should be erected.

Surveillance and Sanctions

Finally, title VIII of Law 24/1988 provides for the creation and functioning of the CNMV with similar purposes, functions and sanctioning power to those of the Securities and Exchange Commission.

Under art 85, the CNMV may oblige complete disclosure of any type of information that is considered necessary to the trading of securities from any individual or entity possessing such information, as well as to investigate such individual or entity whenever the CNMV may deem it appropriate. Furthermore, pursuant to art 89 the CNMV may order any entity (not only the issuers) related to the securities market to make public any relevant information which could affect the trading of securities; should the entity fail to do so, the CNMV is itself entitled to make such information public.[5]

Chapter II of the current Securities Law establishes sanctions for violations of the provisions set forth therein. For example, pursuant to art 99(o) any infringement of the provisions of art 81 (insider trading) would be considered a 'very serious infringement', whereas infringement of art 83 (Chinese Walls) would only be considered a 'serious infringement'.

Sanctions for very serious infringements include:

(I)   Fines of up to five times the benefit obtained as a consequence of the infringement or, in certain cases, up to 5% of the equity of the entity, or 5 million Pesetas.

---

4 Hereinafter 'CNMV'.
5 Article 91 allows the CNMV to refrain from requiring relevant information to be disclosed if it deems such decision to be in the public interest or if it deems that disclosure could cause serious damage to the entity in question, as long as failure to disclose will not lead to 'public error' concerning the related evaluation of the related securities.

(II) Suspension or limitation of the activities of the offender in the securities markets for a period up to five years.

Such sanctions can only be imposed by the Ministry of Economy and Commerce.

15 Switzerland

Dr Hans Rudolf Steiner

NATURE AND EXTENT OF THE BANKERS' DUTY OF CONFIDENCE

Sources and Nature

Non-contractual

The Swiss Civil Code ('CC')[1] generally protects the individual sphere of any person by arts 27 ff. Long before Switzerland had a banking law the Swiss Federal Supreme Court recognised that the private sphere of a person included also information relating to his financial affairs and his personal fortune.[2] Article 28 CC states that a person whose personal sphere has been violated has a right to judicial protection. It is undisputed in Swiss law that confidential information obtained by a bank concerning its clients and their financial affairs is protected by these provisions of the Civil Code.[3] The Civil Code and more particularly the law on protection of the personal sphere is a first pillar of the banking secrecy which is clearly civil in nature.

An intrusion of the personal sphere in breach of CC, art 28 is also qualified as a tort in the sense of arts 41 ff of the Swiss Code of Obligations ('CO').[4] Thus, a breach of banking secrecy may have a civil law aspect even if the bank's confidential information is not covered by a contractual relationship but concerns third parties. Under CC, art 28, the sanctions range from court injunctions to the award of damages. It is important to note that the payment of taxes which the plaintiff was obliged to pay under applicable law may not be considered as a damage in the sense of Swiss law. Penalties payable by the plaintiff for avoidance of taxes may be attributed to the plaintiff's own fault and compensation may therefore not be awarded or only at a reduced amount (CO, art 44).[5]

Contractual

The relationship between a bank and its clients is usually contractual in nature and governed by a variety of provisions of the Code of Obligations. Swiss legal scholars are not unanimous about the qualification of the relationship between

---

1 CC 10 Dec 1907, RS 210.
2 Decision of the Federal Tribunal (hereinafter 'BGE') 64 (1938) II 162.
3 B Kleiner 'Verantwortlichkeits- und Strafbestimmungen' in Bodmer, Kleiner, Lutz: *Kommentar zum Schweizerischen Bankengesetz* (1976/82) (hereinafter 'Kleiner') BkL, art 47; N 2/Art 47 BkL D Guggenheim, 'Die Verträge der Schweizerischen Bankpraxis' [1986] 3 Aufl Zürich (hereinafter 'Guggenheim') p 24.
4 CO 30 March 1911, RS 220; Kleiner N 106/BkL, art 47; Guggenheim, p 24.
5 Kleiner N 105/BkL, art 17.

the bank and the holder of a bank account.[6] However, it is clear that most client relationships contain some elements of a mandate.[7] The key provision in the contract of mandate in the Code of Obligations, CO, art 398 provides that the agent has to execute a mandate faithfully and diligently. Whatever information the client asks the bank to keep secret, the bank has to treat as confidential.[8] The client is master of the 'secret', e g he may ask the bank to make a money transfer 'on behalf of a client' without disclosing his name to the recipient or his bank.

Other contractual relationships between bank and client may not be qualified as mandates under Swiss law but rather as a contract of deposit or loan agreement, in which case it is a question of contract interpretation, whether or not the bank is under a duty of confidentiality. Most legal scholars take the view that a confidentiality covenant is customary and at least implied in such an agreement, unless disclosure is clearly required by the nature of the business in question.[9] This is supported by the fact that the Swiss Federal Banking law ('BkL')[10] in its art 47, clearly prescribes a duty of confidentiality to the bank even though not in a civil law context. Unauthorised disclosure of banking secrets by the bank, therefore, constitutes a breach of contract.

The remedies for breach of contract under Swiss law are either specific performance, which may mean an injunction against disclosure of protected information, or damages. Again[11] losses attributable to the plaintiff's own fault may not be claimed as damages or will at least result in a reduction of the compensation awarded. This may apply to tax amounts and penalties which became payable as a consequence of the unauthorised disclosure of secret information.

Criminal

BkL, art 47 makes breach of banking secrecy a crime. The provision was originally introduced in 1934 at the time when dictatorships in the vicinity of Switzerland introduced arbitrary legislation not only discriminating against people for the mere reason of their race, religion or political belief but also confiscating their property and designed to gain control also of their foreign assets. These objectives were pursued by all kinds of intelligence and espionage and it was necessary to take drastic measures against such intrusion of Swiss sovereignty.

The present wording of art 47 of the BkL is as follows:

'1. Whoever discloses a secret entrusted to him in his capacity as officer, employee, mandatory, liquidator or commissioner of a bank, as a representative of the Banking Commission, officer or employee of a recognised auditing company, or who has become aware of such a secret in this capacity, and whoever tries to induce others to violate professional secrecy, shall be punished by a prison term not to exceed six months or by a fine not exceeding 50,000 francs.

2. If the act has been committed by negligence, the penalty shall be a fine not exceeding 30,000 francs.

---

6 Cf comments M Aubert, J Kerner, H Schönle 'Le secret bancaire suisse' [1982] 2 Aufl Bern (hereinafter 'Aubert') p 33 ff.
7 Guggenheim p 23; O Dunant, M Wassmer 'Swiss Bank Secrecy: Its Limits under Swiss and International Laws' in *Journal of International Law, Vol 20 Nr 2* (Summer 1988) (hereinafter 'Dunant/Wassmer') p 543.
8 Dunant/Wassmer p 543.
9 Kleiner N 2/BkL, art 47; Guggenheim p 21; Aubert p 543.
10 BkL 8 Nov 1934, RS 952.0.
11 Cf above lit a.

3. The violation of professional secrecy remains punishable even after termination of the official or employment relationship or the exercise of the profession.
4. Federal and cantonal regulations concerning the obligation to testify and to furnish information to a government authority shall remain reserved.'

It must be noted that two kinds of information are subject to the provision:

(I)   secrets entrusted to the bank, ie by its clients, and
(II) information which came to the attention of the bank in the course of its business, which may relate also to third persons.

Secrets related to the bank's own business only are not covered by art 47 of the BkL but may be business secrets protected by art 162 of the Swiss Criminal Code.[12]

BkL, art 47 is clearly criminal in nature and its enforcement is not dependent upon a complaint of the damaged party but must take place ex officio. Even negligent breach of banking secrecy is punishable. This shows what importance the Swiss legislature attributes to banking secrecy as compared, for instance, with the attorney-client privilege, a breach of which will be prosecuted only upon complaint of the client and only if the breach was wilful and wanton (cf CP, art 321).

Administrative

Article 23ter of the BkL provides that the Federal Banking Commission may take such measures as it deems appropriate to remedy irregularities in the conduct of a bank. Breach of banking secrecy as provided in art 47 of the BkL may constitute such an irregularity and entail administrative sanctions.[13] These sanctions may range from a warning to the request that the persons who breached banking secrecy be dismissed, or even to a withdrawal of the banking licence. However, the automatic sanction of a withdrawal of the banking licence will be warranted only if softer sanctions do not achieve the desired result. Thus the withdrawal of the licence will hardly ever occur for mere breach of banking secrecy.

Extent

In Time

The duty of confidence continues for as long as the persons whose secrets are involved have a reasonable interest to keep them confidential.[14] Therefore, BkL, art 47, para 3 expressly provides that a breach by a person bound by banking secrecy remains punishable even after termination of his employment or other relationship with the bank. The confidentiality obligation also continues beyond termination of the contractual relationship between the bank and its client for as long as the client may have a reasonable interest in keeping the information confidential.

Territorial Reach

All banks licensed to do business in Switzerland either as Swiss legal entities or branches of foreign banks are subject to the banking secrecy obligation with respect to the business activities of their Swiss offices.[15] However, banking secrecy will not

12 CP 21 Dec 1937, RS 311.0.
13 Kleiner N 108/BkL, art 47; Dunant/Wassmer p 544.
14 Kleiner N 97/BkL, art 47
15 BGE 108 (1982) Ib 519.

prevent a foreign head office from exercising the controls necessary for proper conduct of the business and adequate protection of the banks' creditors, provided that the officers and the personnel of the head office exercising such controls are themselves subject to the Swiss secrecy provisions.

Client relationships of foreign branches of Swiss banks are, however, not protected by the criminal law provision of BkL, art 47.[16]

Swiss legal scholars are disputing the question, whether or not a breach of Swiss banking secrecy by an act of disclosure occurring outside Switzerland is punishable under BkL, art 47.[17] As the provision on criminal protection of banking secrecy would make little sense if anyone could cross the Swiss border and disclose protected information with impunity, we consider such dispute to be of a rather theoretical nature. The real problem is rather the enforcement of the criminal sanctions with regard to offenders residing outside Switzerland.

Persons Bound by Banking Secrecy

The persons bound by the secrecy obligation are all those who in the course of discharging their duties and legal obligations obtain access to protected information (cf the wording of BkL, art 47, para 1). However, apart from criminal sanctions, the applicable sanctions will not be the same for all of them. Thus, an observer appointed by the Federal Banking Commission, independent auditors and some other persons mentioned in BkL, art 47, para 1 will hardly ever become liable to a client under contract law.

Public servants such as the members and officers of the Banking Commission, officers of the Swiss National Bank, Tax Inspectors etc are bound by special confidentiality rules governing their respective offices, which are subject to criminal sanctions as well (cf CP, art 320).

EXCEPTIONS

Customers' Consent

General

As mentioned above, banking secrecy enures to the benefit not only of bank clients in the strict sense of the word but also to the benefit of third persons who had contacts with the clients of the bank or about whom the bank obtained confidential information in the ordinary course of the banking business. However, for simplicity's sake we shall refer to all those persons as 'clients'.

Clients' Consent

As a client is the master of the privileged information, his consent will release the bank from its duty of confidence. However, the bank may be in a conflict if it realises that the consent of the client is not given voluntarily but as a result of pressure exercised by a third party or some Swiss or foreign public authority. In these circumstances banks will usually try to obtain clear evidence that the 'consent' expresses the client's actual intent. Like any communication between the parties to a contract, such a consent will have to be construed in accordance with the 'principle of confidence' established by Swiss court practice and

---

16 Kleiner N 100/BkL, art 47.
17 Affirmative Kleiner N 103/BkL, art 47.

jurisprudence. This means that the communication of the client has to be understood as a correct person would have understood it under the given circumstances in good faith.[18] Given the fact that banking secrecy not only protects a contractual right of the client, but his personal sphere, the test becomes particularly delicate.

Persons Acting in Lieu of the Client

The consent need not be given by the client himself but may be given by any person authorised under applicable law to act on behalf or instead of the client. Thus consent may be given also by agents or proxies appointed by the client, legal representatives such as parents, spouses (if applicable), tutors, officers and directors of a legal entity or successors, heirs and assigns or executors of the client's will. However, such consent may not be effective, if information concerning the client is of a strictly personal nature.

Litigation Involving the Client

If the Client Sues the Bank

BkL, art 47 does not contain an express exception referring to an action of the client against the bank. However, a client who sues the bank but insists that the bank abstain from disclosing facts covered by banking secrecy in defending its position, would act against the general principle of good faith (CC, art 2).[19] Therefore, banks may disclose information necessary or useful for the purpose of such defence without breaching their duty of confidentiality. However, information not directly connected with the subject matter of the dispute remains confidential.

If the Bank Sues the Client

Suing a client requires the bank to balance carefully the interests involved. Thus the bank should abstain from suing a client for a negligible amount or from initiating a frivolous action, because the breach of confidentiality by filing such an action may outweigh by far the interest of the bank. However, in principle the client may not invoke banking secrecy as a defence in an action by the bank for breach of contract, nor will the bank be able to shift its burden of proof to the client by arguing that it is unable to prove its claim due to its secrecy obligation.[20]

The Bank as Third Party Claimant

Very often Swiss banks are involved in litigation between a client and a third party because they hold assets which form the object of the dispute. In these cases the banks have to protect their own interests and must be able to enforce preferential rights such as liens, rights of set-off or other security rights which they may have.[1] According to Swiss jurisprudence, banks must disclose their interests in time if they wish to avoid forfeiture.[2] Therefore, such disclosure is not a breach of banking secrecy.[3] However, in cases of attachments granted by way of

18 Cf BGE 111 (1985) II 279, 110 (1984) II 366 and cases cited there.
19 Kleiner N 91/BkL, art 47.
20 Kleiner N 91/BkL, art 47.
 1 Kleiner N 91/BkL, art 47.
 2 BGE 109 (1983) III 22 ff; 111 (1985) III 21 ff; 112 (1986) III 59 ff; 113 (1987) III 104 ff.
 3 BGE 109 (1983) III 22 ff.

Schnellverfahren

summary proceedings, such disclosure may be contrary to the interests of the client if made prematurely and furnish important information to the other party before it is even certain whether its claim is at all justified.[4]

Compulsion by Law

Civil Proceedings with International Judicial Assistance

Article 47, para 4 of the BkL expressly reserves federal and cantonal provisions on the duty to testify or to disclose information to public authorities.

Thus, based on federal and cantonal statutes, banks may be obligated to testify in court. With respect to civil proceedings three different systems have been adopted by the federal and the cantonal legislatures.[5]

The first expressly excludes testimony from all persons bound by a professional secret, which generally includes banking secrecy. This applies to Aargau, Berne, Geneva, Jura, Neuchatel, St Gallen and Vaud, doubtful: Valais.

The second mentions all professions entitled to refuse testimony without, however, mentioning banks, which means that bank officers are obliged to testify. This applies to Appenzell (AR and AI), Basle (City and Country), Glarus, Grisons, Lucerne (doubtful), Obwalden, Schaffhausen, Solothurn and Thurgau.

The third system requires the judge to weigh the interests involved in each single case and to decide whether or not the bank has to testify. This applies to Fribourg, Nidwalden, Schwyz, Ticino, Uri, Zug and Zurich and also to procedures governed by the Federal Code of Civil Procedure.[6] In the future Lucerne may form part of this group as well.

Usually the obligation of banks to submit documents is subject to analogous rules.[7] Where banking secrecy is protected, the courts may take various measures in order to prevent protected information from being disclosed, such as limiting access of the parties to the file, excluding the public from hearings, covering certain parts of documents, sealing of documents and examination thereof by the judge in the absence of the parties in order to determine whether or not they should be excluded (cf arts 38, 42, paras 1, 2, 3, 51, and 56 of the Federal Code on Civil Procedure and the various cantonal statutes).

Such protective measures raise difficult questions of due process and a careful weighing of the interests involved in each single case.[8]

Arbitrators do not have the power to compel testimony or to subpoena documents.[9] However, by taking recourse to the ordinary courts they may gain access to privileged information and indirectly force banks to give evidence under the applicable local procedural rules (cf art 184 of the Swiss Statute on Private International Law[10] and art 27 of the Concordat on Arbitration[11]).

Switzerland grants judicial assistance in civil proceedings to the members of the Treaty on the Law of Civil Procedure signed in The Hague on 1 March 1954.[12] According to art 11 of such convention, the same coercive measures are applicable as in domestic civil procedures, which means that local procedural

---

4 In detail thereto Kleiner N 38/BkL, art 47.
5 Cf also Guggenheim p 26 ff; Dunant/Wassmer p 548.
6 4 Dec 1947, RS 273.
7 Kleiner N 41/BkL, art 47.
8 Cf Court de Cassation of the Canton of Zurich in ZR 1988 Nos 59 and 60.
9 Kleiner N 40/BkL, art 47.
10 18 Dec 1987, RS 291.
11 27 March 1969, RS 279.
12 RS 0.274.12.

rules are applicable also with regard to protection of banking secrecy. With regard to countries that are not members of the convention, Switzerland will act upon letters rogatory as a matter of comity only and leave it to the cantons whether or not they want to apply coercive measures with regard to depositions of witnesses and submission of documents. The canton of Zurich and most other cantons exclude judicial assistance in fiscal, military and political matters or if it is contrary to Swiss public policy and reserve the possibility to refuse assistance if the foreign state does not grant reciprocity. Upon request of the foreign authority and if the parties agree, evidence can be taken in accordance with foreign procedural rules, however, coercive measures will always be subject to local rules.[13] Each canton has its own rules, however, and it is safe to assume that banking secrecy will at least be protected in the same way as described above.

Collection of Debts and Bankruptcy

Proceedings concerning forced execution of debts and bankruptcy are governed by the Federal Law on Debt and Bankruptcy ('LDB') of 11 April 1889.[14] Once the execution officer has seized a bank account and such seizure has become definitive, the bank cannot refuse information by invoking banking secrecy.[15] Theoretically, banks are obliged to provide information at an early stage of such enforcement proceedings; however, before the seizure becomes definitive no coercive measures can be taken by the authority, and the parties involved in the execution proceedings may sue the bank for damages only.[16] This applies also to attachments which are granted as provisional measures upon summary proceedings without strict proof of a claim.[17] It is relatively easy to obtain attachments against parties not domiciled in Switzerland (LDB, art 271, para 4).

In bankruptcy proceedings the trustee in bankruptcy of a client is entitled to full disclosure of account information.[18] In the bank's own bankruptcy the trustee in bankruptcy or the officially appointed liquidator has full access to all information concerning the bank's business.[19] In spite of some special provisions in the banking law concerning bankruptcy proceedings, creditors of a bankrupt bank or a bank in forced liquidation due to a settlement under bankruptcy law are granted wide access to client-related information for the purpose of protecting their interests in the liquidation proceedings.[20]

Criminal Proceedings

With regard to Swiss criminal proceedings, the situation is rather simple. During the stage of mere preliminary investigations by the police, banking secrecy remains fully protected. However, based on the provisions in BkL, art 47, para 4 the Federal Code of Criminal Procedure,[1] as well as all cantonal statutes on criminal procedure, require banks to testify before official prosecutors and the

---

13 Cf art 11 of the Swiss Statute on Private International Law and Zurich Statute on Organisation of the Judiciary, arts 116–117.
14 LDB, RS 281.1.
15 BGE 112 (1986) III 98, 102 (1974) III 9 ff.
16 Kleiner N 37ff/BkL, art 47.
17 Kleiner N 38/BkL, art 47; BGE 109 (1983) III 24, 112 (1986) III 9.
18 Kleiner N 35/BkL, art 47; Dunant/Wassmer p 549.
19 Kleiner N 94/BkL, art 47.
20 Kleiner N 94, 95/BkL, art 47; BGE 106 (1980) Ib 369.
 1 15 June 1934, RS 312.0.

criminal courts.[2] When testifying bankers may at least have to draw the attention of the judge to the fact that the answer to a question may involve disclosure of secrets of uninvolved third parties. It is then up to the judge or the prosecuting officer to determine whether the information is relevant and necessary for the purposes of the prosecution or not. In criminal proceedings against the bank or any of its officers, secret information relating to clients remains protected and must not be used against them.[3]

Delicate problems may come up for a bank if disclosure of documents and information is requested concerning third parties not involved in the offence. The Federal and Cantonal Code of Criminal Procedure provides for several protective measures, among which are the sealing of documents seized at the bank until a judge or a judicially-appointed expert can screen them and the judge can decide in a formal procedure whether the information is relevant and should be put in evidence. Documents may also be admitted only partially by blocking out parts containing protected information (cf Federal Code of Criminal Procedure, art 69, para 3). As it is not possible to have 'secret files' in Swiss Criminal Procedure, the possibility of making certain documents accessible only to the judge but not to the other parties does not exist and would be contrary to the principles of due process.

International Judicial Assistance in Criminal Matters

International judicial assistance in criminal matters by Swiss authorities has become very important in recent years. Based on the Federal Statute on International Judicial Assistance in Criminal Matters, dated 20 March 1981 (the 'Statute'),[4] the Treaty with the United States dated 25 May 1973,[5] the respective federal statute dated 3 October 1973[6] and the European Convention dated 20 April 1959,[7] bankers can be compelled to testify and to submit documents.

It would exceed the scope of this chapter by far if we were to attempt an exhaustive description of the procedure of granting judicial assistance. However, it is certainly necessary to sum up the most important features.

Whether or not judicial assistance must be granted by Switzerland is determined primarily by applicable treaty provisions. If no treaty applies or if a request is beyond Switzerland's treaty obligations assistance may be granted nevertheless under the Federal Statute of 20 March 1981. This Statute, however, does not impose any obligation upon Switzerland to grant assistance to the requesting state.[8] As Swiss authorities are bound by the provisions of the statute, a refusal of assistance is possible only under applicable treaties or the statute.[9]

The first question is always whether or not the request refers to proceedings in criminal matters. Such term is, however, defined quite broadly (cf art 63, para 3 of the Statute). In the absence of a treaty, Switzerland may refuse judicial assistance if the requesting state does not grant reciprocity, except where a particularly grave offence, national interests, the interest of the incriminated person or of a Swiss victim demand otherwise.[10] On the other hand, assistance

---

2 BGE 95 (1969) I 444, 96 (1970) I 749, 104 (1978) IV 130.
3 BGE 104 (1978) IV 125 ff and 108 (1982) Ib 236/237.
4 RS 351.1.
5 RS 0.351.933.6.
6 RS 351.93.
7 RS 0.351.1.
8 Art 1, para 4 of the Statute.
9 Kleiner N 59/BkL, art 47.
10 Art 8 of the Statute; e g BGE 110 (1984) Ib 176/177.

may be refused when it would be contrary to essential Swiss national interests (art 1, para 2 of the Statute and art 3, para 1(a) of the US Treaty).

No judicial assistance will be granted if the foreign procedure does not adequately provide for protection of human rights or otherwise suffers from grave defects.[11] Furthermore assistance is excluded generally for military offences and offences of a 'predominantly' political character,[12] i e if they were committed in the framework of a struggle for or against the political power or have a close connection with such struggle,[13] except in some grave cases such as genocide or if very detestable means were used[14] (e g hijacking, taking of hostages). The term 'political crime' will be narrowly construed as was shown in the 'Irangate' case, where Switzerland granted judicial assistance.[15]

Finally no assistance will be granted if the offence was aimed at reducing fiscal duties or taxes (except with respect to gambling and traffic in drugs, weapons and explosives as per art 2, para 1(c) US Treaty) or evading regulations concerning currency, trade or economic policy (e g antitrust, cf art 3, para 3 of the Statute and art 2, para 1(c) of the US Treaty).

Judicial assistance will work as an exception to banking secrecy only if coercive measures can be applied by the Swiss authorities, because otherwise the bank is obliged to refuse co-operation. Under the Statute, as well as under the European Convention and the US Treaty, coercive measures are admissible as a rule only if the offence being prosecuted contains the elements (other than intent or negligence) of an offence punishable under Swiss law (requirement of dual criminality), except if the assistance is demanded for exoneration of an incriminated person only (cf art 64, para 1 of the Statute, reservation by Switzerland made under art 5, para 1(a) of the European Convention, art 4, para 2(a) of the US Treaty).

The US Treaty requires in addition that the incriminated offence be one listed in the Annex to the treaty.[16] If the request concerns other crimes, Switzerland may grant assistance and apply coercive measures only under its own law.[17] However, neither the requirement of dual criminality nor the list are applicable with respect to certain cases of organised crime, in which Switzerland will even grant assistance in tax matters if leading figures of organised crime are involved and such assistance is necessary for effective law enforcement (arts 6–7 of the US Treaty). This means that in cases of organised crime it is possible to grant assistance to the US also with respect to offences under tax, antitrust and securities laws.

In order to avoid double jeopardy, Switzerland will normally refuse judicial assistance if the incriminated person is staying in Switzerland and a Swiss procedure concerning the same offence is pending. This applies by analogy to the right of a foreign state to participate in Swiss proceedings as a damaged party (art 66 of the Statute). With respect to the US, the right to refuse assistance in such cases is defined more narrowly (art 3, para 1(b) of the US Treaty).

As Switzerland endeavours to prevent misuse of information furnished by way of judicial assistance, it will request the foreign authority not to use such

---

11 Art 2 of the Statute.
12 Art 3, para 1 of the Statute, art 2, para 1(c) of the US Treaty.
13 BGE 113 (1987) Ib 179/180, 110 (1984) Ib 284/285, 109 (1983) Ib 71, 106 (1980) Ib 309.
14 Art 3, para 2 of the Statute.
15 BGE 113 Ib 180.
16 Art 4, para 2(a) of the US Treaty.
17 Art 4, paras 3 and 4.

information for the prosecution of any offence for which Switzerland would not grant judicial assistance if it were made the object of a separate request.[18] In practice the Swiss authorities require an express confirmation of the requesting state in the absence of a treaty.[19]

Switzerland refuses coercive measures for forcing a witness to appear in proceedings held abroad. Therefore a Swiss banker summoned to appear in foreign proceedings has an obligation not to do so if this would jeopardise the confidentiality of client information (art 69 of the Statute, art 23 ff of the US Treaty and art 8 ff of the European convention).

The Statute as well as the treaties provide for a certain degree of participation by foreign authorities and application of certain procedural rules in the execution of the request for judicial assistance. Thus, foreign judges or prosecutors and similar officers may be present when depositions are taken and when documents are seized. However, even under the treaties, performance of the acts requested is primarily the task of the cantonal authorities who, as far as coercive measures are concerned, apply their own procedural rules (art 16 ff, art 64 of the Statute and art 37, para 2 of the US Treaty) and foreign officers must take a passive role, except where federal law determines otherwise.[20]

In practice the Swiss magistrate is often unable to determine which documents or informations are relevant to a complex case. He will therefore be tempted to consult with his foreign colleague when screening documents and questioning witnesses. Therefore the danger exists that the foreign officer may obtain access to confidential information before his right to such access has been determined in proper proceedings. The Swiss Federal Supreme Court has held that in case of doubt the Swiss magistrate must exclude the presence of foreign representatives in order not to render vain the right of the Swiss authority to determine whether or not certain information should be transmitted to the requesting state.[1]

Measures to protect secret information, where admissible, are the same as provided by the laws on federal and cantonal criminal procedure unless a treaty contains specific rules. This applies to the US. Article 12, paras 3(d) and (e) of the US Treaty provide for exclusion of US representatives until it has been determined whether or not the relevant information can be disclosed. This refers to secret information concerning persons not connected with the incriminated offence. In case such information has to be transmitted to the US under art 10 of the US Treaty, the US government will apply to the relevant court for a protective order excluding the public from access to such information (cf art 15 of the US Treaty and Memorandum of Understanding dated 25 May 1973).

As the term 'third party not concerned by the offence' has been given a very narrow interpretation by the Federal Supreme Court, the rules designed for their protection have no great practical relevance (arts 10, 82 of the Statute and art 10, para 2 of the US Treaty).[2]

The determination of whether or not Switzerland grants judicial assistance is made subject to a special procedure in which the persons concerned, including banks, who are asked to provide information, are granted several possibilities of appeal to cantonal courts and the Federal Supreme Court.

---

18 Art 67 of the Statute, art 5 of the US Treaty.
19 BGE 110 (1984) Ib 177, 107 (1981) Ib 271.
20 BGE 113 (1987) Ib 169, 106 (1980) Ib 261 ff, 103 (1977) Ia 214 ff, cf also art 3, para 1 of the European Convention.
 1 BGE 113 (1987) Ib 169.
 2 BGE 112 (1986) Ib 462 ff and 603.

Regulatory Authorities

With regard to their Swiss business activities, Swiss banks and Swiss branches of foreign banks are subject only to supervision by the Swiss regulatory authorities. In this connection they must fully disclose all information required by the Swiss Federal Banking Commission and the Swiss National Bank acting within the scope of their authority. Officers and functionaries of these two authorities are strictly bound by their own secrecy obligation. Similarly, some cantonal authorities who may have a control function, eg the Zurich Stock Exchange Commission, have access to confidential information but are bound in turn by their own secrecy obligation (cf arts 7, 23 bis, para 2 of the BkL, s 31 of the Zurich Securities Law).

Since customer relationships of foreign branches of Swiss banks are not covered by art 47 of the BkL, disclosure of the relevant information to the competent foreign authorities is not subject to criminal sanctions provided therein and will normally be governed by the relevant foreign law.[3]

There is no legal basis for exchange of customer information between Swiss and foreign regulatory authorities, except the provision of BkL, art 23 bis, para 1, which authorises the Banking Commission to issue all decisions necessary to enforce the Banking Law and to supervise compliance with the statutory regulations. Based on this provision, the Federal Banking Commission co-operates with foreign regulatory authorities in accordance with the concordat of Basle adopted by the so-called 'Cooke Committee' in 1975. In doing so the Swiss Federal Banking Commission has to screen very carefully the information it furnishes to foreign regulatory authorities, because release of customer-related information would require a specific authorisation by Statute (cf Kleiner in *Neue Zürcher Zeitung* 10 August 1983). In this connection it is important to note that the ordinance on foreign banks in Switzerland dated 22 March 1984[4] declares the provisions of the BkL only applicable by analogy to Swiss branches of foreign banks. Thus, one could conclude that to some extent disclosure of information concerning Swiss branches of foreign banks to the regulatory authority of the home country might be admissible if absolutely required for effective supervision of the foreign bank as a whole.

Tax Authorities

With regard to taxes, several problems have to be considered separately.

All Swiss banks, including branches of foreign banks, have to account for stamp duties on purchase and sale of securities, including transactions made for the account of customers, and for withholding taxes on dividends paid to shareholders and interest paid to their clients. The Swiss Federal Tax Authority is entitled to inspect the relevant files and has, therefore, access to the client data contained therein. The Federal Statutes on stamp duties and withholding taxes prohibit the use of client data so obtained for any purpose other than enforcement of the respective taxes.[5] The information may not even be used for assessing other federal taxes.[6] In line with this duty of disclosure, the bank has to testify in criminal proceedings regarding evasion of stamp duties and withholding taxes by

---

3 Kleiner N 100/BkL, art 47.
4 RS 952, 111.
5 Art 37, para 5 of the Federal Law on Stamp Tax, 27 June 1973, RS 641, 10; art 40, para 5 of the Federal Law on Withholding Tax 13 Oct 1965, RS 642, 21.
6 BGE 104 (1978) IV 132.

its clients. Similarly, the bank also has to testify in criminal proceedings concerning the turnover tax (sales tax) and customs duties.[7]

With respect to the bank's own income and wealth taxes, the bank has to disclose the same information to the tax authorities as any other taxpayer. However, the tax authorities have no power to compel disclosure of any information protected by banking secrecy. If such information is directly relevant to the assessment of the bank's taxes, e g reserves for bad debts, compensation for damages paid to clients etc, the bank has to exhaust other means, e g submission of certificates by independent auditors or an independent expert, before disclosing the information to the authorities. Even if such other means fail, the bank may still choose to risk a discretionary assessment by the tax authorities instead of disclosing the information. If the bank discloses privileged information in order to avoid unjustified tax burdens, such disclosure cannot be considered as a breach of banking secrecy. Similar consideration has to be made as in civil proceedings involving the client.[8] Unfortunately, the law is not settled in this area yet, as there has been no decision of the Swiss Supreme Court quite in point.

With regard to income and wealth taxes of the bank's clients, both cantonal and federal tax law require the bank to certify the relevant information to the client only. Thus, the bank cannot be compelled to submit documents or information directly to the tax authorities for the purpose of tax assessment or tax audit.[9] However, in criminal proceedings for tax fraud the bank has to testify as in any other criminal procedure.[10] It must be noted that traditionally tax fraud was defined as:

'an intentional deceit of the tax authorities by means of documents containing untrue information for the purpose of obtaining an illegal tax advantage . . .' (cf BGE 96 I 337 ff)

However, in recent years the definition has been broadened to include other types of 'malicious deceit', such as a 'shady conspiracy of the tax subject with third persons', or 'special machinations, tricks or a whole construction of lies', or even mere silence if it can be foreseen that the victim will not double check given a particular relationship of trust.[11] The latter will hardly ever exist with the tax authorities, whereas the other terms of malicious deceit will work to extend the term 'tax fraud'. The traditional definition still applies with respect to direct federal taxes (cf art 130 bis of the Decree on Direct Federal Tax).[12]

The consequence of this development in domestic Swiss law may be less interesting than the effect in the area of international judicial assistance. However, in the same case in which the Federal Supreme Court seemed to announce a broader definition of 'tax fraud', it tightened the conditions for granting judicial assistance (to Germany under the European Convention) by requesting that in tax fraud cases the request must present a prima facie case and sufficient facts to support a reasonable suspicion, which is contrary to the principle adhered to in other cases of judicial assistance, according to which the facts as presented in the request will be accepted by the Swiss authorities without examination on the merits.[13]

  7 BGE 104 (1978) IV 125.
  8 Kleiner N 46/BkL, art 47.
  9 Kleiner N 45/BkL, art 47; BGE 108 (1982) Ib 56 ff.
10 BGE 108 (1982) Ib 236.
11 BGE 111 (1985) Ib 248.
12 9 Dec 1940, RS 642.11.
13 BGE 111 (1985) Ib 242 ff; 114 (1988) Ib 56 ff.

Normal tax evasion by means of failing to declare certain income items or assets is not considered a crime and, therefore, the bank cannot be compelled to testify in the relevant enforcement proceedings. However, this does not apply to withholding tax and stamp duties.[14] Bank documents may nevertheless find their way into a tax file if the files of criminal proceedings against bank clients which are accessible to the tax authorities furnish strong indications that the persons involved in the criminal proceedings or even third persons may have breached the tax laws.[15]

Based on the treaties concluded by Switzerland concerning avoidance of double taxation, banking secrecy will remain protected.[16]

Other Administrative Authorities

Unless expressly provided by statute, banks have no duty to disclose privileged information in administrative proceedings. A notable exception concerns acquisition of interests in Swiss real estate by foreigners (cf the respective Federal Law dated 16 December 1983, art 22, paras 3 and 31).[17]

If administrative matters are brought before any administrative or other courts, then normally rules corresponding to those applicable in civil proceedings will govern (cf Law on Administrative Procedure of the Canton of Zurich, s 60).

INSIDER DEALING

Since 1 July 1988, insider dealing has been a crime in accordance with art 161 of the Swiss Penal Code. Any director, manager, auditor, attorney or agent of a company or a co-operative or an entity controlling it or controlled by it and any member of the governmental body or agency or a public servant or any auxiliary person thereof may be considered as an insider. Persons directly or indirectly informed by an insider are considered as 'tippees', if they knew or should have known that the information was illegally disclosed by the insider.

Disclosure and use of inside information is punishable only if it refers to shares, participation certificates, bonds, debentures, other negotiable instruments or rights issued by Swiss or foreign companies listed on an official stock exchange or an official second market in Switzerland or if it concerns options for the purchase or sale of such securities. Securities traded merely over the counter are not included. Information is considered as inside information, if it is confidential and concerns a planned rights issue, a merger or a similar occurrence of comparable importance, if it can be foreseen that its disclosure to the public will substantially affect the price of the securities. Apart from disclosure to third persons for the purpose of obtaining a profit, the insider also violates the law if he uses the information to obtain a profit for himself or for a third person. The penalties are stiff and range from a fine to imprisonment of up to three years.

The consequence of introduction of art 161 into the Swiss Penal Code is that banking secrecy can be lifted in domestic insider cases of a criminal nature as well as in judicial assistance proceedings concerning foreign insider cases.

Under the treaty on mutual judicial assistance in criminal matters with the United States, the two governments signed a memorandum of understanding

---

14 Kleiner N 50/BkL, art 47.
15 BGE 108 Ib 474 and Steuerrevue 1/89 p 27 ff and 3/89 p 134 ff.
16 Kleiner N 88/BkL, art 47; Dunant/Wassmer p 553.
17 RS 211.412.4.

dated 10 November 1987,[18] by which Switzerland agreed to grant assistance also in so-called 'civil proceedings' concerning insider dealing conducted by the Securities and Exchange Commission.

The memorandum of understanding constitutes an example of how two countries with entirely different legal systems try to harmonise their enforcement proceedings.

CONFLICTS OF INTEREST

Where a bank is in a contractual relationship with each of the parties to a transaction or a dispute and possesses confidential information on one or both of them which might be interesting to the other, the duty of loyalty and trust forming part of the contractual relationship with clients prevents the bank from assisting one party against the other by using such confidential information. To provide such confidential information would be an outright breach of BkL, art 47.

It is not certain whether Swiss courts would prevent a bank from assisting one party by merely financing it for the purpose of a transaction which may be contrary to the interests of the other party. However, cases can be imagined in which the terms of such financing may be influenced by confidential information about the other party, which could involve a misuse of confidential information, short of a breach of BkL, art 47 but in breach of contractual duties. Unfortunately there are practically no published court decisions dealing with this problem.

If a bank acts in such a case of conflict of interests, it may also violate the terms of its banking licence which require that the bank conduct its business in an impeccable way. The Banking Commission has to determine what constitutes improper conduct. In the past, cases of conflict of interests were rare, but it is to be expected that a bank would face disciplinary measures if it were to misuse confidential information about one client in favour of another client, even short of outright disclosure.

MISUSE OF BANKING SECRECY

Responding to discrete pressure by the Swiss authorities, the members of the Swiss Bankers' Association entered into a private Convention on Due Diligence to be applied by banks. The present version dates from 1 July 1987 and forces the banks to identify their clients carefully and the beneficial owners (if any) behind their actual clients.

Even lawyers opening accounts on behalf of clients have to disclose the name of the beneficial owner unless the account is closely connected to legal work. Thus, if the lawyer is used only for the purpose of protecting the identity of the beneficial owner by the attorney-client privilege as an additional screen, the Due Diligence Convention does not allow the bank to open an account or to lease a safe deposit box without disclosure.[19]

The Convention also forbids banks from actively assisting clients in capital flights from countries with currency controls and to avoid taxes by rendering false or incomplete statements.[20]

By making sure that banks know not only their actual clients, but the beneficial owners of assets held in their accounts or deposit boxes, banks are put into a

18 RS 0.351.933.65.
19 Dunant/Wassmer p 572/573, Jahresbericht EBK 1987 p 26/27.
20 Dunant/Wassmer p 573.

position to furnish quite comprehensive information whenever they are legally required to do so. Ironically the industry, which by law has to protect confidential client information much more strictly than any other in Switzerland, is also obliged to keep a much more complete file on its clients and their background than others.

The Convention must be seen as Switzerland's response to criticism frequently uttered abroad that it is a haven for funds from all kinds of criminal sources.[1] Given the combination of the Due Diligence Convention with the legislation of international judicial assistance in criminal matters, international delinquents will not be able to sleep well with a numbered Swiss bank account.[2]

FINAL REMARK

As can be seen from the above, Swiss banking secrecy is by no means as absolute as some people outside Switzerland tend to believe. The difficult problem, which is being constantly re-examined by the Swiss authorities, is the balance between the interests of the individual in the protection of his private sphere and the interests of the society as a whole in enforcement of the laws. It is natural that changing circumstances will also produce new solutions. There is definitely a tendency to lift banking secrecy more easily than in the past, particularly in view of the growing need for international co-operation in combating international and organised crime, which is evidenced again by a recent proposal of the Swiss Government to introduce criminal provisions against money laundering.

1 Dunant/Wassmer p 569.
2 Dunant/Wassmer p 574.

16 United States

David R Slade and Lynn E Stofan

INTRODUCTION

When the Miami, Florida branch of the Canadian-based Bank of Nova Scotia was served several years ago with a grand jury subpoena calling for the production of documents from the bank's branches in the Bahamas and the Cayman Islands, the bank believed it was in a terrible bind. If it complied with the subpoena and produced the requested materials it contended that the secrecy laws of both the Bahamas and the Cayman Islands would be violated. Nonetheless, when the bank failed to comply with the subpoena it was held in contempt of court and fined $1,825,000. And, on appeal, a federal circuit court ruled that both the enforcement of the subpoena and the sanctions imposed were proper. *In re Grand Jury Proceedings Bank of Nova Scotia* 740 F 2d 817 [11th Cir 1984], *cert den, Bank of Nova Scotia v United States*, 469 US 1106 [1985].

This case and others like it draw into sharp contrast the basic differences between United States law and foreign law on the confidentiality of bank records. As the United States continues to expand its extraterritorial reach for confidential customer information, that conflict is likely to grow, putting banks and individual bankers into increasingly difficult positions as they endeavour to protect customer information in compliance with foreign law.

Banks doing business in the United States face a second type of conflict involving their customers' confidential information. This, though, is an internal conflict relating to the ability of a bank to use that information for its own business purposes. These purposes may differ from those for which the bank was given the information in the first place; indeed, they may even be contrary to the interests of the customer. The question thus arises whether the bank has a legal responsibility not to use the information for such purposes.

This chapter will first focus on the common law duty of bank confidentiality in the United States. Then it will analyse statutory law in the United States affecting this duty. Finally, the chapter will discuss the duty in terms of the two conflicts mentioned above: that between the United States government's interest in obtaining customer information and foreign laws that protect it, and conflicts of interest involving the ability of banks to use that information for their own business purposes.

CASE LAW

General Scope of Duty

The basic thrust of court decisions in the United States relating to bank confidentiality of customer information is to protect the reasonable expectations of customers. To determine whether a customer's desire for confidentiality is reasonable in any particular instance, courts are likely to look to the kind of information that the customer wants to be protected, the circumstances (including the relationship with the bank) in which the information was furnished by the customer, the identity of the third party seeking the information and the third party's reasons for doing so.

These factors were all-important in one of the first significant United States decisions specifically holding that a bank owes a duty of confidentiality to its customer. That case arose after a bank manager told a customer's employer without the customer's knowledge or consent that a number of the customer's cheques had been returned for insufficient funds. The customer brought suit against the bank and the trial court granted the bank's motion to dismiss. The Idaho Supreme Court reversed that decision, holding that '[i]t is implicit in the contract of the bank with its customer or depositor that no information may be disclosed by the bank or its employees concerning the customer's or depositor's account, and that, unless authorised by law or by the customer or depositor, the bank must be held liable for breach of the implied contract' *Peterson v Idaho First National Bank* 367 P 2d 294 [Idaho 1961].

In a case several years later, a depositor alleged that a bank divulged confidential information to various third parties concerning the amount the depositor had on deposit in its account, allowing the third parties to use that information to obtain court orders freezing the account. An intermediate appellate court found an 'implied duty on the part of a national bank not to disclose information negligently, wilfully or maliciously or intentionally to third parties, concerning the depositor's account' and after surveying several cases and commentators' views determined that 'a qualified duty of non-disclosure appears to be evolving in both England and America' *Milohnich v First National Bank of Miami Springs* 224 So 2d 759 [Fla Dist CA 1969].

The precise scope of that common law duty remains unclear and varies from state to state. While disclosure of a depositor's account information to private third parties without consent as a general rule are forbidden, disclosures of that information to the government under subpoena or other compulsion of law are in most cases permitted. The courts in many states will further allow banks to disclose information to protect the bank's own interests or to protect the interests of the public, but the availability and scope of these exceptions is less clear. For example, in *Indiana National Bank v Chapman* 482 NE 2d 474 [Ind CA 1985], the Indiana Court of Appeals reversed a trial court decision holding a bank liable for common law damages to a customer who was arrested on charges of arson (later dismissed) based in part on information furnished by the bank pursuant to a police request. The court held that information furnished to the police pursuant to a legitimate law enforcement inquiry falls within a 'public duty' exception to the bank's implied contract not to disclose. On the other hand, in *Suburban Trust Co v Waller*, 44 Md App 335, 408 A 2d 758 [Md Ct Spec App 1979], the Maryland Court of Special Appeals held a bank liable for disclosing customer information to the police upon becoming suspicious that a crime had been committed, expressly rejecting any public duty exception to the implied contract of confidentiality. The court felt the 'vast area of discretion' that such an exception would confer on the bank would erode the duty to the point of being meaningless, and therefore adopted the more stringent rule that 'absent compulsion by law, a bank may not make any disclosures concerning a depositor's account without the express or implied consent of the depositor'.

Duty to Borrowers

There are two decisions by courts in the State of New York suggesting that the bank duty of confidentiality owed to borrowers in that state may be more limited than the duty owed to depositors.

In one case, a borrower alleged that the bank violated a duty of confidentiality when it told another bank and an owner who intended to sell property on credit to the borrower that the borrower had failed to repay a loan when due. As a result of those statements, the other bank refused to extend credit to the borrower and the owner of the property refused to sell. The trial court, focusing on the borrower's reasonable expectations as to confidentiality, ruled against the borrower, holding that a breach of a loan agreement 'was not information that the borrower would normally expect would be kept confidential' *Graney Development Corp v Taksen* 400 NYS 2d 717 [1978], affirmed 411 NYS 2d 756 [App Div 1978].

A borrower in a more recent case also complained that a bank breached its duty of confidentiality by disclosing that its loan was in default to another bank, a business competitor and the borrower's insurance agent. The court disagreed, simply stating that 'New York recognises an implied duty of confidentiality between a bank and its depositors . . . but not between a bank and its borrowers' *Sharma v Skaarup Ship Management Corp* 699 F Supp 440 [SDNY 1988].

Despite this categorical statement by the court in *Sharma*, it would be unwise for banks to assume that there is no duty of confidentiality owed to borrowers in the State of New York (not to mention other states). Both *Graney* and *Sharma* are cases involving information about loan defaults rather than confidential information about a borrower's business or financial affairs revealed to the lender in the course of the lending relationship. Because it may be argued that a borrower has a more reasonable expectation that its financial information will be kept confidential than it has in relation to the fact that it has defaulted on a loan, courts may be more likely to construe the duty of confidentiality as protecting that type of information. This view is supported by dicta in an earlier decision by a federal court in New York, *Humana, Inc v American Medicorp, Inc* [1977–78 Transfer Binder] CCH Fed Sec L Rep paras 96, 286 [SDNY 1978], involving the question whether confidential financial information of a loan customer may be used by a bank in financing a hostile takeover of that customer (discussed below). In a general statement of the duty owed by banks to such customers under New York law the court observed that 'a special relationship which may be designated fiduciary or confidential, does exist between a prospective borrower and its bank which should preclude the bank from disseminating or using the [confidential] information for improper purposes'.

Constitutional Interpretations

A number of state courts have found that provisions in their state constitutions offer customers certain rights of protection against disclosure by banks of their confidential information. For example, the California Supreme Court has found, based on the prohibitions of that state's constitution against unreasonable searches and seizures, that bank customers have a reasonable and legally protectable expectation that their financial records will be kept confidential, thus requiring that customers be notified and have an opportunity to challenge any requested disclosure to state or local government agencies. *Burrows v Superior Court* 529 P 2d 590 [Cal 1974]. Courts in Illinois, Pennsylvania and Colorado have similarly interpreted the search and seizure provisions of their state constitutions. Based on a separate provision of the California constitution guaranteeing rights of privacy, the courts of that state have further extended these rights of notice and challenge to requests for disclosure by private third parties pursuant to discovery in civil litigation. *Valley Bank v Superior Court* 542 P 2d 977 [Cal 1975].

The United States Supreme Court has reached a different conclusion with respect to the search and seizure provisions of the United States Constitution. In *United States v Miller* 425 US 435 [1976], a bank customer charged with federal tax law and other violations objected to the use by the government of bank records obtained by subpoenas issued by the US attorney and served on the bank without any judicial supervision. The Court held that the Fourth Amendment to the Constitution, which protects '[t]he right of the people to be secure in their persons, houses, papers, and effects, against unreasonable searches and seizures' by the government, afforded no protection to the customer. The Court reasoned that bank customers have no reasonable expectation of privacy in bank records, which they neither own nor possess, and that in revealing information to banks they assume the risk that the banks may convey those records to the federal government. This decision, it is important to note, overrules neither court opinions basing a duty of confidentiality on an implied contract nor the decisions relying on provisions of state constitutions; it says only that the Fourth Amendment to the United States Constitution may not be used to support any duty of confidentiality by banks to their customers.

STATUTORY LAW

In the United States, unlike the case in many civil law countries, the primary aim of statutory law relating to bank customer information is not to maintain secrecy of the information, but rather to facilitate law enforcement. In recognition of the value of bank records in enforcing laws, the statutes thus mandate that information be recorded in a certain level of detail and be disclosed in certain circumstances to the government. Only after the Supreme Court's decision in *Miller* did Congress and a number of state legislatures decide to enact statutes designed to protect bank customers against potential abuses by the government in obtaining that disclosure.

The Bank Secrecy Act of 1970

Despite its name, the purpose of the Bank Secrecy Act is not to establish requirements for keeping bank records secret. Instead, this law generally requires each office, agency or branch located within the United States of both US and foreign banks to maintain certain records of customer transactions and to submit reports to the federal government based on those records.

The Bank Secrecy Act directs the Secretary of the Treasury to promulgate regulations requiring banks and other financial institutions to maintain records deemed by the Secretary to have a high degree of usefulness in criminal, tax or regulatory investigations or proceedings. The records required to be kept under these regulations generally include the identity of persons having accounts and, with certain exceptions, copies of all cheques, drafts and other instruments in excess of $100 drawn on or received by the bank, together with an identification of the person to whose account they are to be posted. Further, banks are generally required to record each extension of credit exceeding $10,000 (unless secured by an interest in real property), each remittance or transfer of funds or instruments exceeding $10,000 to a person, account or place outside of the United States, and each receipt of funds or instruments exceeding $10,000 directly (ie not through another domestic financial institution) from a bank, broker or foreign exchange dealer outside the United States.

Based on these records the regulations under the Bank Secrecy Act require banks to file reports with the Internal Revenue Service of each deposit, withdrawal, currency exchange or other payment or transfer involving more than $10,000, whether by, through or to the bank and whether the transaction is domestic or foreign. There are certain exceptions to these reporting requirements, including certain intrabank transactions, certain transactions between banks and transactions with an established customer maintaining a deposit relationship with the bank in amounts which the bank reasonably concludes are commensurate with the customary conduct of the customer's business. Each report must be filed within 15 days of the transaction to which it relates.

Banks and bank officers failing to comply with these record-keeping and reporting requirements face potential civil and criminal liability including fines of up to $1,000 and imprisonment for up to a year in case of wilful violations of the record-keeping requirements, and fines of up to $250,000 and imprisonment for up to five years in case of violations of the reporting requirements.

While the record-keeping requirements of the Bank Secrecy Act may not appear at first blush to affect customers' privacy interests, to the extent they make information available for disclosure to the government or private third parties that would not otherwise exist, they indirectly have that effect. In fact, the recording-keeping requirements were enacted for that very purpose. In 1970, when the law was enacted, Congress was concerned at the number of banks that were discontinuing their prior practice of retaining copies of cheques and other customer records, and wished to ensure that appropriate records continued to be maintained for law enforcement purposes. Similarly, the reports submitted by banks to the Secretary can more broadly affect a customer's privacy interests than would at first seem to be the case. In addition to being used by the Treasury Department, these reports generally are available to any other agency or department of the federal government and to any state, local or foreign government that submits a written request for them to the Treasury, The Act does provide, however, that the reports are exempt from disclosure under the Freedom of Information Act (which generally provides for public access to information held by federal government agencies).

The Right to Financial Privacy Act

When the United States Supreme Court decided in *United States v Miller* (above) that bank customers have no constitutionally protected expectation of privacy in bank records, it did so in relation to records and other information maintained by a bank pursuant to the Bank Secrecy Act. Congressional concern over that decision led the very next year to the enactment of the Right to Financial Privacy Act of 1978.

The Privacy Act imposes certain restrictions on the circumstances in which a bank may disclose customer information to the government. The scope of the Privacy Act, however, is limited in two very significant respects. First, the bank customers entitled to its protection include only individuals and partnerships of up to five individuals, so that the information of corporate customers is not protected. Second, the Privacy Act relates solely to attempts by agencies and departments of the United States government to obtain customer information, and does not apply to such attempts by state or local governments or private third parties.

Procedures

Within this scope, the Privacy Act generally prohibits banks in the United States from disclosing customer information to the government without customer consent unless the government issues or obtains an authorised subpoena or search warrant (or uses another 'means of access' authorised under the Act), the customer is first notified by the government, and a waiting period has elapsed during which the customer may try to prevent the disclosure in the courts. There are few grounds for customers to challenge disclosure, however, and those attempting to do so are typically unsuccessful.

Even the requirement for prior notice to the customer is not without exception. The government may obtain a court order authorising a delay in notification for up to 90 days (with the possibility of further extensions of up to 90 days) upon a showing that records are relevant to an investigation within the lawful jurisdiction of the governmental agency seeking them, and that there is reason to believe that delivery of the notice will jeopardise the investigation or result in certain other types of serious harm. If a delay is granted by the court, the bank will be subject to a 'gag' order prohibiting it from disclosing to its customer that records have been obtained or that a request for the records has been made. In addition, if the means of access used by the government to obtain disclosure is a search warrant issued by a court in accordance with the federal rules of criminal procedure, then the government is not obliged to give notice to the customer until 90 days after the warrant is served on the bank (with the possibility of further 90-day delays as described above), and there is no requirement for a waiting period before the search can commence.

Banks are specifically prohibited from releasing the financial records of a customer to the government under the Privacy Act until the government has certified in writing to the bank that the government has complied with the applicable procedures prescribed by the Privacy Act and that any applicable waiting period has expired. A bank that discloses a customer's financial records in violation of the Privacy Act is liable to its customer for civil penalties, including $100 per violation, actual damages sustained by the customer as a result of the disclosure and court costs and legal fees. Punitive damages may be awarded where a violation is wilful or intentional, and a customer also may obtain injunctive relief to require compliance with the Privacy Act. On the other hand, the Privacy Act expressly provides that a bank that makes disclosure in good faith reliance on a compliance certificate has no liability to its customers for the disclosure.

One of the 'means of access' to bank records authorised under the Privacy Act is a formal written request. A government agency is authorised to use this means only if it lacks the statutory power to issue a subpoena and has promulgated regulatory procedures authorising the issuance of such requests. Whereas in the case of subpoenas and search warrants the bank upon receipt of a certificate of compliance from the government must grant disclosure, in the case of information sought pursuant to a formal written request disclosure by the bank is discretionary. In view of this discretion, where there is any question concerning compliance by the government with the provisions of the Privacy Act or concerning the possibility of a state law violation resulting from disclosure, some banks have chosen not to disclose information pursuant to a formal written request. Although as indicated above, banks making disclosure in good faith reliance on a compliance certificate are protected by the Privacy Act against liability to their customer, banks must consider whether disclosure in these circumstances would be viewed by the courts as having been made in good faith.

Access to records obtained by one agency of the government under the Privacy Act is not limited to that agency. The records may be transferred to another agency in most cases if the government certifies in writing that there is reason to believe that the records are relevant to a legitimate law enforcement inquiry within the jurisdiction of the receiving agency and if the government sends a copy of the certification to the customer within 14 days after the transfer together with a notice describing the nature of the law enforcement inquiry.

Exceptions

Besides being limited in scope, the Privacy Act contains a number of important exceptions to its general requirements. One of the most significant exceptions provides that the Privacy Act's notice, waiting period and challenge procedures do not apply to customer information sought pursuant to a federal grand jury subpoena. The Act's requirements are also inapplicable to subpoenas obtained by a government agency in connection with litigation or adjudicative administrative proceedings to which both the government agency and the customer are party.

Another important exception allows a bank to notify the federal government that it has information that may be relevant to a possible violation of any statute or regulation without having to alert its customer to the fact that it is doing so. Recent amendments to the Privacy Act by the Money Laundering Control Act of 1986, which made the laundering of proceeds from illegal activities a criminal offence, clarify the types of information banks may supply to the government under this exception. Under this law, banks may provide the government with the names of the individuals conducting a suspect transaction and other identifying information concerning the individuals involved, the account number or other identifying information concerning the account, and the nature of the suspected illegal activity. Banks are not merely permitted to disclose this information to the government; Congress, the Treasury Department and federal bank regulators have actively encouraged them to do so. And because banks are potentially liable for criminal prosecution under the Money Laundering Control Act as aiders and abetters, they have an incentive to disclose information in their possession to dispel any notion that they may have had knowledge of and participated in the perpetration of the crime. In addition, the Money Laundering Control Act specifically provides that banks that disclose this information to the federal government may not be held liable to their customers for breach of any confidentiality duty.

Other provisions of the Privacy Act exclude information requests in connection with bank examinations from its requirements, and permit the Internal Revenue Service (IRS) and the Securities and Exchange Commission (SEC) to obtain financial records using procedures other than those provided in the Privacy Act.

The SEC and the IRS

The SEC is permitted to use special procedures provided in the Securities Exchange Act of 1934 (as amended) to obtain financial records in the course of certain securities investigations. Generally, these special procedures permit the SEC to obtain records using its subpoenas without providing prior notice to a bank's customer and without the customer having a chance to challenge the requested disclosure if the SEC is able to obtain court approval for this process after an ex parte hearing. Because these procedures are not part of the Privacy Act, the bank will not receive a compliance certificate from the SEC. The bank may, however, request a copy of the court order obtained by the SEC.

The Internal Revenue Code contains privacy provisions that authorise the IRS to examine bank records for the purposes of ascertaining the correctness of tax returns, determining tax liability and certain related purposes. These provisions are broadly similar to the procedures of the Privacy Act. Thus, the IRS must provide notice to the taxpayer of any summons requesting information from a bank, there is a waiting period during which the taxpayer may attempt through the courts to prevent disclosure and banks are exonerated from liability to the customer for any disclosure made in good faith reliance on a certificate of compliance received from the IRS. As in the case of the Privacy Act, the IRS is able to avoid the prior notice and waiting period requirements if it obtains a court determination that such notice could jeopardise an investigation or result in certain other types of serious harm. A significant difference between the provisions of the Code and those of the Privacy Act is that the tax provisions protect corporations as well as individuals and partnerships.

State Financial Privacy Laws

A number of states, including California and Illinois but not including New York, have enacted statutory schemes that are generally similar to the Privacy Act and prevent a bank from disclosing financial information to state and local government agencies unless similar procedural safeguards are complied with. Unlike the federal Privacy Act, these statutes typically protect corporations and other legal entities in addition to individuals and small partnerships. Moreover, financial privacy statutes in some states, including Illinois, apply to information requests from any 'person', without specifically confining their coverage to requests from government authorities. Because the scope and procedural requirements of these state statutes may differ from the federal Privacy Act and vary significantly from state to state, banks must carefully analyse the laws of the particular state in which they operate in order to ascertain their full responsibilities and potential for liability with respect to any request for disclosure of customer information.

CONFLICT WITH FOREIGN BANK SECRECY LAWS

When the United States government investigates transactions involving the international flow of funds for possible violations of US law, the US laws relating to bank customer information, with their emphasis on disclosure, often conflict with foreign bank secrecy laws.

Negotiations

The Anti-Drug Abuse Act of 1988 reflects an effort by Congress to limit that conflict by requiring the Secretary of the Treasury to negotiate with foreign bank regulators and other officials to ensure that foreign banks and other financial institutions are required to maintain records of all United States currency transactions over $10,000 and to ensure that, upon request, such records will be made available to US law enforcement officials. While the Secretary is required to negotiate with all foreign countries, he must give the highest negotiating priority to those countries 'whose financial institutions the Secretary determines, in consultation with the Attorney General and the National Director of Drug Policy, may be engaging in currency transactions involving the proceeds of international narcotics trafficking, particularly US currency derived from drug sales in the United States'. Within two years, the Secretary must issue a final report to Congress and the President on the outcome of the negotiations. The Secretary must identify those countries with jurisdiction over financial institutions participating in currency transactions that affect the United States involving the proceeds of international narcotics sales. It is then the responsibility of the President to impose temporary or permanent sanctions on the countries in that group that have not reached agreement with the United States for developing a mechanism for exchanging adequate records on international currency transactions involved in narcotics investigations and have not negotiated in good faith to reach such agreement. The sanctions may include prohibiting financial institutions in those countries from maintaining accounts at United States banking institutions and from participating in any United States dollar clearing or wire transfer systems.

Treaties

The US federal government also has attempted to avoid confrontation with foreign bank secrecy laws through the use of tax treaties and Mutual Legal Assistance Treaties ('assistance treaties').

To a limited extent, the United States government can obtain financial records through the information exchange provisions of tax treaties. Tax treaties often contain provisions to share information where necessary to prevent double taxation and to prevent fraud in relation to the taxes covered by the treaty. However, the information exchange provisions in tax treaties generally provide a means to obtain information protected by bank secrecy laws only to the extent that the foreign tax authority named in the treaty could obtain the information if it were investigating a breach of the tax laws it administers.

In addition, the United States has entered into assistance treaties with a number of countries, including Switzerland, Italy and the Netherlands. Assistance treaties with the Cayman Islands and West Germany have been signed but are not yet in force.

From the point of view of the United States, an assistance treaty generally requires that the central government of the treaty counterparty obtain information on behalf of the United States government, thus enabling the United States to obtain the benefit of a typical exception to foreign bank secrecy laws: disclosure to a country's government authorities. Of course, these treaties also open up the possibility of foreign governments obtaining bank records located in the United States through the intervention of the United States government.

The scope of an assistance treaty is typically limited to investigations and proceedings related to activities that are crimes in both countries and as a consequence often excludes offences under the US securities, antitrust and tax laws. For example, the only offences related to violations of United States tax law that are covered by the assistance treaty with Switzerland are tax fraud, tax offences committed in furtherance of the purposes of an organised crime group and other tax offences that constitute crimes under Swiss law. While the assistance treaty between the United States and Switzerland covers violations of United States securities laws which are also crimes in Switzerland, until recently the United States government's ability to use the assistance treaty in investigations of insider trading was limited because insider trading was not a crime in Switzerland. In an attempt to remedy that situation, the United States and Switzerland entered into a non-binding Memorandum of Understanding establishing special procedures to enable the SEC to obtain certain information in connection with insider trading investigations. Recently, however, the Swiss enacted a new law criminalising insider trading, thus permitting the United States to proceed through the basic provisions of the assistance treaty itself.

Assistance treaties typically contain a provision relating to the obligation of the treaty parties to use the treaty as opposed to other methods of obtaining information, such as subpoenas served on offices of the counterparty's banks located in the requesting party's country. These provisions vary significantly from treaty to treaty, and it is generally difficult to ascertain whether their legal effect is to render the treaty the exclusive or even the first means to be used by a party seeking to obtain information in the other party's jurisdiction. In any event, since assistance treaties generally expressly foreclose standing for private parties to allege treaty violations, these provisions are likely to be of little comfort to a bank in circumstances where the US government has served the bank's US office with a subpoena seeking information from its foreign branch, notwithstanding the existence of a treaty between the US and the foreign country in which the branch is located.

Litigation

Perhaps no litigation puts a bank in a more precarious position than where disclosure of information that is sought from a bank by a United States grand jury or other government body could arguably lead to a violation of law in another country in which the bank is also doing business. Many American courts have noted that that conflict alone does not preclude the United States from requiring disclosure of the specified information. As one court wrote in similar circumstances, 'If the Bank cannot, as it were, serve two masters and comply with the lawful requirements both of the United States and Panama, perhaps it should surrender to one sovereign or the other the privileges received therefrom' *First National City Bank of New York v Internal Revenue Service*, 271 F 2d 616 [2d Cir 1959], *cert den*, 361 US 948 [1960].

In *Garpeg Ltd v United States*, 583 F Supp 789 [SDNY 1984], the IRS issued a summons for records from the Hong Kong branch of the Chase Manhattan Bank while the bank and its customers sought to quash the summons on the grounds that disclosure of the records would violate Hong Kong bank secrecy laws. The bank's customers had obtained an interim injunction from a Hong Kong court prohibiting the bank from producing the requested records. The federal court in New York nevertheless required that the records be produced after it applied a balancing test. The test, which is based on the test set forth in s 40 of the Restatement (Second) of Foreign Relations Laws for determining the scope of the United States government's enforcement jurisdiction, weighs the vital national interests of each nation (including, the importance of the investigation), the extent and nature of the hardship that inconsistent enforcement actions would impose upon the person against whom enforcement of the United States law is brought, the extent to which the required conduct is to take place on the territory of the foreign state, the nationality of the person against whom enforcement is sought and the extent to which enforcement can reasonably be expected to achieve compliance with the law in question.

The court in *Garpeg* determined that the first factor of the test was the most significant and, in applying the test to the facts, decided that the interests of the United States in enforcing its tax laws significantly outweighed Hong Kong's interest in preserving bank secrecy. 'The vital interest of the United States, or any state for that matter, in enforcement of its tax laws is unquestionable', the court said, noting that, on the other hand, 'the interest of Hong Kong in maintaining its banking secrecy doctrine, a commercial concern, does not directly involve an express statutory concern vital to the government itself'. As for the second factor of the test, the court recognised that Chase could be placed in an 'untenable legal quandary' if it were permanently enjoined in Hong Kong from disclosing the information sought by the summons, but observed that this argument had been rejected repeatedly by United States courts in prior decisions.

As indicated by *In re Grand Jury Proceedings Bank of Nova Scotia* (above), the Restatement's balancing test has also been applied in cases where the US government has sought to compel foreign banks through their US offices to produce records located abroad. In deciding to enforce the sanctions against Bank of Nova Scotia for failing to produce foreign records, the court in that case also focused on the first factor of the test, and concluded that the importance of the grand jury's investigation of possible tax and narcotics law violations outweighed the bank secrecy interests of the Bahamas and the Cayman Islands. It then observed that, as the government of each foreign country had authorised release of the documents within days of commencement of the sanctions, the bank in fact suffered no hardship as a result of inconsistent enforcement actions. As for the bank's contention that it was unfair for the sanctions to have been imposed in the first place, since the consequence at the time was to force the bank to choose between the conflicting demands of foreign sovereigns, the court simply noted that 'such occasions will arise and a bank will have to choose'.

Individual foreign bankers have also found themselves in the difficult position of being faced with contempt charges from United States courts for refusing to disclose information, while at the same time facing possible civil or criminal charges in a foreign jurisdiction if the disclosure is made. In *United States v Field*, 532 F 2d 404 [5th Cir 1976], *cert den*, 429 US 940 [1976], the officer of a Cayman Islands bank, a Canadian citizen, while in transit through the Miami International Airport was served with a subpoena to testify before a grand jury investigating possible criminal violations of tax laws. He refused to answer questions concerning the bank and its clients on the grounds, among others, that to do so would violate the bank secrecy laws of the Cayman Islands. The court noted that ordering the officer to testify would subject him to prosecution in the Cayman Islands, but decided that in light of the serious nature of the crime under investigation, the United States interests in enforcing its laws outweighed the foreign bank secrecy laws. See also *In re Sealed Case* 825 F 2d 494 [DC Cir 1987], *cert den sub nom Roe v United States* 108 S Ct 451 [1987] (where the manager of the US agency of a foreign bank was ordered to be sent to prison for refusing before a federal grand jury to give testimony concerning foreign transactions relevant to a money laundering scheme, even though the testimony would have subjected him to criminal prosecution overseas for the violation of foreign bank secrecy laws).

While the majority of most recent court decisions in the US have required production of bank records in these circumstances despite foreign bank secrecy laws, at least two courts have reached a different result when applying the balancing test. The court in *United States v First National Bank of Chicago* 699 F 2d 341 [7th Cir 1983], focusing primarily on the second factor of the test relating to the hardship that inconsistent enforcement would impose, reversed a district court decision to enforce an IRS summons seeking documents from the Athens branch of a United States bank. And in *In re Sealed Case* (above), the court (despite holding the individual manager in contempt for refusing to give oral testimony) decided not to enforce a grand jury subpoena served on the US agency of a foreign bank seeking records from an overseas branch because the court, focusing on the third factor of the test, felt that the grand jury's need for information was not as important as the principle that United States law should not compel a foreign person (ie the bank) to violate the laws of a foreign country in its own territory.

As is evident from the foregoing discussion, the decision rendered by US courts confronted with foreign bank secrecy laws have not been entirely consistent. The courts generally have applied a balancing test, and the results of their decisions appear to depend on which factors of the test they consider the most significant. Those courts focusing on the first factor, not surprisingly, have decided in favour of giving effect to the stated national interests of the United States and thus have enforced subpoenas requesting information from foreign sources despite the hardship caused by inconsistent enforcement action against the bank for the violation of foreign bank secrecy laws and regardless of the extent of the conduct in the territory of the foreign state required to comply with the subpoena. Those courts focusing on the second and third tests, of course, have decided the other way.

INTERNAL CONFLICTS OF INTEREST

In certain circumstances, a bank may be tempted to use a customer's confidential financial information for its own business purposes, thus giving rise to important issues of conflicts of interests.

Chinese Walls

Frequently, the commercial loan departments of banks or departments engaged in underwriting, private placements, trading and other securities activities possess non-public information about companies that could be material to decisions by the bank's trust department to purchase or sell those companies' securities. Federal securities law generally prohibits use of that inside information by the trust department. As a consequence, the SEC has recommended that all financial institutions in possession of material inside information adopt internal procedures designed to ensure that the information remains in the department of the bank where it originated and is used solely for the purposes originally intended, rather than flowing to and being misused by other departments making investment or trading decisions about publicly traded securities. These procedures, which ordinarily include written policy statements, restricted access to files and physical separation of personnel, have become known as 'Chinese Walls'.

The sufficiency of Chinese Walls to protect an institution from charges of insider trading was questioned in *Slade v Shearson, Hamill & Co Inc* [1973–1974 Transfer Binder] CCH Fed Sec L Rep, para 94,329, remanded 517 F 2d 398 [2d Cir 1974], where Shearson's brokerage customers alleged that Shearson had violated the securities laws by continuing to recommend a company's securities while its investment banking department possessed adverse inside information on the company. Shearson argued that its Chinese Wall prevented the investment banking department from providing the information to the brokerage department and that, in any event, the brokerage department was precluded by the securities laws from using that information. Although the case was settled prior to resolution of the issue whether a securities law violation had occurred, the case led the SEC to recommend that Chinese Walls be reinforced by 'restricted lists' to provide additional safeguards against misuse of inside information. Restricted lists typically preclude a firm from recommending the purchase of securities of a company for which it possesses material inside information and from investing in such securities for its own account. Firms have also developed 'watch lists', which indicate the need to monitor the firm's activity involving securities of a company for which the firm might possess material inside information, as a preliminary but less dramatic step to placing securities on a restricted list. These procedures are used by both commercial banks and investment banks in the United States.

Recognising the potential for violations of the securities laws and in furtherance of their own duty to regulate unsafe and unsound banking practices, federal bank regulators have also adopted regulations and guidelines regarding use of material inside information. For example, the Comptroller of the Currency requires that every national bank exercising trust powers adopt written policies to ensure that the trust department does not use material inside information in connection with any decision or recommendation to purchase or sell any security. Similarly, the Federal Reserve Board has stated that because of the potential exposure of state member banks to civil and criminal proceedings under the securities laws resulting from misuse of material inside information, it views the use of material inside information in connection with any decision or recommendation to purchase or sell securities as an unsafe and unsound banking practice. State member banks are thus expected to adopt written policies and procedures, suitable to each bank's particular circumstances, to ensure that such information in its possession is not misused.

More elaborate structures known as 'firewalls' have most recently been advocated by the Federal Reserve Board in the context of expanding the permitted securities activities of United States banks and bank holding companies. In 1987, the Federal Reserve Board permitted non-bank subsidiaries of United States bank holding companies to engage in certain limited securities underwriting and dealing activities, conditioning the exercise of those expanded powers on the creation by the holding company of strict policies and procedures designed to insulate its banking and lending subsidiaries from the risks associated with the activities of the securities subsidiary. These firewalls are in part designed to prevent the misuse of customer information, and prohibit any lending affiliate from disclosing to the securities company any non-public customer information (including evaluations of creditworthiness) without the customer's consent. Similar kinds of firewalls have been included in many of the bills that Congress has considered during the last few years proposing to expand the securities activities of banks and bank holding companies.

Customer Take-overs

A different type of conflict of interest may arise whenever a bank is asked by one customer to provide financing or financial advice in connection with a hostile bid for the stock of another customer. In this situation, questions arise first as to whether the bank's relationship with the target company entirely precludes the bank from acting for the bidding company and, if not, as to whether the bank can actually utilise information that it possesses on the target company in acting for the bidder.

In *American Medicorp Inc v Continental Illinois National Bank* 475 F Supp 5 [ND Ill 1977], a commercial loan customer of a bank argued that since it had provided the bank with non-public financial information in connection with its loans, the bank owed it a fiduciary duty absolutely precluding it from making a loan to finance a hostile take-over of the customer, and that in any event the bank had breached a duty to the customer by actually using the information in determining whether to make the loan. The court held that a bank is not in all circumstances precluded from making a loan to facilitate the take-over of a customer so long as it does not use or rely on confidential information in its files relating to the customer in determining whether or not to make the loan, and that since there was no material evidence of such use in this case the bank was free to make the loan. In another lawsuit stemming from the same take-over battle, a New York court stated even more clearly that a bank may be precluded from using confidential customer information for improper purposes, including such use to determine whether to finance a hostile take-over. However, since it found no evidence of such use it refused to enjoin the bank's participation in the take-over financing: *Humana Inc v American Medicorp Inc.*

In the only appellate court decision to address these issues, the court of appeals for the Third Circuit similarly found that neither a bank's capacity as lender to a target customer nor its receipt of confidential information in that capacity imposes on the bank an absolute duty not to act adversely to the interests of the customer, and that the bank, absent any evidence of use of that information, is free to extend credit to a hostile bidder for the customer. This court took the analysis one step further in favour of the bank, however, by expressing the view that the bank would not have breached any duty to the customer even if it had consulted and used confidential information about the customer in determining whether to extend the credit. The court considered that a duty absolutely precluding such use could force banks to make loans blindly (in possible violation of their fiduciary duty to depositors) and might also restrict the availability of bank capital for take-over finance: *Washington Steel Corp v TW Corp*, 602 F 2d 594 [3d Cir 1979]. This dictum has been widely criticised by legal commentators and is not generally relied upon by banks. Instead, banks generally proceed upon the assumption that while they are not absolutely precluded from acting for a hostile bidder against an existing customer (absent any agreement with the existing customer to the contrary), any use of confidential information obtained from the customer should be avoided because some courts may impose liability for such use. In order to demonstrate the absence of such use, many banks erect a Chinese Wall within the loan department immediately upon commencement of a take-over financing between the officers in charge of that financing and any files of bank personnel associated with prior loans to the target customer.

The question whether banks are able to use customer information for their own purposes in financing a hostile take-over of the customer should not be permitted to obscure the basic legal principle underlying this article. Even assuming such use were permitted, any bank taking the further step of disclosing that information to the bidder runs a grave risk of liability to the customer for breach of its implied contract not to disclose the information to third parties.

Index